Glimpses Into
The
Spirit Realm

Moving From The Physical

World Into The Eternal

William Morford

True Potential
REACH THE WORLD

Scripture taken from the *One New Man Bible*, copyright © 2011 William J. Morford. Used by permission of True Potential Publishing, Inc.

Glimpses Into The Spirit Realm

Cover and Interior page design by True Potential, Inc.

ISBN: (paperback): 9781953247636
ISBN: (e-book): 9781953247643
LCCN: 2021950199

True Potential
REACH THE WORLD

True Potential, Inc.
PO Box 904, Travelers Rest, SC 29690
www.truepotentialmedia.com
Printed in the United States of America.

Contents

INTRODUCTION

Eternal Life is not physical, as some may think. Living in the Spirit Realm will be very different from life on Earth, for instance the food in ETERNAL LIFE is Spiritual! *For the* Kingdom of God *is* not food and drink, but righteousness and peace and joy in the Holy Spirit: (Roman 14:17)

> Deuteronomy 8:3. *And He humbled you and allowed you to hunger and fed you with manna, which you had not known, neither did your fathers know,* **so He could make you know that man does not live by bread alone, (Luke 4:4) but man lives by everything that proceeds from the mouth of the LORD*.**

Consider the Marriage Festival in Heaven

> Revelation 19:7. *Let us rejoice and be glad*
> *and we will give Him the glory,*
> *because the* marriage festival *of the* Lamb *has come*
> *and His wife has prepared herself*
> 8. and it was given to her that she would be clothed
> *in* brilliant pure fine linen:

The Marriage Festival of the Lamb is Spiritual, not a big sit-down feast of roast beef and mashed potatoes at the long table seen in illustrations of the meal. Our food will be Spiritual, not physical. It will be Righteousness, Peace, and Joy in the Holy Spirit!

Romans 14:17 *For the* Kingdom of God *is* not *food and drink, but* righteousness and peace and joy in (the) Holy Spirit:

Our food in ETERAL LIFE will be the Word of God!

When you read Ezekiel with the dry bones coming together, growing flesh and breathing; realize that is allegorical not literal.

> Ezekiel 37:4. *Again He said to me, Prophesy over, in the direction of these bones and say to **them** (the people), O you dry bones, Listen! Obey the word of the LORD*! 5. Thus says Adonai, the LORD* toward these bones, Behold, I AM will cause breath to enter you and you will live, (Rev. 11:11) 6. And I shall lay sinews upon you and will bring up flesh upon you and cover you with skin and put a Spirit in you, and you will live, and you will know that I AM the LORD*.*

The pronoun Them does not refer to bones, but to the people who formerly used the bones. Bones, 'atsam'ot' in Hebrew, is a feminine noun, while the pronoun, 'alaihem' is masculine. All the pronouns in verses 5, 6, 8, through 14, every "you" is masculine plural, meaning that this passage is allegorical, not literal. The masculine pronoun applies to both men and women because ancient Israel was like the United States prior to political correctness, which started in the 1970s, when it became necessary to address women separately. The word "Chairman" could apply to a woman who headed a group just well as to a man who headed a group.

We naturally think of being in the physical sense because we live in the Physical world and that is what we know. We have to learn about the Spiritual. Reading the Word daily brings us closer to the Spiritual.

> 1 Corinthians 15:42. *So also the resurrection of the dead. It is sown in corruption, it is raised incorruptible: 43. It is sown in dishonor, it is raised in magnificence: it is sown in weakness, it is raised in power: 44. **A body is sown fleshly, it is raised a spiritual body. If there is a fleshly body, there is also a spiritual.** 45. And so it has been written, "The first man was Adam in living life," (Gen. 2:7) the last Adam has become a life-giving **spirit**. 46. But **the spiritual was not first but the physical, then the spiritual.** 47. The first man is from dust of the earth, the second man out of **heaven**. 48. What sort of earthly man, and such as these earthly ones, and what sort of the heavenly One, then such as these born of the heavenly nature: 49. And just as we bore constantly the image of the earthly, **we will bear constantly also the <u>image</u> of the heavenly One.***

The First Man was made in the flesh, physical. Y'shua was made both Physical and Spiritual. We are made in His image. We are to become more and more like Him, the One Who now lives in the Spirit. Angels appear many times in this compilation, most often to one or maybe two, but sometimes an angel or two will appear to a crowd, as in Genesis 19 where the men of Sodom see them. Someone's eyes need to be opened Spiritually to be able see Angels so God opened the Spiritual Eyes of the men of Sodom, making them able to see the two angels who came to rescue Lot. The Spirit Realm is three-dimensional, so all the Angels and God Himself are three-dimensional, as are the Third Temple and New Jerusalem!

This book details much of the interaction of our Physical Realm with the Spirit Realm, with the Spiritual coming to interact with us, often with a prophet, but also often with just an average human being. Sometimes the LORD* Himself intervenes, with the chapter Our Sovereign God detailing those. We think of the Physical world as the Real world, but the Spirit world is every bit as Real as the Physical. We have to Trust to understand the Spiritual:

Hebrews 11:1. *And Trust is being confident of things hoped for, proof of things not seen.*

OUR HEAVENLY FATHER DESIRES RELATIONSHIP

Each person is to have a relationship with our heavenly Father, just as He walked with Adam and Eve, with Enoch, and with Noah. He wants to walk with you every day.

> Genesis 3:8. *And they heard the **voice of the LORD* God walking** in the garden in the cool of the day, and **Adam** and his **wife hid** themselves from the presence of the LORD* God among the trees of the garden. 9. And the LORD* God called to Adam and said to him, "Where are you?" 10. And he said, "I **heard Your voice** in the garden and I was awed because I was naked, and I hid myself." 11. And He said, "Who told you that you were naked? Have you eaten of the tree of which I commanded you that you should not eat?" 12. And the man said, "The woman whom You gave to be with me, she gave me of the tree and I did eat."*

God wants to walk with you too, so be careful what you do and what you think as you walk in repentance with Him.

> Genesis 4:3. *And in process of time it came to pass that **Cain** brought an offering to the LORD* from the fruit of the ground. 4. And **Abel** also brought from the **firstlings** of his flock and from its fat. And the LORD* turned to **Abel** and **his offering**, 5. but He **did not turn** to **Cain** and to **his offering**. And **Cain** was very, very angry and his countenance fell. 6. And the **LORD*** said to **Cain**, "Why are you so angry? And why has your countenance fallen? 7. Behold, if you do well, you will be accepted. And if you do not do well, **sin** sits waiting at the door, and **its desire** is to **(possess)** you, but you can rule over it."* (Num. 32:23)

The difference between the offerings of Cain and Abel is that Cain did not bring his First Fruits but Abel did bring his First Fruits. Verse seven has the first mention of Sin in the Bible.

God Walks with Enoch

> Genesis 5:21. *And **Enoch** lived sixty-five years and begot Methuselah. 22. And **Enoch walked with God** three hundred years after he begot Methuselah, and begot sons and daughters. 23. And all the days of **Enoch** were three hundred sixty-five years. 24. And **Enoch walked with God**, then **he was not**, for **God took him**.*

'Was not' can mean either Enoch died or that God simply Took him to Heaven.

God Walks with Noah

> Genesis 6:9. *These are the generations of **Noah**: **Noah** was a just man, perfect in his generations. **Noah walked with God**. 10. And **Noah** begot three sons, Shem, Ham, and Japheth. 11. The whole earth was corrupt before **God** and the earth was filled with violence. 12. And **God** looked upon the earth and, behold, it was corrupt, for all flesh had corrupted their way upon the earth.*

God Establishes His First Covenant with Mankind

> Genesis 6:18. *"But with you I shall **establish**, ratify, **My covenant** and you will **come** into the box, you, your sons, your wife, and your sons' wives with you. 19. And of every living thing of all flesh, you will bring two of every sort into the box, to keep alive with you; they will be male and female. 20. Of fowls after their kind, and of cattle after their kind, of every creeping thing of the earth after its kind, two of every sort will come to you, to keep alive. 21. And take for yourself of all food that is eaten, and you will gather it for yourself, and it will be for food for you and for them." 22. And **Noah** did so. According to all that **God** commanded him, so he did.*

Having this Covenant with Noah, God firmly states His desire for long term relationship, which He wants with you Too! This was a given Covenant, with no offering involved.

After the Flood Noah Builds the First Altar to the LORD*

> Genesis 8:20. *And **Noah** built an altar to the LORD* and took of every clean beast and of every clean fowl, and offered burnt offerings on the altar. 21. And the LORD* smelled a sweet savor and the LORD* said in His*

*heart, "I shall not again curse the ground any more for man's sake, for the **imagination of man's heart is bad from his youth**. (Jer. 32:30) Neither will I again any longer strike everything living, as I have done. 22. While the earth remains, seedtime and harvest, and cold and heat, and summer and winter, and day and night will not cease."*

Man's heart is bad from his Youth; although Mankind is born Pure, each is later corrupted by the older generations.

*Genesis 9.1. And **God** blessed **Noah** and his sons and said to them, "Be fruitful and multiply and replenish the earth. 2. And the awe of you and the dread of you will be upon every beast of the earth and upon every fowl of the air, upon all that moves upon the earth and upon all the fishes of the sea. They are delivered into your hand. 3. Every moving thing that lives will be food for you, even as the green herb. I have given you everything. 4. But **you will not eat flesh with its life, which is in its blood!** 5. And surely your blood of your lives will I require, at the hand of every beast I shall require it, and at the hand of man. At the hand of every man's brother I shall require the life of man. 6. **Whoever sheds man's blood, by man will his blood be shed, for He made man in the image of God.** 7. And you, be fruitful and multiply. Bring forth abundantly in the earth and multiply in it."*

God Establishes a Second Covenant with Noah

*Genesis 9:8. And **God** spoke to **Noah** and to **his sons** with him saying, 9. "And behold, I AM **Establishing (Ratifying) My covenant** with you and with your seed after you, 10. and with every living creature that is with you, of the fowl, of the cattle, and of every beast of the earth with you; from all that go out of the box, to every beast of the earth. 11. And I will **confirm My covenant with you**. Neither will all flesh be cut off any more by the waters of a flood, nor will there any more be a flood to destroy the earth." 12. And God said, "This is the token of the covenant which I AM giving between Me and you and every living creature that is with you, for perpetual generations: 13. I have set My **rainbow** in the cloud, and it will be for a token of a covenant between Me and the earth. 14. And it will be, when I bring a cloud over the earth, that the rainbow will be seen in the cloud, 15. and I shall remember My **covenant**, which is between Me and you and every living creature of all flesh: and the waters will no longer become a flood to destroy all flesh. 16. And the bow will be in the cloud, and I shall look upon it, so I can remember the everlasting **covenant** between **God** and **every living creature** of all flesh* *that is upon the earth." 17. And **God** said to **Noah**, "This is the token of the **covenant**, which I have **established** between Me and all flesh that is upon the earth."*

The rainbow, having all the colors, represents God's concern over all of His creation. All the colors being in the covenant also shows there will be more covenants. See *Covenants* in the One New Man Bible Glossary.

God Speaks to Abram, ordering him to get going to Canaan

> Genesis 12:1. *Now the LORD* had said to Abram, "**Get yourself out of here!** From your country and from your kindred and from your father's house to a land that I shall show you. (Acts 7:3) 2. And I shall make a great nation of you, and I shall bless you and **make your name great** and you will be a **blessing**. 3. And I shall **bless** those who **bless you** and **curse** the one who **curses you**: and in you will all families of the earth be **blessed**." (Num. 24:9, Gal. 3:8) 4. So **Abram** departed, as the **LORD*** had spoken to him and Lot went with him, and **Abram** was seventy-five years old when he left Haran. 5. And **Abram** took **Sarai** his wife and **Lot** his brother's son and all their possessions that they had gathered, and the **souls** that they had made in Haran: and they left to go into the land of **Canaan**, and they came into the land of **Canaan**. (Heb. 11:8) 6. And **Abram** passed through the land to the place of **Shechem**, to the oak of Moreh. And the Canaanites were then in the land.*

The LORD* had earlier ordered Abram to go to Canaan, but he stayed in Haran for years; then the LORD* ordered him emphatically to Get going!

Abram was the world's first Evangelist, bringing his entire flock of converts along with his flocks of sheep and goats, and herds of cattle. The LORD* orders Abram to get on with it, continue to Canaan, but Canaan is a large area so Abram goes in faith, not knowing the final destination. He takes all the Souls, Disciples he had made in Haran.

The LORD* Appears to Abram

> Genesis 12:7. *And the LORD* **appeared** to **Abram** and said, "I shall give this land to your seed." (Acts 7:5) And he built an **altar** there to the **LORD***, Who **appeared** to him. 8. And he went from there to a mountain on the east of Beit-El and pitched his tent, having Beit-El on the west and Ai on the east, and there he built an **altar** to the LORD* and called upon the name of the LORD*. 9. And **Abram** journeyed, still going on toward the south.*

Abram's relationship with the LORD* is shown by the LORD*'s Appearance to Abram. Each Relationship with the LORD* is shown by the way the person behaves, whether or not the LORD* appears to the person.

God Gives the Land to Abram

> Genesis 13:14. *And the **LORD*** said to **Abram**, after **Lot** was separated from him, "Now lift up your eyes and look northward from the place where you are, then southward and eastward and westward, 15. for I shall give to you and to your seed forever **all the land that you see**. (Acts 7:5) 16. And I shall make your **seed** as the dust of the earth, so that if a man can number the dust of the earth, then your **seed** will also be **numbered**. 17. **Arise**, walk through the land in the **length** of it and in the **breadth** of it, for I shall give it to you." 18. Then **Abram** removed his tent and came and lived in the plain of Mamre, which is in Hebron, and there he built an **altar** to the **LORD***.*

The LORD* promises to make Abram's descendants as numerous as the dust of the earth. Now that Lot has separated from Abram, the LORD* again speaks to Abram; Looking eastward gave Abram the land to which Lot went. See Joshua 13:5, 2 Corinthians 6:14.

Abram Has a Vision

> Genesis 15.1. *After these things the word of the **LORD*** came to **Abram** in a **vision**, saying, "**Do not be in awe, Abram! I AM your Shield!** Your reward will be exceedingly great." 2. And **Abram** said, "Adonai, **LORD***, what will You give me, seeing I go childless and the steward of my house is this Eliezer of Damascus?" 3. And Abram said, "Behold, to me You have given no seed, and one born in my house is my heir." 4. And, behold, the word of the **LORD*** came to him saying, "This one will not be your heir, but he that will come out of your own being will be your heir." 5. And He brought him outside, and said, "Look now toward the heavens and count the stars, if you are able to number them." And He said to him, "So will your seed be." (Rom. 4:18) 6. And he believed in the **LORD***, and He counted it to him for acts of loving kindness. (Rom. 4:3, Gal. 3:6, Jcb. 2:24) 7. And He said to him, "I AM the **LORD*** Who brought you out of Ur of the Chaldees, to give you this **land** to inherit it. 8. And he said, "Adonai, **LORD***, how will I know that I shall inherit it?"*

In verse one the Hebrew word for I AM is Anokhi, showing the LORD* is very deliberate, a very purposeful application of the shield. The your is singular, so your Heavenly Father sets Himself as the Protector of each one of us. When

Anokhi is used, I AM is in bold type. The I AM promises to bless Abram with descendants too numerous to count, and also to give him all the land that could be seen from the high lookout, from the Mediterranean to the Euphrates River. The LORD* then cuts a Covenant with Abram.

Covenant Between the Parts

> Genesis 15:9. *And He said to him, "Take a heifer for Me, three years old, and a three year old she-goat, and a three year old ram, a turtle-dove, and a young pigeon." 10. And he took all these to Him, and divided them down the middle, and laid each piece one opposite another, but* **he did not divide the bird.**

The word for Bird, Tsipor, is a collective singular, referring to both birds, showing the inherent lesson that Israel's generations (mother and child) are one unit, not to be divided. The Two Birds are released, representing the Two Witnesses, Revelation 11:3, going forth to bring God's love to the whole world. See that in the chapter on Revelation.

> Genesis 15:11. *And when the* **birds of prey** *came down upon the carcasses,* **Abram** *drove them away. 12. And when the sun was going down, a deep sleep fell upon* **Abram***, and behold, a horror of great darkness fell upon him. 13. And* **He** *said to* **Abram***, "Know of a surety that your seed will be a* **stranger** *in a* **land** *that is not theirs and* **will serve them** *and they* **will afflict them four hundred years.**

The four hundred years is the Egyptian captivity.

> Genesis 15:14. *And also that* **I AM** *will judge that nation whom they will serve, and afterward* **they will come out** *with* **great possessions***. (Exod. 11:2, Acts 7:6,7) 15. And you will go to your fathers in peace: you will be buried in a good old age. 16. But in the fourth generation they will return here again, for the* **iniquity of the Amorite is not yet full.***"

The Israelites did go to Egypt, then after being slaves, left Egypt with great Wealth, much of which was used for the Tabernacle. The Amorites were the most powerful of the Canaanite tribes, so here they represent all Canaanite peoples. Their Iniquity being full shows God's patience as He gave the Amorites ample time to Repent but they failed to Repent.

> Genesis 15:17. *And it was that when the sun went down and it was dark, there was a smoking furnace and a burning flame that passed between those pieces. 18. On the same day the LORD*** cut** *a covenant with Abram saying,*

"To your seed I have given this land, from the river of Egypt to the great river, the river Euphrates: 19. the Kenite, the Kenizite, the Kadmonite, 20. the Hittite, the Perizzite, the Rephaim, 21. the Amorite, the Canaanite, the Gergashite, and the Jebusite."

The LORD* Cut this Covenant with Abram announcing that all the land from the eastern border of Sinai to the Euphrates would be Abram's. Next, He sends an Angel to comfort Hagar, telling her to return to Sarai.

Genesis 16:7. *And an **angel** of the LORD* found her by a fountain of water in the wilderness, by the fountain on the way to Shur. 8. And he said, "**Hagar, Sarai's maid**, where did you come from? And where will you go?" And she said, "I am fleeing from the face of my mistress **Sarai**." 9. And the **angel** of the LORD* said to her, "**Return** to your mistress and submit yourself to her." 10. And the **angel** of the LORD* said to her, "I shall multiply your seed exceedingly, that it will not be numbered for multitude." 11. And the **angel** of the LORD* said to her, "Behold, you are with **child** and will **bear a son**, and will call his name **Ishmael** because the LORD* **has heard** your affliction. 12. And (**Ishmael**) will be a wild man. His hand will be **against every man** and every man's hand against him, and he will dwell in the presence of all his brothers." 13. And she called the name of the LORD* that spoke to her, "You are **El-Ro'i**," for she said, "Have I also here looked after **Him Who sees me**? 14. Therefore the well was called "**Beer-Lakhai-Ro'i**." Behold, it is between Kadesh and Bered. 15. And **Hagar** bore **Abram** a **son**, and **Abram** called his son's name that **Hagar** bore, **Ishmael**. 16. And **Abram** was eighty-six years old when **Hagar** bore **Ishmael** to **Abram**.*

Hagar is ordered to return to Sarai and submit to her. Then He promises to multiply Ishmael exceedingly although Ismael will be a wild man. El-Roi means God Sees Me. Hagar names the place, Well of the Living One Who Sees Me. She does bear a son and names him Ishmael, God will hear.

The LORD* Gives a Covenant, Appearing to Abram

Genesis 17.1. *And when **Abram** was ninety-nine years old, the **LORD*** **appeared** to **Abram**, and said to him, "**I AM Almighty God!** Walk before Me and be innocent. 2. And I will **Give** My covenant between **Me** and **you** and will **multiply** you exceedingly." 3. And **Abram** fell on his face and **God** talked with him saying, 4. "As for Me, behold, **My covenant is with you**, and you will be a **father** of many nations."*

The Hebrew text has El-Shaddai, which means Almighty God. Some say El-Shaddai means many breasted, but that is not correct. The Root verb of Shaddai is Shadad which means "to deal violently with." God Gives this Covenant, making it Unconditional; so, no matter what, this Covenant will remain in effect.

Name Changed to Abraham

> Genesis 17:5. *"Neither shall your name any more be called **Avram**, but your name shall be **Avraham**; for I have made you a **father of many nations**. 6. And I will make you exceeding fruitful, and I will make nations of you, and kings shall come out of you. 7. And I will **establish** My covenant between **Me** and **you** and **your seed** after you in their generations for an **everlasting covenant**, to be a **God** to **you**, and to **your seed** after you. 8. And I will give to **you**, and to **your seed** after you, the **land** in which **you are a stranger**, all the **land of Canaan**, for an everlasting possession; and I will be their **God**."*

Avram and Avraham are the correct transliterations from the Hebrew text, not the traditional transliterations, which are from the Latin text. God Establishes, ratifies, this Covenant, making it Unconditional. All Canaan belongs to Israel and God will be the only God in Canaan.

God Cuts a Covenant with Israel, ordering Circumcision

> Genesis 17:9. And **God** said to **Avraham**, *"Therefore you shall keep My covenant, you, and your seed after you in their generations. 10. This is **My covenant**, which you will keep, between **Me** and **you** and **your seed** after you. Every **man child** among you will be **circumcised**. (Acts 7:8) 11. And you will **circumcise** the **flesh of your foreskin** and it will be a **token** of the **covenant between Me and you**. 12. And he that is **eight days old** will be **circumcised** among you, every **male** in your generations, he that is born in the house or bought with money from any stranger who is not of your seed. 13. He that is **born** in your house and he that is **bought** with your money must definitely be **circumcised**. And **My covenant** will be in your **flesh** for an **everlasting covenant**. 14. And the uncircumcised male whose flesh of his foreskin is not circumcised, that soul will be cut off from his people; he has broken My covenant."*

Every Cut Covenant requires Blood, which in this instance is the Blood from the Circumcision. Every Cut covenant is Conditional.

Sarai Changed to Sarah

> Genesis 17:15. *And **God** said to **Abraham**, "As for **Sarai** your wife, you will not call her name **Sarai**, but her name will be **Sarah**. 16. And I shall **bless her** and give you a **son** also from **her**. Yes, I will **bless** her and she will be a **mother of nations**; kings of peoples will be of her."*

Sarai means My Princess, while Sarah simply means Princess so she will now be a Princess in her own Right. She is now Abraham's equal – the way every marriage should be.

> Genesis 17:17. *Then **Abraham** fell upon his face and **laughed**, and said in his heart, "Will a child be born to him that is a **hundred** years old? And will **Sarah**, who is **ninety** years old, bear (a **child**)?" 18. And **Abraham** said to **God**, "Oh! That **Ishmael** might live before You!" 19. And **God** said, "**Sarah** your wife will indeed bear a **son** for you; and you will call his name **Isaac**. And I shall **establish My covenant** with him for an **everlasting covenant**, (and) with his seed after him. (Heb. 11:11) 20. And as for **Ishmael**, I have heard you. Behold, I have **blessed** him and will make him fruitful and will multiply him exceedingly. He will beget **twelve princes** and I shall make him a great nation. 21. But I shall **ratify**, **(establish)**, My covenant with **Isaac**, whom **Sarah** will bear to you at this set time in the next year."22. And He left off talking with him and **God** went up from **Abraham**.*

God enjoys the laughter of Abraham and Sarah, showing His pleasure by naming the boy, Isaac, which means Laughter. Isaac will have an unconditional covenant with the LORD*. Our Heavenly FATHER Relishes His relationship with Abraham.

The LORD* Appears Again to Abraham

> Genesis 18.1. ***And** the LORD* **appeared** to him in the plains of Mamre and he was sitting in the tent door in the heat of the day. 2. And he lifted up his eyes and looked, and there were **three men** standing by him. And when he saw them, he ran from the tent door to meet them and he bowed toward the ground 3. and said, "My Lord, if now I have found favor in **Your** sight, do not pass by, I pray **You**, from **Your** servant:*

The pronouns You and Your are capitalized because they are singular as Abraham recognized the LORD* separately from the others. The next pronouns are plural.

> Genesis 18:4. *Let a little water, I pray **you**, be brought and wash **your** feet and rest **yourselves** under the tree. 5. And I shall get a morsel of bread and*

comfort your hearts for **you**. *After that* **you** *will pass on, for that is why* **you** *have come to* **your** *servant." And they said, "So do as you have said." 6. And* **Abraham** *hastened into the tent to* **Sarah** *and said, "Make ready quickly* **three measures** *of fine meal, knead it and make cakes." 7. And* **Abraham** *ran to the herd and fetched a good,* **tender calf** *and gave it to a young man and he hastened to dress it. 8. And he took* **butter**, **milk**, *and the* **calf** *which he had dressed and set it before them, and he stood by them under the tree and they ate.*

The three measures are about twenty-one quarts of grain to make bread, so Abraham prepares a huge banquet for so few people. He does not rush; preparing the calf and cooking it took quite a long time.

Genesis 18:9. *And they said to him, "Where is* **Sarah** *your wife?" And he said, "There – in the tent." 10. And* **He** *said, "***I shall certainly return to you at this time next year** *and, see,* **Sarah** *your wife will have a* **son**.*" (Rom. 9:9) And Sarah listened in the tent door, which was behind him. 11. Now* **Abraham** *and* **Sarah** *were old and well up in age: the manner of women had ceased to be with* **Sarah**. *12. Therefore* **Sarah** *laughed within herself saying, "After I have grown old will I have pleasure, my lord being old also?" 13. And the* **LORD*** *said to* **Abraham**, *"Why did* **Sarah** *laugh saying, 'Will I, who am old, a surety bear a child?' 14. Is anything too hard for the LORD*? (Jer. 32:17, Matt. 19:26, Luke 1:37) At the time appointed I shall return to you, about this time next year, and* **Sarah** *will have a son." (Rom. 9:9) 15. Then* **Sarah** *denied it saying, "I did* **not laugh**,*" for she was afraid. And* **He** *said, "***No, but you did laugh**.*"*

Sarah tried to no effect to contradict the LORD*, but contradicting Him never works.

Genesis 18:16. *And the men rose up from there and looked toward Sodom and* **Abraham** *went with them to bring them on the way. 17. And the* **LORD*** *said, "Will I hide from* **Abraham** *that thing which I am (about to) do, 18. seeing that* **Abraham** *will surely become a great and mighty nation and* <u>*all the nations of the earth will be blessed in him*</u>*? 19. For I know him, that he will command his children and his household after him and they will keep the* **Way of the LORD***, *to do acts of loving kindness and judgment, so the LORD* may bring upon* **Abraham** *that which He has spoken of him." 20. And the LORD* said, "Because the cry of Sodom and Gomorrah is great and because their sin is very grievous, 21. I shall go down now and see whether they have done everything I told them, which has come* *to Me. And if not, I shall know." 22. And the men turned their faces from there and went toward Sodom, but **Abraham** still stood before the **LORD***. 23. And **Abraham** drew near and said, "Will You also destroy the righteous with the wicked? 24. If there are fifty righteous within the city will You also destroy and not spare the place for the fifty righteous that are there? 25. Far be it from You to do after this manner, to slay the righteous with the wicked and that the righteous should be like the wicked: far be that from You. Will not the Judge of all the earth do right?" 26. And the **LORD*** said, "If I find in Sodom fifty righteous within the city, then I shall spare the entire place for their sake." 27. And **Abraham** answered and said, "Behold now, I, who am but dust and ashes, have taken upon me to speak to the **LORD***. 28. If by chance there will lack five of the fifty righteous, will You destroy the whole city for lack of five?" And He said, "If I find forty-five there, I shall not destroy it." 29. And he spoke to Him yet again and said, "If by chance there will be forty found there?" And He said, "I shall not do it for forty's sake." 30. And he said to Him, "Oh do not let the **LORD*** be angry, and I shall speak: If by chance thirty will be found there?" And He said, "I shall not do it, if I find thirty there." 31. And he said, "Behold now, I have taken upon myself to speak to the **LORD***: If by chance twenty will be found there?" And He said, I shall not destroy it for twenty's sake." 32. And he said, "Oh please, let not the **LORD*** be angry, and I shall speak yet but this once: If by chance ten will be found there?" And He said, "I shall not destroy it for ten's sake." 33. And the **LORD*** went His way, as soon as He had left speaking with **Abraham**, and **Abraham** returned to his place.*

Verse nineteen is the first use of Way in the Bible, referring to a walk with the LORD*; a Way of life dedicated to the LORD* is an expression used more than sixty times in the Hebrew Scriptures, about twelve times in the New Testament.

Lot Rescued

Genesis 19.1. *And **two angels** came to **Sodom** in the evening and **Lot** was sitting in the gate of **Sodom**. And when **Lot** saw them he rose up to meet them and he bowed himself with his face toward the ground. 2. And he said, "Behold now, my lords, turn in, I pray you, into your servant's house and tarry all night and wash your feet and you will rise up early and go on your way." And they said, "No. But we will stay in the street all night." 3. And he pressed upon them greatly and they went in with him and entered his **house** and he made a **feast** for them and baked unleavened bread and they ate.*

Two Angels bring the Spirit Realm to Lot

Genesis 19:4. *But before they lay down, the men of the city, the **men of Sodom**, surrounded the house, both old and young, all the people from every quarter. 5. And they called to **Lot** and said to him, "Where are the men who came in to you tonight? Bring them out to us, so **we can know them**." 6. And **Lot** went out to them at the door and shut the door behind him 7. and said, "I pray you, brothers, do not behave so wickedly. 8. Behold now, I have two daughters who have not known a man: let me, I pray you, bring them out to you and you do to them as is good in your eyes. Only to these men do nothing, for therefore they came under the shadow of my roof." 9. And they said, "Stand back!" And they said again, "This one came in to sojourn and he thinks he is a judge. Now we will deal worse with you than with them." And they pressed sore upon the man, **Lot**, and came near to break the door. 10. But the **men (Angels)** put forth their hand and pulled **Lot** into the house to them and shut the door. 11. And **they** struck the **men** with **blindness** that were at the **door of the house**, both small and great, so that they wearied themselves to find the **door**. 12. And the men said to **Lot**, "Do you have here any besides yourself? **Sons-in-law**, your **sons**, your **daughters**, and whoever you have in the city, **bring them out of this place**, 13. for we will **destroy** this place, because their cry has become great before the face of the **LORD***, and the **LORD*** has sent **us** to **destroy** it."*

Lot was the most Righteous in Sodom but he was less than stellar; well, none of us is perfect either.

The Sons-in-Law Opt Out of Being Rescued

Genesis 19:14. *And **Lot** went out and spoke to his **sons-in-law**, who **married** his **daughters**, and said, "Get up, get out of this place, for the **LORD*** will **destroy** this city." But he seemed like one who teased to his **sons-in-law**. 15. And when the morning came, then the **angels** hastened **Lot** saying, "Arise, take your **wife** and your **two daughters** that are here, so you will **not be consumed** in the **iniquity** of the **city**." 16. And while he lingered, the **men** laid hold upon his hand and upon the hand of his **wife** and upon the hand of his **two daughters**. The **LORD*** had pity on him and they brought him out and set him **outside** the **city**. 17. And it was, when they had brought them out, that he said, "**Escape** for your **life**! **Do not look behind you! Do not stay anywhere in the plain! Escape** to the **mountain**, so you will not be **consumed**." 18. And **Lot** said to them, "Oh, **not so**, my lord. 19. Behold now your servant has found favor in your sight and you have magnified your loving kindness, which you have shown to me in **saving** my life. And I **cannot escape** to the mountain, lest something **evil*** *overtake me and I die. 20. Behold now, this **city** is near to flee to and it is a little one. Oh, let me **escape** there, (is it not a little one?) and my soul will live." 21. And he said to him, "See, I have **accepted** you concerning **this** thing also, that I shall not **overthrow** this **city** of which you have spoken. 22. Quick! **Escape** there, for I cannot do anything until you have come there." Therefore the name of the city was called **Zoar**.*

The Iniquity of verse fifteen is intentional sin, showing that the men of Sodom knew that homosexuality was sin, but did it anyway. Zoar means Insignificant, so Lot goes to that little town.

Sodom Gets What it Deserves

*Genesis 19:23. The sun had risen upon the earth when **Lot** entered **Zoar**. 24. Then the **LORD* rained brimstone** and **fire** from the **LORD*** out of heaven upon **Sodom** and upon Gomorrah. (Rev. 14:10; 20:10; 21:8) 25. And he overthrew those **cities**, and all the **plain** and all the inhabitants of the cities and that which grew upon the ground. 26. But his **wife** looked **back** from behind him and she became a **pillar of salt**.*

Looking back, living in the past, is never fruitful. It is essential to look ahead, planning and moving on with life.

Sarah and Isaac

*Genesis 21.1. And the **LORD*** visited **Sarah** as He had said and the **LORD*** did for **Sarah** what He had spoken. (Gen. 18:10) 2. For **Sarah** **conceived** and **bore Abraham** a **son** in his old age, at the set time of which God had spoken to him. (Heb. 11:11) 3. And **Abraham** called the name of his son that was born to him, whom **Sarah** bore to him, **Isaac**. 4. And **Abraham** circumcised his son **Isaac** when he was eight days old, as God had commanded him. 5. And **Abraham** was a hundred years old when his son **Isaac** was born to him.*

The long-sought child will finally be a reality; the second Patriarch will arrive on time – in God's timing that is.

God's Promised Son is Named Isaac, meaning Laughter.

*Genesis 21:6. And **Sarah** said, "God has made **laughter** for me, so that all who hear will **laugh with me**." 7. And she said, "Who would have said to **Abraham** that **Sarah** should be given children to nurse? For I have borne him a son in his old age." 8. And the child grew and was weaned, and*

*Abraham made a great feast the day that **Isaac** was weaned. 9. And **Sarah** saw the **son** of **Hagar** the Egyptian, whom she had borne to **Abraham**, <u>scornful</u>. 10. So she said to **Abraham**, "Cast out this bondwoman and her son, for the son of this bondwoman will not be heir with my son, with **Isaac**."* (Gal. 4:30, Heb. 11:17)

The word translated scornful has been discussed at length in commentary. The interpretations, which are all negative, range from playing around to murder, so Sarah was very concerned about the situation.

Abraham was reassured by the LORD* that He would protect Ishmael, and that Isaac would be Abraham's heir.

Genesis 21:11. *And the thing was very grievous in Abraham's sight because of his son. 12. And **God** said to Abraham, "**Do not be distressed** in your sight because of the lad and because of your bondwoman. In all that Sarah has said to you, listen to her voice because **your seed will be called in Isaac**. (Rom. 9:7, Heb. 11:18) 13. And of the son of the bondwoman I shall also make a nation, because he is your seed." 14. And **Abraham** rose up early in the morning and took **bread** and a **skin-bottle of water** and gave it to **Hagar**, putting it on her shoulder, and the **boy**, and sent her away. And she left and wandered in the wilderness of Beer-Sheba. 15. And the water was spent in the bottle and she put the **boy** under one of the shrubs. 16. And she went and sat down opposite, a good way off, about a bowshot, for she said, "Let me not see the death of the **boy**." And she was sitting opposite (him) and lifted up her voice and wept. 17. And **God** heard the voice of the **lad**, and an **angel** of **God** called to **Hagar** out of heaven and said to her, "What troubles you, **Hagar**? **Do not be in awe!** **God** has heard the voice of the **lad** where he is. 18. Arise, lift up the **lad** and hold him in your hand, for I shall make a great nation of him. 19. And **God opened** her eyes and **she** saw a **well of water**, and **she** went and filled the bottle with water and gave the **lad** a drink.*

The LORD* keeps watch on each of us, shown by the Priestly Blessing.

Numbers 6:22. *And the LORD* spoke to Moses saying, 23. "Speak to Aaron and to his sons saying, In this way you will bless the children of **Israel**, saying to them, 24. 'The LORD* will bless you and He will keep you. 25. The LORD* will make His face to shine upon you and He will be gracious to you. 26. The **LORD* will lift His countenance to you** and He will establish Shalom for you.' (1 Chr. 23:13) 27. And they will put **My name upon the children of Israel** and **I will bless them**."*

21

This is the literal translation, not the weak, iffy, "May the LORD* bless you." Be very thankful that you are in the LORD*'s eye every moment. If you are not Jewish, you are grafted in!

Abraham's Ultimate Test

> Genesis 22.1. *And it happened after these things that* **God** *tested* **Abraham** *and said to him,* **"Abraham."** *And he said, "Here I am." 2. And* **He** *said, "Now take your* **son***, your* **only son Isaac***, whom you love! Get yourself into the land of* **Moriah***! Offer him there as an offering upon one of the mountains of which I shall tell you!"*

Moriah, meaning "Yah (God) is *the* Teacher," speaks of the future Jerusalem, the seat of Jewish teachings. This passage is called the Akeidah, the Binding.

> Genesis 22:3. *And* **Abraham** *rose early in the morning and saddled his donkey and took two of his young men with him and* **Isaac** *his son, and split the wood for the offering and rose up and went to the place of which God had told him. 4. Then on the third day* **Abraham** *lifted up his eyes and saw the place afar off. 5. And* **Abraham** *said to his young men, "You stay here with the donkey and I and the* **lad** *will go yonder and worship, and come again to you." 6. And* **Abraham** *took the wood of the burnt offering and laid it upon* **Isaac** *his son, and he took the fire in his hand and a knife, and they went, both of them together.*

Isaac was thirty-seven years old at this time.

Isaac Asks "Where is the Lamb?"

> Genesis 22:7. *And* **Isaac** *spoke to* **Abraham** *his father and said, "My father." and he said, "Here I am, my son." And he said, "Here are the fire and the wood, but* **where is the lamb** *for a burnt offering?" 8. And* **Abraham** *said, "My son,* **God will see to it***, (providing) a* **lamb** *for a burnt offering for Himself." so they went, both of them together. 9. And they came to the place which* **God** *had told him about, and* **Abraham** *built an altar there and laid the wood in order and* **bound Isaac** *his son, and laid him on the altar upon the wood. 10. And* **Abraham** *stretched forth his hand and took the knife to slay his son. 11. Then the* **angel** *of the* **LORD*** *called to him out of heaven and said, "Abraham. Abraham!" And he said, "Here I am." 12. And He said,* **"Do not lay your hand on the lad! Do not do anything to him!** *For now I know that you* **revere God***, seeing you have* **not** *withheld* **your son, your only son** *from Me." 13. And* **Abraham** *lifted up his eyes and looked,*

*and behind him there was a **ram** caught in a thicket by his horns, and **Abraham** went and took the **ram** and offered it up for a burnt offering **in the place of** his son. 14. And **Abraham** called the name of that place "The **LORD*** **Will See (to it)**" as it is said to this day, "The **LORD*** Will Show Himself on the mountain."*

The preposition Tahat, in verse thirteen translated in the place of his son, has the primary meaning of Under. See *Two Interpretations of the Same Scripture* in *Companion Volume II.*

*Genesis 22:15. And the **angel** of the LORD* called to **Abraham** out of heaven the second time 16. and said, "By Myself I have sworn," says the **LORD***, "For because you have done this thing and have not withheld your son, your only son, 17. that I shall greatly **bless you,** and I shall **multiply** your **seed** as the **stars** of the heaven and as the **sand** on the seashore, (Heb. 6:14; 11:12) and your **seed** will **possess** the **gate** of his enemies, 18. and in your **seed** will all the **nations** of the earth be **blessed** because you have **obeyed** My voice."*

God still honors His promises to Abraham, as we see Him blessing Israel in these times, winning wars, building the economy, and now establishing relations with Arab countries. The Spirit Realm is forever involved with Israel.

Genesis 22:19. *"So* Abraham *returned to his young men and they rose up and went together to* Beer-Sheba *and* Abraham *stayed at* Beer-Sheba.*"*

Where is Isaac? Did only Abraham and the servants return? Abraham went to stay in Beer Sheba, but Sarah lived in Kariat-Arba, which is Hebron, explained in the next passage of Chapter 23 in the Bible.

Jacob Dreams, Seeing the Gate of Heaven

*Genesis 28:10. And **Jacob went out** from **Beer-Sheba** and went toward Haran. 11. And he lighted upon a certain place and tarried there all night, because the sun had set. And he took one of the stones of that place and put it under his head and lay down in that place to sleep. 12. And he dreamed, and there was a **ladder** set up on the earth, and the top of it reached to **heaven** and, behold, the **angels of God** were **ascending** and **descending** on it. 13. And, behold, the **LORD*** stood above it and said, "**I AM the LORD***, the **God of Abraham your father**, and the **God of Isaac**: the **land** on which you are lying, to **you will I give it**, and to **your seed**. 14. And your **seed** will be as the **dust** of the earth and you will break out to the **west**, to the **east**, to the **north**, and to the **south**: (Mic. 2:13) and in you and in your **seed** will* *all the **families** of the earth be **blessed**. 15. And, behold, **I AM** with you and will keep you in all places where you go and will bring you again into this land. I will not leave you until I have done that which I have spoken about to you." 16. And **Jacob** awakened from his sleep and he said, "Surely the **LORD*** is in this place, but I did not know it." 17. And he was in awe and said, "How awesome is this place! This is none other but the **House of God**, and this is the **gate of heaven**."*

What a wonderful Word from the LORD* at the start of Jacob's trip to Seek his Wife! Notice that the Angels Ascended first, then Descended, showing that the Angels were with Jacob on the earth to begin with.

Jacob Told to Return, Doing so with Great Wealth

*Genesis 31.1. And he heard the words of **Laban's** sons, saying, "**Jacob** has taken away all that was our father's, and of that which was our father's he has gotten all this wealth." 2. And **Jacob** beheld the countenance of **Laban** and, behold, it was not toward him as before. 3. And the **LORD*** said to **Jacob**, "**Return** to the land of your fathers and to your kindred, and **I shall be with you**." 4. And **Jacob** sent and called **Rachel** and **Leah** to the field to his flock, 5. and said to them, "I see that your **father's countenance** is **not toward me** as before, but the **God of my father** has been with me. 6. And you know that I have served your father with all my power. 7. And your father has deceived me and changed my wages ten times, but **God** did not allow him to hurt me. 8. If he would say, 'The speckled will be your wages,' then the whole flock bore speckled, and if he would say, 'The ring-streaked will be your pay,' then the whole flock bore ring-streaked. 9. Thus **God** has taken away your father's livestock and given them to me. 10. And it was at the time that the livestock conceived, that I lifted up my eyes and saw in a dream and, behold, the rams which leaped upon the sheep were ring-streaked, speckled, and spotted. 11. And the **angel** of **God** spoke to me in a dream, '**Jacob**!' And I said, 'Here I am.' 12. And he said, 'Lift up your eyes and see, all the rams which leap upon the flock are ring-streaked, speckled, and spotted, for **I have seen all that Laban does to you**. 13. **I AM** the **God of Beit-El**, where you anointed the pillar, where you vowed a vow to Me. Now **arise! Get out** from this land! **Return** to the land of your kindred!'" 14. And **Rachel** and **Leah** answered and said to him, "Is there still any portion or inheritance for us in our father's house? 15. Are we not counted by him as strangers? For he has sold us and has also quite devoured our money. 16. For all the riches which **God** has taken from our father, that is ours, and our children's: now then, whatever **God** has said to you, do."*

First, God shows Jacob how to get the animals to produce the ring-streaked, speckled, and spotted, greatly increasing Jacob's fortune. Then the Family leaves with their eleven sons.

On the way to the Land of his Fathers, Jacob Wrestles with God

Jacob Wrestles

> Genesis 32:25. And **Jacob** *was left alone, and a* **Man** *wrestled with him there until the breaking of the day. 26. And when the* **Man** *saw that He did* **not prevail** *against him, He touched the* **socket** *of his* **hip***, and the* **socket** *of* **Jacob's thigh** *was out of joint as he wrestled with* **Him***. 27. And* **He** *said, "Let* **Me** *go, for the day is breaking." And (***Jacob***) said, "I shall* **not** *let* **You** *go until* **You bless me***." 28. And (the* **Man***) said to him, "What is your name?" And he said, "***Jacob***." 29. And He said,* **"Your name will no longer be called Jacob, but Israel***, for as a* **prince** *you have* **power** *with* **God** *and with* **men***, and you have* **prevailed***." 30. And* **Jacob** *asked and said, "Tell me, I pray You,* **Your name***." And He said, "Why do you ask after* **My name***?" And* **He blessed** *him there. 31. And* **Jacob** *called the name of the place* **Peniel***, for "I have seen* **God** *face to face and my life is preserved." 32. And as he passed over* **Peniel** *the sun rose upon him, and he was limping on account of his hip.*

The Hebrew word in verse twenty-five for **Man, Ish,** could also be translated **Husband**: He is our **Bridegroom**. Jeremiah 3:14 says **He** married **Israel. Jacob,** Yaakov in Hebrew, and **Israel**; both names are related: Yaakov means Follow Close After, to heed (God's will) and **Israel** means **Prevailing with God**. God continues to lead Jacob and his family where He wants them in order to bless them.

From Shechem to Beit-El

> Genesis 35.1. *Then* **God** *said to* **Jacob***, "Arise, go up to* **Beit-El***, and live there and there make an* **altar** *to* **God***, Who* **appeared to you** *when you fled from the face of Esau your brother." 2. Then* **Jacob** *said to his household and to all that were with him, "***Put away the strange gods** *that are among you! And be clean and change your garments. 3. And let us rise and go up to* **Beit-El***, and there I shall make an* **altar** *to* **God***, Who answered me in the day of my distress and was with me in the way which I went." 4. And they gave to* **Jacob** *all the* **strange gods** *which were in their hand and the rings which were in their ears, and* **Jacob** *hid them under the oak which was by* **Shechem***. 5. And they journeyed and the terror of* **God** *was upon the cities that were all around them, and they did not pursue after the sons of* **Jacob***.*

*6. So **Jacob** came to **Luz**, which is in the land of Canaan that is **Beit-El**, he and all the people with him. 7. And he built an altar there and called the place **El Beit-El** because God appeared to him there, when he fled from the face of his brother. 8. And **Deborah**, **Rebeccah's nurse** died, and she was buried below **Beit-El** under an oak, and the name of it was called **Allon-bakhut** (Oak of Weeping).*

The Strange gods were brought with the captives of Shechem who were with the sons of Jacob after Simeon and Levi killed all the men of Shechem. It would have been better to destroy the gods rather than hide them, but at least the gods were not available for the Canaanites who were with Jacob to pray to. The LORD* spoke with each of the Patriarchs of Israel, showing a close relationship with each one; that relationship that He also wants with each of us. None of them was perfect just as none of us is perfect.

The Lord Appears to Jacob and Prophesies to Him

*Genesis 35:9. And **God** appeared to **Jacob** again, when he came out of **Padan-Aram**, and blessed him. 10. And **God** said to him, "Your name is **Jacob**. Your name will **not** be called **Jacob** any more, but your name will be **Israel**: and He called his name **Israel**." 11. And **God** said to him, "**I AM El Shaddai (God Almighty)**! Be fruitful and multiply! A nation and a company of nations will be out from you, and kings will come out of your loins. 12. And I shall give to you the **land** which I gave **Abraham** and **Isaac**, and I shall give the land to **your seed** after you." 13. And **God** went up from him in the place where He talked with him. 14. And **Jacob** set up a pillar in the place where he talked with Him, a pillar of stone, and he poured a drink offering on it and he poured oil on it. 15. And **Jacob** called the name of the place where **God** spoke with him, **Beit-El**.*

This is the second time, Genesis 32:29 the first, the name of Jacob has been changed to Israel, but unlike any other name changes, such as for Abraham and Sarah, the name Jacob is still used often in the Hebrew Text.

Just as God desired and fostered Relationship with Abraham, Isaac, and Jacob, He Seeks Relationship with you and each one of us:

They See the God of Israel

*Exodus 24:9. Then **Moses** and **Aaron**, **Nadab** and **Abihu**, and **seventy** of the **elders of Israel** went up. 10. And **they saw** the **God of Israel** and there was **under His feet** as it were a paved work of **brilliant sapphire** (Ezek.*

*1:26, Rev. 4:2) and as it were the **body of heaven** in its clearness. 11. And He did not lay His hand upon the **nobles of the children of Israel**: they also **saw God**, then they ate and drank.*

All those people actually saw the LORD*! This book is an extensive listing of the ones who had a relationship with the LORD*, but is not an exhaustive listing. As you go through Scripture you will find other examples of experiences with the Spirit Realm which are not listed in this book, so make note of them.

ELOHIM BRINGS THE SPIRIT REALM

Luke 17:20. *And having been asked by the Pharisees when the Kingdom of God is coming He answered them and said,* "**The Kingdom of God does not come by means of, or in company with, close observation,** *21. And will they not say, 'Behold it is here,' 'There it is,' for behold* **the Kingdom of God is within you.**"

The Kingdom of God is here now! The Kingdom of God is within you! You, yourself have the Kingdom now! What we see in the natural is our practice world. The coming world is the Real world, the spirit world. Judgment Day is a spiritual Day in which the Saints are privileged to experience the fulness of the Spirit Realm. The Spirit Realm is not physical, but it is REAL Joshua learned this by staying in the Tent of Meeting which was outside the camp.

Joshua Spends Time with God

Exodus 33:7. *And (Moses) took the tent and pitched it* **outside** *the camp, afar off from the camp and called it the* **tent of meeting***. And it was that everyone who sought the LORD* went out to the* **tent of meeting***, which was* **outside** *the camp. 8. And it was, when Moses went out to the tent that all the people rose up and stood, each man at his tent entrance, and watched Moses until he went into the tent. 9. And it happened, as Moses entered the tent, the* **cloudy pillar descended and stood at the entrance of the tent and He talked with Moses***. 10. And* **all the people saw the cloudy pillar** *stand at the tent entrance, and all the people rose up and worshipped, each man at his tent entrance. 11. And the* **LORD* spoke to Moses face to face***, as a man speaks to his friend. And Moses returned again to the camp, but his servant* **Joshua, the son of Nun, a young man, did not leave the tent.**

That time with the LORD* prepared Joshua for leadership, teaching him to converse with the LORD* so Joshua could always work the LORD*'s plan not Joshua's plan. Joshua paid a penalty each time he failed to check with the LORD* for a battle plan. You too can be in the Presence of the LORD* continuously without the cloudy pillar, just like Joshua.

After Disaster at Ai, Prayer

> Joshua 7:6. *And **Joshua** tore his clothes and fell to the earth on his face in front of the Ark of the LORD* until evening, he and the elders of Israel, and put dust upon their heads. 7. And **Joshua** said, Alas, **Adonai**, **LORD***, why have You even brought this people over the Jordan to deliver us into the hand of the Amorite to destroy us? Would to God we had been content and stayed on the other side of the Jordan! 8. O my Lord, what will I say when Israel has turned their backs before their enemies! 9. For the Canaanites and all the inhabitants of the land will hear of it and will surround us and cut off our name from the earth, and what will You do about Your great name?*

First, Deal with Sin

> Joshua 7:10. *And the **LORD*** said to **Joshua**, **Get yourself up!** Why are you lying like this on your face? 11. **Israel has sinned** and they have also **trespassed My covenant** which I commanded them for they have even taken of the **accursed thing** and have also **stolen** and **denied** also and they have put it even among their own things. 12. Therefore **the children of Israel could not stand before their enemies**, but turned their backs before their enemies because they were accursed. Neither will I be with you any more, unless you destroy the accursed from among you. 13. **Get up! Sanctify the people!** Say, **Sanctify yourselves** against tomorrow! For thus says the **LORD*** God of Israel, There is an **accursed thing** among you. O **Israel**, you cannot stand before your enemies until you take away the **accursed thing** from among you. 14. In the morning therefore you will be brought near according to your tribes and it will be that the tribe which the LORD* takes will come near according to their families, and the family which the LORD* will take will come near by households, and the household which the LORD* will take will come near man by man. 15. And it will be, that **he that is taken with the accursed thing** will be burned with fire, he and all that he has, because he has transgressed the covenant of the LORD*, and because he has committed villainy in Israel.*

Saying the guilty one will be burned with fire means he will be burned in the Spiritual sense, that is he will be killed, but not burned alive or cremated. The burning here is by ritual cleansing, not literal burning, but refers to purging the sin. See Leviticus 20:14. See *Burning* in the One New Man Bible Glossary.

Joshua Does it Again:

Again, Israel Fails to Pray

> Joshua 9:7. *And the men of Israel said to the Hivite, Perhaps you will stay among us, so how will we cut a covenant with you? 8. And they said to Joshua, We are your servants. And **Joshua** said to them, Who are you? And from where have you come? 9. And they said to him, **Your servants have come from a very far country because of the name of the LORD* your God, for we have heard of His fame and all that He did in Egypt,** 10. And all that He did to the two kings of the Amorite, who were beyond the Jordan, to Sihon king of Heshbon and to Og king of Bashan, who was at Ashtarot. 11. Therefore our elders and all the inhabitants of our country spoke to us saying, Take provisions with you for the journey and go to meet them and say to them, **We are your servants**, therefore now cut a covenant with us. 12. This is our bread we took for our provision, hot out of our houses on the day we came out to go to you, but now, look, it is dry and it is moldy, 13. And these wineskins, which we filled, were new and, look, they are torn and these our garments and our sandals have become old because of the very long journey. 14. And the men took of their provisions, but **did not ask counsel at the mouth of the LORD***. 15. And **Joshua** made peace with them and **cut a covenant** with them, to let them live, and the princes of the congregation swore to them.* (2 Sam. 21:1)

Joshua Learns too Late

> Joshua 9:16. *And it happened at the **end of three days after they had cut a covenant with them**, that they heard that **they were their neighbors** and they lived among them. 17. And the children of Israel traveled and came to their cities on the third day. Now their cities were **Gibeon, Chephira, Beeroth, and Kiriat-Jearim**. 18. And the **children of Israel did not strike them, because the princes of the congregation had sworn to them by the LORD* God of Israel**. And the whole congregation murmured against the princes. 19. But all the princes said to the whole congregation, We have sworn to them by the LORD* God of Israel, therefore now **we may not touch them**. 20. We will do this to them, we will let them live, or else wrath will be upon us because of the oath which we swore to them.*

So, Israel was stuck with their oath to accept the Gibeonites. That the Gibeonites had lied to them did not remove Israel's oath. Joshua and all Israel paid a price for doing something major without praying first. No one of us can assume that because of a close walk with God, we automatically know what He would have us do. Each one of must continually walk in repentance and in touch with God.

Sin in the Camp

Exodus 34:29. *And it happened when* **Moses** *came down from Mount Sinai with the* **two tablets of Testimony** *in* **Moses'** *hand, when he came down from the mountain, that* **Moses** *did not know that the* **skin of his face shone** *while he talked with Him. 30. And when Aaron and all the children of Israel saw* **Moses**, *behold, the* **skin of his face shone**, *and they were awed to come near him. 31. And* **Moses** *called to them and Aaron and all the rulers of the congregation returned to him, and* **Moses** *talked with them. 32. And afterward all the children of Israel came near and he gave them in commandment all that the* **LORD*** *had spoken with him in Mount Sinai. 33. And until* **Moses** *had finished speaking with them, he put a veil on his face. 34. But when* **Moses** *went in before the* **LORD*** *to speak with Him, he took the veil off until he came out. And he came out and spoke to the children of Israel that which he was commanded. 35. And the children of Israel saw that the* **skin of Moses' face shone and Moses put the veil on his face again, until he went in to speak with Him.**

Moses was in the Spirit Realm as he spent time with God – and it showed. Then Moses taught the people the full Word that God had written on the tablets, not listed in the summary, which we call The Ten Commandments.

Exodus 35:1. *And* **Moses** *assembled the whole congregation of the children of Israel together and said to them, "These are the words which the LORD* has commanded, that you should do them. 2.* **Six days will work be done**, *but on the* **seventh** *day there will be a* **holy day** *for you, a* **Sabbath** *of rest to the LORD*:* **whoever does work on it will be put to death. 3. You will kindle no fire throughout your habitations on the Sabbath.**"

In those verses Moses gave commandments that were not in the Ten Statements of Exodus Twenty, reinforcing the statement that all the words of Torah were written on both sides of the two tablets.

Mankind occasionally enters the Spiritual. Paul wrote of confirming the Spiritual Heaven:

2 Corinthians 12:1. *It is necessary to boast, even though it doesn't help, but I shall go on to visions and revelations of the Lord. 2. I know a man who was in Messiah more than fourteen years ago, whether in the body I do not know, God knows, or outside the body I do not know, this one was taken away up to the third heaven. 3. And I know such as this man, whether in the body or without the body I do not know, God knows, 4. That **he was taken away into Paradise** and he heard inexpressible words, which are not permissible for a man to speak.*

Heaven is Spiritual, not natural, not physical, but REAL.

The Spiritual occasionally enters the natural.

The LORD* appears to Abram:

Genesis 12:7. *And the* LORD* *appeared to Abram and said, "I shall give this land to your seed."*

Genesis 17.1. *And when Abram was ninety-nine years old, the* LORD* *appeared to Abram, and said to him, "I AM Almighty God! Walk before Me and be innocent.*

Genesis 18.1. *And the* LORD* *appeared to him in the plains of Mamre and he was sitting in the tent door in the heat of the day.*

The LORD* appears to Isaac:

Genesis 26.1. *And there was a famine in the land, besides the first famine that was in the days of Abraham. And Isaac went to Abimelech king of the Philistines to Gerar. 2. And the **LORD*** **appeared to him** and said, "**Do not go down into Egypt. Stay in the land which I shall tell you about**.*

Genesis 26:24. *And the **LORD*** **appeared to him the same night and said, "I AM the God of Abraham your father. Do not be in awe! I AM** with you and **will bless you and multiply your seed for My servant Abraham's sake**."*

The LORD* Appears to Jacob

Genesis 28:10. ***And** Jacob **went out** from Beer-Sheba and went toward Haran. 11. And he lighted upon a certain place and tarried there all night, because the sun had set. And he took one of the stones of that place and put it under his head and lay down in that place to sleep. 12. And he dreamed, and there was a **ladder** set up on the earth, and the top of it reached to heaven and, behold, the **angels** of God were ascending and descending on it. 13.*

And, behold, the **LORD* stood above it and said, "I AM the LORD*, the God of Abraham your father, and the God of Isaac: the land on which you are lying, to you will I give it, and to your seed.**

Genesis 35:9. *And* **God appeared to Jacob again,** *when he came out of Padan-Aram, and blessed him. 10. And God said to him, "Your name is* **Jacob.** *Your name will not be called Jacob any more, but your name will be* **Israel:** *and He called his name* **Israel."** *11. And God said to him, "***I AM El Shaddai (God Almighty)!** *Be fruitful and multiply! A nation and a company of nations will be out from you, and kings will come out of your loins. 12. And I shall give to you the land which I gave Abraham and Isaac, and I shall give the land to your seed after you."*

Moses is Visited by the LORD*

Exodus 3.1. *Now* **Moses** *kept the flock of Jethro, his father-in-law the priest of Midian, and he led the flock to the far side of the wilderness and came to the mountain of God, to Horeb. 2. And the* **angel of the LORD* appeared to him in a flame of fire out of the midst of a bush** *and he looked and, behold, the bush burned with fire, yet the bush was not consumed. (Acts 7:30) 3. And Moses said, "I shall now turn aside and see this great sight, why the bush is not burned." 4. And when the* **LORD* saw that he turned aside to look, God called to him out of the midst of the bush and said, "Moses. Moses!"** *And he said, "Here I am." 5. And He said, "***Do not draw near to here.** *Take off your shoes from your feet, for the place where you are standing is holy ground." (Josh. 5:15) 6. Moreover He said, "***I AM** *the God of your father, the God of Abraham, the God of Isaac, and the God of Jacob." (Matt. 22:32, Acts 3:13) And Moses hid his face, for he was awed to look upon God.*

Exodus 3:14. *And* God said to Moses, "I AM WHO I AM!"

This is Ehyeh Asher Ehyeh, literally "I WILL BE AS I WILL BE."

And He said, "Thus will you say to the children of Israel, I AM has sent me to you.

I AM is literally, I WILL BE. This is a statement that He is now and forever will be the Power, always the same.

Exodus 3:15. *And God said further to Moses, "Thus will you say to the children of Israel, 'The* **LORD* God of your fathers, the God of Abraham, the God of Isaac, and the God of Jacob** *(Acts 3:13) has sent me to you.* **This is My name forever,** *and this is My memorial to all generations.' 16.* **Go!** **Gather the elders of Israel** *together and say to them, 'The* **LORD***

*God, the **LORD*** of your fathers, the **God of Abraham, of Isaac, and of Jacob appeared** to me saying, I have surely visited you and seen what has been done to you in Egypt. 17. And I have said, I shall bring you up out of the **affliction of Egypt** to the land of the Canaanite, the Hittite, the Amorite, the Perizzite, the Hivite, and the Jebusite, to a land flowing with milk and honey.' 18. And they will heed your voice and you will come, you and the elders of Israel, to the king of Egypt and you will say to him, 'The **LORD*** God of the **Hebrews** has met with us and now let us go, we beseech you, three days' journey into the wilderness, so we can sacrifice to the **LORD*** our God.' 19. And I AM sure that the king of Egypt will not let you go, no, not by a mighty hand. 20. And I shall stretch out My hand, and **strike Egypt with all My wonders** which I shall do in the midst of it, and after that he will send you. 21. And I shall give this people favor in the sight of the Egyptians, and it will be that, when you go, you will **not go empty**, 22. But every woman will ask from her neighbor and from anyone who stays in her house, jewels of silver, jewels of gold, and raiment. And you will put them upon your sons and upon your daughters, and you will plunder Egypt."*

Moses is given precise instructions by the LORD* for sending the Hebrew children from Egypt. Later, on the mountain, Moses is given the Torah, including the moral teachings that have been and are still so frequently violated today. All the Plagues brought the Spiritual Realm to Pharaoh and the Egyptian people. The LORD* showed His Power and His love for the Hebrew People.

The LORD* Orders the Tabernacle

Exodus 35:30. *And **Moses** said to the children of Israel, "See, the **LORD*** has called by name **Bezalel** the son of Uri, the son of Hur, of the tribe of Judah, 31. And **He has filled him with the Spirit of God, in wisdom, in understanding, in knowledge, and in all manner of workmanship, 32. And to devise astute works, to work in gold, in silver, and in bronze, 33. And in the cutting of stones, to set them, and in carving of wood, to make any manner of skillful work.***

Bezalel, Aholiab, and others were filled with the Spirit of God to build the Tabernacle, making everything needed; The Tent, the Altars, Lavers, Furnishings, Curtains, and Tools.

The Glory of the LORD* Appears to all the People

Leviticus 9:23. *And Moses and Aaron came in the Tent of Meeting, then went out and blessed the people, and the **glory of the LORD*** **appeared*** *to all the people.* 24. *And a fire came out from before the* **LORD*** *and consumed the burnt offering and the fat on the altar and all the people saw it, and they shouted and fell on their faces.*

This Appearance of the Glory is the culmination of the eight-day installation of Aaron and his sons as the first Priests of Israel! This installation of Priests began with repentance by the Priests, ending with the Fire of the LORD* consuming the offering.

Gideon Called

Judges 6:11. *And an* **angel** *of the* **LORD*** *came and sat under an oak which was in Afrah that belonged to Joash the Abiezrite, and his son* **Gideon** *threshed wheat by the wine press, to hide it from the Midianites.* 12. *And the* **angel** *of the* **LORD*** *appeared to him and said to him, the* **LORD*** *is with you, you mighty man of valor.* 13. *And* **Gideon** *said to him, Oh my lord, if the* **LORD*** *is with us, why then has all this befallen us? And where are all His miracles which our fathers told us about, saying, Did not the* **LORD*** *bring us up from Egypt? But now the* **LORD*** *has forsaken us and delivered us into the hands of the Midianites.* 14. *And the* **LORD*** *looked at him and said, Go in this your might and you will save Israel from the hand of Midian! Have I not sent you?* 15. *And he said to Him, Oh my Lord, With what will I save Israel? See, my family is poor in Manasseh and I am the least in my father's house.* 16. *And the* **LORD*** *said to him, Surely* **I shall be with you and you will strike Midian as one man**. 17. *And he said to Him, If now I have found favor in Your sight, then show me a sign that You are talking with me.* 18. *Now, please! Do not leave from here until I come to You and bring forth my offering and set it before You.*

And He said, **I AM** *staying until you come again.* 19. *And* **Gideon** *went in and made ready a kid and unleavened cakes of an ephah of flour. He put the flesh in a basket and he put the broth in a pot and brought it out to Him under the oak, and presented it.*

So, Gideon, the least in his family among the poor of Manasseh, goes on to defeat the entire Midianite army with 300 unarmed men! Here the Anokhi, the Bold I AM, shows that the LORD* is very deliberate in waiting for the offering, after which He will bring a great miracle to Israel. The LORD* wants you, too, to do something for which you think you are not qualified to do! Say Yes! when He calls you!

Fire from Heaven

> Judges 6:20. *And the **angel of God** said to him, Take the flesh and the unleavened cakes and lay them upon this rock and pour out the broth. And he did so. 21. Then the **angel of the LORD*** put forth the end of the staff that was in his hand and touched the flesh and the unleavened cakes and there **rose up fire out of the rock**, and consumed the flesh and the unleavened cakes. Then the **angel of the LORD*** departed from his sight.*

The Angel caused the fire to rise from the rock, consuming Gideon's offering.

> Judges 6:22. *And when* Gideon *perceived that he was an* angel of the LORD*, *Gideon said, Alas, my Lord,* LORD*! *Because I have seen an* angel of the LORD* *face to face.*

Then the LORD* puts His Spirit on Gideon.

> Judges 6:33. *Then all of Midian and Amalek and the children of the east were gathered together and went over and pitched in the valley of Jezreel. 34. But **the Spirit of the LORD*** came upon Gideon *and he blew a shofar, and **Abiezer** was gathered after him. 35. And he sent messengers throughout all Manasseh who also gathered after him: and he sent messengers to Asher and to Zebulun and to Naphtali and they came up to meet them.*

Abiezer was Gideon's father's clan. Gideon's having the Spirit of the LORD* brings victory over more than 120,000 Midianites by 300 unarmed Israelites! Nothing is too hard for God!

An Angel announces the Coming birth of Samson

> Judges 13:2. *And there was a certain man of Zarah of the family of the Danites, whose name was **Manoah**, and his wife was barren and had not borne. 3. And an **angel** of the **LORD*** appeared to the woman and said to her, Behold now, you are barren and have not borne, but you will conceive and bear a son. 4. Now therefore beware, I pray you, and, **Do not drink wine or strong drink!** And **Do not eat any unclean thing!** 5. For, behold, you will conceive and bear a son and no razor will come on his head, for the child will be a **Nazirite** to God from the womb, and he will begin to deliver Israel out of the hand of the Philistines.*

The vow of a Nazirite is not in way related to the city we now know as Nazareth because the Hebrew name of the city is Natsrat. The root verb of Nazirite, N-Z-R means to dedicate, separate, the source of the name of the vow.

Judges 13:6. *And the woman came and told her husband saying, A **man of God** came to me and his countenance was like the countenance of an **angel of God**, very awesome, but I did not ask him where he was from, neither did he tell me his name. 7. But he said to me, Behold, you will conceive and bear a son and now, **Do not drink wine or strong drink! Do not eat any unclean thing!** For the child will be a **Nazirite** to God from the womb to the day of his death. 8. Then Manoah entreated the LORD* and said, O my Lord, **let the man of God whom you sent come to us again and teach us what we will do with the child** that will be born. 9. And God heard the voice of Manoah and the **angel of God** came to the woman again as she sat in the field, but **Manoah** her husband was not with her. 10. And the woman made haste and ran and told her husband and said to him, Behold, the man who came to me that day has appeared to me.*

Elizabeth is given the same instructions as Manoah's wife when she is carrying John the Immerser over one thousand years later.

Luke 1:13. *And the angel said to him, "Do not fear, Zechariah, because your entreaty has been listened to and your wife **Elizabeth** will bear a son to you and you will call his name **John**. 14. And for you there will be joy and gladness and many will rejoice over his birth. 15. For he will be great before the Lord, and **he should not drink wine or strong drink, and he will be filled with the Holy Spirit while he is still in his mother's womb**,*

Judges 13:11. *And Manoah got up and went after his wife and came to the man and said to him, Are you the man who spoke to my wife? And he said, I am.*

Judges 13:12. *And **Manoah** said, Now let your words come to pass. What will be done with the child and his work? 13. And the **angel** of the **LORD*** said to **Manoah**, Of all that I said to the woman let her beware. 14. She may not eat of anything that comes from the vine. **She will not drink wine or strong drink! She will not eat any unclean thing! She will observe all that I commanded her!** 15. And **Manoah** said to the **angel** of the **LORD***, I pray you, let us detain you until we make ready a kid for you.*

Manoah makes a sacrificial offering to the Angel of the LORD*, as had Gideon earlier, with this Angel going up in the flame to Heaven!

Angel Ascends in the Flame

Judges 13:16. *And the **angel** of the LORD* said to **Manoah**, Though you detain me, I shall not eat of your bread and if you will offer a burnt offering,* *you must offer it to the **LORD***. For **Manoah** did not know that he was an* ***angel*** *of the LORD*. 17. And **Manoah** said to the **angel** of the **LORD***, What is your name, so when your sayings come to pass we can honor you? 18. And the **angel** of the **LORD*** said to him, Why do you ask this about my name, seeing it is **Miracle**? 19. So **Manoah** took a kid with a grain offering and offered it to the **LORD*** on a rock, and the **angel** did wondrously, and **Manoah** and his **wife** looked on. 20. For it happened when the flame went up toward heaven from the altar, that the **angel** of the **LORD*** ascended in the flame of the altar. And **Manoah** and his **wife** looked at it and fell to the ground on their faces.*

The Angel appeared to be a man. His name was Peli, meaning Wonder, Miraculous, Amazing, Marvelous, Astounding.

Isaiah 9:5. *For unto us a child is born, unto us a Son is given, and the government is upon His shoulder, and His name will be called **Wonder**, Counselor, Mighty God, Eternal Father, Prince of Peace. 6. Of the increase of His government and Shalom there will be no end, upon the throne of David and upon His kingdom, to order it, and to establish it with judgment and with acts of loving kindness from now even forevermore. (John 12:34) The zeal of the LORD* of Hosts will perform this.*

This is also Peli, here describing Y'shua!

Judges 13:21. *And the **angel** of the LORD* did not appear any more to **Manoah** and to his wife. Then **Manoah** knew that he was an **angel** of the **LORD***. 22. And **Manoah** said to his wife, We will surely die, because **we have seen God**. 23. But his wife said to him, If the **LORD*** were pleased to kill us, He would not have taken a burnt offering and a grain offering at our hands, neither would He have shown us all these things nor would he have told us such things as these at this time.*

Manoah's wife was correct! It is astonishing that our pure, Holy Heavenly Father would choose to assign Samson with his faults to save Israel, but our Heavenly Father has only imperfect people to use for His assignments. None of us is Perfect.

Samuel is anointed, called to function as a true Prophet!

1 Samuel 3.1. *And the young man* Samuel *ministered to the LORD* before* Eli. *And the word of the LORD* was rare in those days. There was no frequent vision.*

Eli and his sons were not in tune with the LORD* so there was no prophetic input and Israel was beset by enemies. The LORD* had to appoint Samuel to lead Israel to again establish the Word of the LORD* in Israel. Samuel was young, but was not a toddler as some suppose when he was brought to Eli. He would have been at least eleven, but could have been early teens. It was years later, when Samuel was at least thirty that he heard the LORD*. Samuel was sleeping in the Holy Place; a Priest had to be over thirty years old to be in the Holy Place.

> 1 Samuel 3:3. *And the lamp of God had not yet gone out and Samuel was lying down in the* **Temple of the LORD***, where the Ark of God was. 4. The* **LORD*** *called* **Samuel** *and he answered, Here I am. 5. And he ran to* **Eli** *and said, Here I am, for you called me.*

Although called the Temple, this is the Tabernacle.

> 1 Samuel 3:5b. *And he said, I did not call. Lie down again. And he went and lay down. 6. And the* **LORD*** *called yet again,* **Samuel***! And* **Samuel** *got up and went to* **Eli** *and said, Here I am, for you did call me.*

> *And he answered, I did not call, my son. Lie down again.*

The next passage shows that Eli had not taught Samuel about communication with the LORD*.

> 1 Samuel 3:7. *Now* **Samuel** *did not yet know the* **LORD***, neither was the word of the* **LORD*** *yet revealed to him. 8. And the* **LORD*** *called* **Samuel** *again the third time. And he got up and went to* **Eli** *and said, Here I am, for you did call me. And* **Eli** *understood that the* **LORD*** *had called the young man.*

> 1 Samuel 3:9. *Therefore Eli said to* **Samuel***, Go, lie down and it will be, if He calls you, that you will say, Speak,* **LORD***, for Your servant is listening.*

> *So* **Samuel** *went and lay down in his place. 10. And the* **LORD*** **came and stood, and called as at other times, Samuel. Samuel***!*

> *Then* **Samuel** *answered, Speak, for Your servant is listening.*

The LORD* actually came and stood by Samuel, then called Samuel twice to really get his attention.

> 1 Samuel 3:11. *And the* **LORD*** *said to* **Samuel***, Behold,* **I AM** *doing a thing in Israel at which both the ears of everyone who hears will tingle. 12. In that day* **I shall perform against Eli all things which I have spoken concerning his house, from beginning to end***. 13. For I AM has told him that I shall judge his house forever for the iniquity which he knows because his*

*sons made themselves vile, and he did not restrain them. 14. And therefore I have sworn to the house of **Eli** that the **iniquity of Eli's house will not ever be purged with a sacrifice or an offering**.*

That was a hard message for Samuel to have to give for his first prophetic message, but Eli should have been expecting it! After Samuel's judging, David comes on the scene.

2 Samuel has the LORD*'s Army on the Mulberry trees

2 Samuel 14:11. *So they came up to Baal-Perazim and **David** smote them there. Then **David** said, God has broken forth upon my enemies by my hand like the breaking forth of waters, therefore they called the name of that place **Baal-Perazim**.*

David destroys the false gods, as Baal-Perazim means Breaking forth on Baal, the false god of Canaan.

David Burns the False gods

2 Samuel 14:12. *And when they had left their gods there, **David** gave a command and they were **burned** with fire. 13. Then the Philistines yet again spread themselves abroad in the valley. 14. Therefore David **inquired again of God** and God said to him, **Do not go up after them!** Turn away from them and **come upon them by the mulberry trees**. 15. And it will be, when **you hear a sound of marching in the tops of the mulberry trees, then you will go out to battle**, for **God has gone out before you to strike the army of the Philistines**. 16. David therefore did as He commanded him and **they struck the army of the Philistines from Gibeon even to Gezer**. 17. And **David's** reputation went out into all lands and the **LORD*** brought that fear of him upon all the nations.*

God gave David the strategy for victory over the Philistines, establishing David as the leader of Israel, which makes Israel feared!

Unnamed Prophet brings a True Word to Jeroboam

1 Kings 13.1. *And, behold, a **man of God came out of Judah** by the **word of the LORD*** to Beit-El, and **Jeroboam** stood by the altar to burn incense. 2. And he cried against the altar by the word of the LORD* and said, **O altar, altar, thus says the LORD***, Behold, a **child will be born to the house of David, Josiah** by name, and he will offer upon you the priests of the high places who burn incense upon you, and **men's bones will***

*be burned upon you. 3. And he gave a **sign** the same day saying, This is the* ***sign** which the **LORD*** has spoken, Behold, the **altar will be split and the*** ***ashes that are upon it will be poured out.***

The Prophecy concerning Josiah was given about 290 years before Josiah began to reign. The second prophecy, about the altar splitting, came immediately, with the Altar splitting and the ashes pouring out. The Presence of the LORD* was even felt by the apostate king (Jeroboam) who had made the gold calves.

*1 Kings 13:4. And it happened, when king **Jeroboam** heard the saying of the man of God, who had cried against the altar in Beit-El, that **he put*** ***forth his hand from the altar saying, Lay hold of him.** And his **hand**,* *which he put out against him, **dried up**, so that he could not draw it back to himself. 5. The **altar** also **was split and the ashes poured out** from the altar, according to the **sign** which the man of God had given by the word of the **LORD***. 6. And the king answered and said to the man of God, Now,* ***please, plead** with the **presence of the LORD* your God** and pray for me, so my hand can be restored to me again. And the **man of God prayed to the*** ***LORD***, and the **king's hand was restored** to him again and became as it was before. 7. And the king said to the **man of God, Come** home with me and **refresh yourself**, and I shall give a **reward**.*

The Man of God resisted the temptation to go with the king who enticed him with a reward.

*1 Kings 13:8. And the **man of God** said to the king, If you will give me half your house, I shall **not go in with you**, neither will **I eat bread nor drink*** ***water** in this place: 9. For so was it charged to me by the word of the **LORD**** *saying, **Eat no bread, nor drink water, nor return by the same way that*** ***you came.** 10. So he went another way and did not return by the way that he came to **Beit-El**.*

The Unnamed Prophet Failed in the Next Test of His Resolve.

*1 Kings 13:11. Now there lived an **old prophet in Beit-El**; and his sons came and told him all the works that the **man of God** had done that day in* ***Beit-El**: they also told to their father the words which he had spoken to the king. 12. And their father said to them, What way did he go? For his sons had seen which way the **man of God** who had come from Judah went. 13. And he said to his sons, Saddle the donkey for me. So they saddled the donkey for him and he rode on it, 14. And went after the **man of God**, and found him sitting under an oak: and he said to him, Are you the **man of God** who* *came from Judah? And he said, I am. 15. Then he said to him, Come home with me and **eat a meal**.*

The Price of Disobedience

*1 Kings 13:16. And he said, **I may not return with you or go in with you: I will neither eat a meal nor drink water with you in this place**, 17. For it was said to me by the word of the LORD*, You will eat no bread or drink no water there, or turn back to go by the way that you came. 18. He said to him, I am a **prophet** also like you are and an **angel** spoke to me by the **word of the LORD*** saying, **Bring him back** with you to your house, so he can eat bread and drink water. But **he lied** to him. 19. So he went back with him, and ate a meal in his house, and drank water.*

Anyone receiving a prophecy is responsible to discern and witness in the Spirit that the Word is True. People have married, relocated, or changed jobs based on a prophetic Word that was not a Word of God, and paid a price for their error. So, this un-named Prophet who gave such a good Word, paid the highest price for not obeying the LORD*

*1 Kings 13:20. And it happened, as they sat at the table, that the **word of the LORD*** came to the **prophet** who **brought** him back. 21. And he cried to the **man of God** who came from Judah saying, Thus says the **LORD***, Since you have **disobeyed the mouth of the LORD*** and have not kept the commandment which the **LORD* your God** commanded you, 22. But you came back and ate bread and drank water in the place of which the LORD* said to you, **Do not eat a meal or drink any water, or your carcass will not come to your fathers' sepulcher**.*

The old prophet who talked him into coming for a meal, now gave a true Word of the LORD*, telling the man that he had disobeyed the LORD*.

Now the Man of God Finds the Cost of Disobedience:

*1 Kings 13:23. And it was, after he had eaten a meal and after he had drunk, that he saddled the donkey for him, for the **prophet** whom he had brought back. 24. And when he had gone, a **lion** met him on the way and **slew him**, and his corpse was cast in the road and the donkey stood by it. The **lion** also stood by the corpse. 25. And, behold, men passed by and saw the corpse cast in the way and the **lion** standing by the corpse and they came and told in the city where the old prophet lived. 26. And when the prophet who brought him back from the way heard, he said, It is the **man of God*** *who was **disobedient** to the **word of the LORD***, therefore the **LORD*** has delivered him to the **lion**, which has torn him and slain him according to the word of the LORD*, which He spoke to him. 27. And he spoke to his sons saying, Saddle the donkey for me. And they saddled it. 28. And he went and found his **corpse** cast on the road and the **donkey** and the **lion** standing by the **corpse**. The **lion** had not eaten the corpse or torn the donkey. 29. And the prophet took the **corpse** of the **man of God** and laid it on the donkey and brought it back, and the **old prophet** came to the city to mourn and to bury him. 30. And he laid his **corpse** in his own grave and they mourned over him saying, **Alas, my brother!***

The Final Words of the Old Prophet

*1 Kings 13:31. And it was, after he had buried him, that he spoke to his sons saying, When I am dead, then **bury me in the sepulcher where the man of God** is buried. Lay my bones beside his bones, 32. For **the saying will surely come to pass which he cried by the word of the LORD* against the altar in Beit-El and against all the houses of the high places which are in the cities of Samaria.***

The Old Prophet had apparently been used by the LORD* to test the Unnamed Prophet.

The LORD* Appears to Solomon:

1 Kings 3:5. In Gibeon the LORD **appeared to Solomon** in a dream by night and **God** said, Ask what I shall give you. 6. And **Solomon** said, You have shown great loving kindness to Your servant **David** my father, according as he walked before You in truth and in acts of loving kindness and in uprightness of heart with You, and You have kept this great loving kindness for him, that You have given him a son to sit on his throne, as it is this day. 7. And now, **LORD*** my **God**, You have made Your servant king instead of **David** my father and I am but a **little lad**:*

Solomon was seventeen when he became king, being asked by the LORD* what Solomon wants; his answer pleases the LORD*.

1 Kings 3:7b I do not know how to go out or come in. 8. And Your servant is in the midst of Your people whom You have chosen, a great people, that cannot be numbered or counted for multitude. 9. Therefore give Your servant an understanding heart to judge Your people, so I can discern between good and bad, for who is able to judge this Your so great a people? 10. And the *speech was **pleasing in the eyes of Adonai**, that **Solomon** had asked this thing. 11. And **God** said to him,*

*Because you have asked this thing and have **not** asked **long life** for yourself. Neither have you asked **riches** for yourself, nor have you asked the **life of your enemies**, but have asked for yourself **understanding to discern judgment**. 12. Behold, I have done according to your words. See, I have given you a wise and an understanding heart, so that there was no one like you before you, neither after you will any arise like you. 13. And **I have also given you that which you have not asked**, both **riches** and **honor**, so that there will not be any among the kings like you all your days. 14. And **if you will walk in My Ways, to keep My statutes and My commandments**, as your father **David** walked, then **I shall lengthen your days**.*

Solomon did NOT always walk in the Ways of the LORD*, but fell away to the gods of his foreign wives, dying at the age of fifty-seven.

The LORD* appears to Solomon a Second Time:

*1 Kings 9.1. And it was, when **Solomon** had finished the building of the **House of the LORD*** and the king's house, and all **Solomon's** desire which he was pleased to do, 2. That the **LORD*** appeared to **Solomon** the second time, as He had appeared to him at **Gibeon**.*

Gibeon was the location of the Tabernacle at that time. When Solomon's Temple was completed, the Tabernacle was carried to Jerusalem, then stored in the First Temple. The first half of Solomon's reign was Godly, but after that his faith faded quickly and precipitously.

1 Kings 9:3. And the LORD said to him, **I have heard your prayer and your supplication that you have made before Me**. I have **sanctified this House**, which you have built, to put **My name there forever** and **My eyes and My heart will be there perpetually**. 4. And if you will walk before Me, as David your father walked, in integrity of heart and in uprightness, to do according to all that I have commanded you, and will keep My statutes and My judgments, 5. Then **I shall establish the throne of your kingdom over Israel forever**, as I promised David your father saying, There will not fail for you to have a man on the throne of Israel. 6. But **if you will at all turn from following Me**, you or your children, and will **not keep My commandments and My statutes** which I have set before you, but go and serve other gods and worship them, 7. Then I will **cut off Israel from the land** which I have given them, and this House, which I have sanctified* *for My name, I shall cast out of My sight and Israel will be a proverb and a byword among all peoples. 8. And at this House, which is high, everyone who passes by it will be astonished and will hiss and they will say, Why has the LORD* done thus to this land and to this House? 9. And they will answer, **Because they forsook the LORD* their God**, Who brought their fathers out of the land of Egypt and have taken hold of other gods and have worshipped them and served them: therefore the LORD* has brought all this evil upon them.*

Of course, Solomon did not keep his end of this bargain; by following his flesh, marrying foreign wives, and making altars to their foreign gods, thereby guaranteeing Israel's Captivity and Exile. Those sins kept Solomon from living the long-life God had promised him at the beginning of his reign.

Elijah Calls Down Fire

*1 Kings 18:25. And **Elijah** said to the **prophets of Baal**, Choose for yourselves one bull and dress it first, for you are many. Then call on the name of your **gods**, but put **no fire** under it. 26. And they took the bull which was given them and they dressed it and called on the name of **Baal** from morning even until noon saying, O **Baal**, hear us. But there was **no voice**, nor any that answered. And they leaped about the altar which was made. 27. And it was at noon that Elijah mocked them and said, Shout! For he is a **god**. Either he is talking, or he is relieving himself, or he is on a journey, or perhaps he is sleeping and must be awakened. 28. And they cried aloud and cut themselves as was their custom with knives and lancets until the blood gushed out of them. 29. And it happened when midday was past, and they prophesied until the **time of the offering of the (afternoon) sacrifice**, that there was neither voice, nor any to answer, nor any attention.*

It was about 3:00 PM when the prophets of Baal gave up, after starting in the morning hours! Six hours of calling to Baalim were to no avail. Then Elijah rebuilt the Altar of the LORD* with twelve stones representing the Tribes of Israel.

*1 Kings 18:30. And **Elijah** said to all the people, Come near to me. And all the people came near to him. And he repaired the **altar** of the **LORD*** that was broken down. 31. And **Elijah** took **twelve stones**, according to the number of the **tribes of the sons of Jacob**, to whom the word of the **LORD*** came saying, **Israel** will be your name. 32. And he built an **altar** with the stones in the **name** of the **LORD***, and he made a **trench** around the **altar**, as great as would hold **two measures** of seed. 33. And he put the wood in order and cut the bull in pieces and laid it on the wood 34. and he said, Fill* *four jars with **water** and let them pour it on the **burnt offering** and on the **wood**. And he said, Do it the **second time**. And they did it the **second time**. And he said, Do it the **third time**. And they did it the **third time**. 35. And the **water** ran over the **altar**, and he also filled the **trench** with **water**.*

After the pagans fail to get any fire going, Elijah has three and a half gallons of water poured on his offering, then fills the trench with water.

The Fire of the LORD* Confirms Elijah

1 Kings 18:36. *And it was at the **time** of the **afternoon burnt offering** that **Elijah** the prophet came near and said, **LORD* God of Abraham, Isaac, and of Israel**, let it be known this day that **You** are **God in Israel**, and that I am **Your servant** and I have done all these things at Your word. 37. Answer me, **LORD***. Answer me, so this people can know that **You** are the **LORD* God**, and You have **turned their heart back** again. 38. Then the **fire** of the **LORD*** fell and consumed the **burnt sacrifice**, the **wood**, the **stones**, the **dust**, and licked up the **water** that was in the **trench**.* (Rev. 13:13)

Elijah's call brought instant Fire! Not just the Fire to consume the offering – his fire consumed the Altar, the Stones, and the Water! There was nothing left!

*1 Kings 18:39. And when all the people saw it, they fell on their faces, and they said, The **LORD***, He is the **God**. The **LORD***, He is the **God**.*

'The God' means He is the Only God!

Elijah Orders the People to Catch the Prophets of Baal

1 Kings 18:40. *And* Elijah *said to them,* Catch *the* prophets of Baal*! Do not let one of them escape! And they took them and* Elijah *brought them down to the brook Kishon and* slew *them there.*

The Prophets of Baal got their Just Desserts!

Jezebel Threatens Elijah, Making him Escape to Mount Sinai

1 Kings 19:3. *And when he saw that, he got up and went for his life and came to **Beer-Sheba**, which belongs to Judah, and left his servant there. 4. But he himself went a **day's journey** into the **wilderness** and came and sat down under a juniper tree, and he **requested for himself** that he might **die** and said, It is enough! Now, LORD*, take away my life, for I am not better than my fathers.*

Elijah followed his extraordinary victory with the Fire, by running away in despair! But God took care of him when Elijah lost hope! That was an exceptionally long trip, hundreds of miles through desert and mountains.

> 1 Kings 19:5. *And as he lay and slept under a juniper tree, behold, then an **angel** touched him and said to him, Arise! Eat! 6. And he looked and, behold, there was a **cake** baked on the coals and a **cruse** of **water** at his head. And he ate and drank and laid down again. 7. And the **angel** of the **LORD***came again the second time and touched him and said, **Arise! Eat!** The journey is too great for you. 8. So he got up and **ate** and **drank**, and went in the strength of that **meal forty days** and **forty nights** to **Horeb**, the **mountain of God**.*

The Angel gave Elijah anointed food and water that carried Elijah for forty days of rigorous travel,

1 Kings 19:9. *And he came to a cave there and stayed there and, behold, the word of the* LORD* *came to him and He said to him, What are you doing here,* Elijah?

> 1 Kings 19:10. *And he said, I have been very zealous for the **LORD*** **God of Hosts** *for the children of Israel have forsaken Your covenant, thrown down Your altars, and slain Your prophets with the sword. And **only I** am left and they seek my life, to take it away.* (Rom. 11:3)

Even with the support from the Angel, Elijah still feels sorry for himself, thinking he is the only Godly man remaining, but the LORD* still supports him.

Voice of the Lord

> 1 Kings 19:11. *And **He** said, **Go out** and stand on the mountain before the **LORD***. *And, look, the **LORD*** passed by, and a great and strong **wind** tore the mountains and broke the rocks in pieces before the **LORD***, *but the **LORD*** was **not** in the **wind**. And after the wind an **earthquake**, but the **LORD*** was **not** in the **earthquake**. 12. And after the **earthquake** a **fire**, but the **LORD*** was **not** in the **fire**. And after the **fire** a **still small voice**. 13. And it was so, when **Elijah** heard, that he wrapped his face in his **mantle** and went out and stood in the entrance of the cave. And, behold, a **voice** came to him and said, What are you doing here, **Elijah**?*

Elijah's Mantle is his Prayer Shawl!

> 1 Kings 19:14. *And he said, I have been very **zealous** for the **LORD*** **God of Hosts** because the children of Israel have forsaken Your covenant, thrown*

*down Your altars, and slain Your prophets with the sword. And **only I** am left, and they are seeking to take my life.* (Rom. 11:3)

Elijah even after being fed and given water, then hearing the voice of the LORD* is still feeling sorry for himself, saying Only I am left. The LORD* then gives Elijah a new assignment.

1 Kings 19:15. *And the **LORD*** said to him, Go! **Return** on your way to the wilderness of **Damascus**, and when you come, anoint **Hazael** to be **king** over **Syria**. 16. And **you** will anoint **Jehu** the son of Nimshi **king over Israel**.*

The LORD* has more assignments for him, but takes Elijah to Heaven before Elijah can complete them, to anoint Hazael king of Syria or Jehu king of Israel; so, Elisha gets to complete the tasks, ordering another prophet to anoint Hazael.

Elijah Calls Down Fire two more Times

2 Kings 1:9. *Then the king sent to him a captain of fifty with his fifty. And he went up to him and, behold, he was sitting on the top of a hill. And he spoke to him, You! Man of God, the king has said, Come down! 10. And Elijah answered and said to the captain of fifty, If I am a man of God, then let **fire come down from heaven and consume you and your fifty**. And **fire** from heaven came down and **consumed him and his fifty**.* (Rev. 11:5; 20:9)

Elijah Calls Down Fire a Third Time

2 Kings 1:11. *And again he sent another captain of fifty with his fifty to him. And he answered and said to him, O man of God, thus has the king said, Come down quickly! 12. And **Elijah** answered and said to them, If I am a man of God, let **fire** come down from heaven and consume you and your fifty. And the **fire of God came down** from heaven and **consumed him and his fifty**.*

Adding these two, Elijah called down fire from Heaven a total of Three times!

Elisha Appointed by the LORD*

1 Kings 19:16b *And you will anoint **Elisha** the son of Shafat from Abel Meholah to be **prophet** in your place. 17. And it will be, **Jehu** will slay the one who escapes the sword of **Hazael** and **Elisha** will slay the one who escapes from the sword of **Jehu**. 18. Yet I have **seven thousand** left in **Israel**, all the knees which have not **bowed to Baal**, and every mouth which has **not kissed** him.* (Rom. 11:4)

The mouth that Praises and Worships Baal, Kisses Baal. Elisha goes on to receive double Elijah's anointing! Those who today praise and worship Evil things, are actually Kissing Baal!

Elisha Sees a Supernatural Ascension:

> 2 Kings 2:7. *And fifty men of the sons of the prophets went and stood opposite them afar off, and they two stood by the Jordan. 8. And **Elijah** took his mantle, (prayer shawl), and wrapped it together and struck the waters and they were divided here and there, so that the two went over on dry ground. 9. And it was when they had gone over, that **Elijah** said to **Elisha**, Ask what I shall do for you, before I am taken away from you. And **Elisha** said, I pray you, let a **double portion** of your spirit be upon me. 10. And he said, You have asked a hard thing, but if you see me when I am taken from you, it will be so for you, but if not, it will not be so. 11. And it was, as they still went on and talked; that, behold, a **chariot of fire and horses of fire appeared and divided them both**, and **Elijah** went up by a **whirlwind into heaven**. (Rev. 11:12) 12. And **Elisha** saw it and he cried, My father, My father! The chariot of Israel and its horsemen! Then he saw him no more and he took hold of his own clothes and tore them in two pieces. 13. He also took up the **mantle (prayer shawl)** of **Elijah** that fell from him and went back and stood by the bank of the Jordan. 14. And he took the **mantle of Elijah** that fell from him and **struck** the waters and said, **Where is the LORD* God of Elijah?** And when he also had **struck** the waters, they parted here and there and **Elisha** went over.*

Elisha does get double Elijah's anointing! When he returns to the Jordan River, he strikes the river with his new prayer shawl – Elijah's prayer shawl – and the river splits, leaving dry ground for Elisha.

Elisha Sees in the Spirit, The Chariot of Fire was Spiritual, not physical, yet Elisha was able to witness entire event when the Physical body of Elijah was transformed into his Spiritual Body as Elijah was taken to Heaven.

At that, even Elisha was not always in contact with the LORD*!

> 2 Kings 4:27. *And when she came to the man of God at the hill, she caught him by his feet, but **Gehazi** came near to push her away. And the man of God said, Let her alone, for her soul is vexed within her and the **LORD* has hidden it from me and has not told me**. 28. Then she said, Did I desire a son from my lord? Did I not say, Do not deceive me? 29. Then he said to **Gehazi**, Gird up your loins and take my staff in your hand and go your way.*

*If you meet anyone, do not greet him, and if anyone greets you, do not answer him, and lay my staff on the face of the young man. 30. And the mother of the young man said, As the **LORD*** lives and as your soul lives, I shall not leave you. And he got up and followed her.*

This not seeing in the Spirit is unusual for Elisha.

Elisha, Seeing into the Spirit Realm, Sees Gehazi Taking Gifts

2 Kings 5:22. *And he (**Gehazi**) said, All is well. My master has sent me saying, Behold, even now there are coming to me two young men of the sons of the prophets from Mount Ephraim. Please give them a talent of silver, and two changes of garments.*

Gehazi flat out lies to Naaman, asking for seventy-five pounds of silver – about $30,000 in today's prices – a not insignificant gift. Naaman offers $60,000, which Gahazi accepts, not knowing that Elisha is watching the entire scene. Nothing is hidden from God and His Agent Elisha!

2 Kings 5:23. *And **Naaman** said, Be content, take **two talents**. And he urged him and bound **two talents** of silver in two bags, with two changes of garments and laid them upon two of his young men, and they bore them before him. 24. And. When he came to the hill, he took them from their hand and deposited them in the house, then he let the men go and they departed.*

Gehazi chose to put his loot in a place that he knew Elisha could not see. He never gave a thought to Elisha's ability to see into the Spirit Realm.

2 Kings 5:25. *Then he came and stood before his master. And* Elisha *said to him, Where were you,* Gehazi? *And he said, Your servant went neither here nor there.*

Another Bold-Face lie by Gehazi but this one is answered quickly by Elisha!

2 Kings 5:26. *And he said to him, Was not my heart with you, when the man turned from his carriage to meet you? Is it a time to take money and to take garments, olive trees, vineyards, sheep, oxen, men servants, and maid servants? 27. Therefore the **leprosy of Naaman** will **cling to you** and to your seed forever. And he went out from his presence a **leper** as white as snow.*

Leprosy was high price to pay for Gehazi's ill-gotten money!

Elisha sees into the Spirit Realm at Dothan:

2 Kings 6:13. *And he (king of Syria) said, Go and spy where he is so I can send and fetch him. And he was told saying, Behold, he is in* **Dothan.** *14. Therefore he sent horses and chariots and a great army there, and they came by night and surrounded the city. 15. And when the* **young man** *of the man of God had risen early and gone out, behold, an* **army surrounded the city with horses and chariots.** *And his* **young man** *said to him, Alas, my master! What will we do?*

The young man was Elisha's servant who had replaced Gehazi. This is a really scary situation in the natural! Elisha is calm as can be because he sees in the Spirit Realm! Elisha knows God is in control. We need that assurance too.

2 Kings 6:16. *And he answered,* **Do not be in awe!** *For* **those who are with us are more than those with them.** *17. And* **Elisha prayed** *and said,* **LORD***, now please,* **open his eyes so he can see.** *And the* **LORD*** *opened the eyes of the young man, and he saw and, there! The* **mountain was full of horses and chariots of fire** *all around* **Elisha.** *18. And when they came down to him,* **Elisha** *prayed to the* **LORD*** *and said, Strike this* **heathen people,** *I pray you, with* **blindness!** *And He struck them with* **blindness** *according to the word of* **Elisha.** *19. And* **Elisha** *said to them, This is not the way, neither is this the city. Follow me, and I shall bring you to the man whom you seek. And* **he led them to Samaria.**

Samaria was the capital of Israel, where the Israeli army was headquartered.

2 Kings 6:20. *And it was, when they had come into* **Samaria** *that* **Elisha** *said, LORD*,* **open the eyes of these men so they can see.** *And the* **LORD*** **opened their eyes and they saw and, behold, they were in the midst of Samaria.** *21. And the king of Israel said to* **Elisha** *when he saw them, My father, will I strike them? Will I strike them, my father?*

Elisha commands mercy; feed the troops!

2 Kings 6:22. *And he answered,* **You will not strike them.** *Would you strike those whom you have taken captive with your sword and with your bow?* **Set bread and water before them,** *so they can eat and drink and go to their master. 23. And* **he prepared great provision for them, and when they had eaten and drunk he sent them away and they went to their master.** *So the bands of* **Syria no longer came into the land of Israel.**

To set bread and water before them meant to be hospitable, so they had great provision, far more than bread and water!

Isaiah sees into the Spirit Realm:

Isaiah 6.1. *In the year that king Uzziah died* I saw the Lord sitting on a throne, high and lifted up, *(Rev. 4:2,9; 7:10) and* His train filled the palace.

The word translated palace is 'haihal' and can be translated either Temple or Palace. If the throne is in the heavenly Temple, this would be in the Holy of Holies on the Ark of the Covenant, where no one could see it except the High Priest on Yom Kippur. There is no throne or throne room in the Tabernacle, the First Temple, the Second Temple, or Ezekiel's Third Temple. Uzziah is another name for Azariah, 2 Kings 15:1.

> Isaiah 6:2. *Above Him stood the seraphim: each one had six wings, with two he covered his face, with two he covered his feet, and with two he flew. 3. And one cried to another and said,* **Holy! Holy! Holy is the LORD* of Hosts!** *(Rev. 4:8) The whole earth is full of His* **glory***! 4. And the posts of the door moved at the voice of the one who cried, and the house was filled with smoke. (Rev. 15:8)*

Isaiah sees and hears the Seraphim. He might have been surprised by this vision as he says that he is a man of unclean lips – not worthy of this Spiritual sight.

> Isaiah 6:5. *Then I said, Woe is me! For I am undone because I am a man of* **unclean lips** *and I live in the* **midst** *of a people of* **unclean lips***, for my* **eyes** *have* **seen** *the* **King***, the* **LORD* of Hosts***. 6. Then one of the seraphim flew to me, having a live coal in his hand, which he had taken with the tongs from off the altar: 7. and he laid it on my mouth and said, Lo, this has touched* **your lips** *and* **your iniquity** *is* **taken away***, and your* **sin** *is* **purged***.*

God cleansed Isaiah so he could report this vision!

Isaiah 6:8. *Also I heard the voice of the Lord saying, Whom shall I send, and who will go for us?*

> *Then I said,* Here I am! Send me!

Isaiah is eager for his new assignment.

Micaiah Sees onto the Spirit Realm

> 1 Kings 22:19. *And he said, Therefore listen to the word of the LORD*!* **I saw the LORD* sitting on His throne** *and all the host of heaven standing by Him on His right hand and on His left. (Rev. 4:2,9; 7:10) 20. And the* **LORD*** *said, Who will persuade Ahab, so he will go up and fall at Ramot*

Gilead? And one said in this manner and another said in that manner. 21. And there came forth a spirit and stood before the LORD and said, I shall persuade him. And the LORD* said to him, How? 22. And he said, <u>I shall go out and I shall be a lying spirit in the mouth of all his prophets. And He said, You will persuade him and prevail also. Go and do so. 23. Now therefore, behold, the LORD* has put a **lying spirit** in the mouth of all these your prophets and the LORD* has spoken evil concerning you.</u>*

When Micaiah saw the LORD* sitting on His throne he was authorized to put a lying spirit in the mouth of each prophet who prophesied to Ahab, thus, the Spirit Realm brought God's plan for Ahab.

Shadrach, Meshach, and Abednego are transposed into their Spiritual Bodies:

*Daniel 3:12. There are certain Jews whom you have set over the affairs of the province of Babylon; **Shadrach, Meshach, and Abednego**. These men, O king, have not paid attention to you: **they do not serve your gods or worship the golden image which you have set up.***

Other Leaders were jealous of the status of Shadrach, Meshach, and Abednego so they found a way to get rid of them, by reporting that they ignored the worship of the false gods; but that attempt failed miserably.

*Daniel 3:13. Then Nebuchadnezzar in rage and fury commanded to bring **Shadrach, Meshach, and Abednego**. Then they brought these men before the king. 14. Nebuchadnezzar spoke and said to them, Is it true, O **Shadrach, Meshach, and Abednego**, that you do **not serve my gods** or **worship the golden image** which I have set up? 15. Now if you are ready that at what time you hear the sound of the horn, flute, harp, sambuke, psaltery, and double pipe, and all kinds of music, you fall down and worship the image which I have made, well, but **if you do not worship, you will be cast the same hour into the midst of a burning fiery furnace**, and who is the God that will deliver you out of my hands?*

The threat of the painful punishment of being burned to death does not deter the three from their devotion to the LORD*.

*Daniel 3:16. **Shadrach, Meshach, and Abednego** answered and said to king Nebuchadnezzar, we have no need to answer you in this matter. 17. Behold, **our God Whom we serve is able to deliver us from the burning fiery furnace and He will deliver us out of your hand, O king**. 18. But if not, be it known to you, O king, that we will **not serve your gods** or **worship the golden image** which you have set up.*

They stand resolute!

> Daniel 3:19. *Then Nebuchadnezzar was full of fury and the form of his visage was changed against* **Shadrach, Meshach, and Abednego***; therefore he spoke and commanded that they should* **heat the furnace seven times more than it would normally be heated***. 20. And he commanded the mightiest men that were in his army to bind* **Shadrach, Meshach, and Abednego***, and to cast them into the burning fiery furnace. 21. Then these men were* **bound** *in their* **cloaks***, their tunics, their turbans, and their other garments, and* **were cast into the midst of the burning fiery furnace***. 22. Therefore because the king's commandment was urgent and the furnace exceedingly hot, the flame of the fire slew those men who took up* **Shadrach, Meshach, and Abednego***. 23. And these three men,* **Shadrach, Meshach, and Abednego***, fell down bound into the midst of the burning fiery furnace.*

Their Cloaks were their Prayer Shawls. The three have been transformed and are now heat-resistant, wrapped in their Prayer Shawls! Their Prayer Shawls provided extra protection, a sign to all, including the king, satraps, governors, captains, and especially the King of the Universe Who did protect those who worship Him and only Him.

> Daniel 3:24. *Then* **Nebuchadnezzar** *the king was alarmed and stood up in haste, spoke and said to his counsellors, Did we* **not cast three men** *bound into the midst of the fire? They answered and said to the king,* **True***, O king.*

The king is startled!

Daniel 3:25. *He answered and said, Lo, I see* four men loose, *walking in the midst of the* fire *and they have* no hurt! *And the form of the* fourth *is like a* Son of God.

God has sent a Comforter to accompany Shadrach, Meshach, and Abednego.

> Daniel 3:26. *Then Nebuchadnezzar came near to the door of the burning fiery furnace and spoke, and said,* **Shadrach, Meshach, and Abednego***, you servants of the* **Most High God***, come forth, and come here. Then* **Shadrach, Meshach, and Abednego***, came out of the midst of the* **fire***. 27. The satraps, governors and captains and the king's counsellors, being gathered together, saw these men,* **upon whose bodies the fire had no power***, nor was the hair of their head* **singed***, neither were their* **cloaks changed***, nor the* **smell of fire** *had passed on them. 28. Nebuchadnezzar spoke and said,* **Blessed be the God of Shadrach, Meshach, and Abednego***, Who has sent* **His angel** *and* **delivered His servants who trusted in Him** *and have changed the king's word and yielded their bodies, so they could* **not serve** *or* **worship**

*any god except their own God. 29. Therefore I make a decree, That **every** **people, nation, and language that speaks anything amiss against the** **God of Shadrack, Meshach, and Abednego, will be cut in pieces and** **their houses will be made a dunghill because there is no other God that** **can deliver after this sort**.*

After the miracle, the three return to their physical bodies! They had been instantly transformed into their Spiritual Bodies, then as they came out of the Fire they were instantly transformed back to their natural physical bodies. Next Daniel gets a personal miracle to save his life.

Daniel 6:14. *Then they answered and said before the king, That **Daniel**, who is of the children of the captivity of Judah, does **not regard you, O king**, or the interdict that you have signed, but makes his **petition (Prayer)** **three times a day**. 15. Then the king, when he heard these words, was sore displeased with himself, and set his heart on **Daniel** to deliver him and he labored till the going down of the sun to deliver him. 16. Then these men assembled to the king and said to the king, Know, O king, that the law of the Medes and Persians is, That no interdict or statute which the king establishes may be changed. 17. Then the king commanded, and they brought **Daniel** and cast him into the den of **lions**. Now the king spoke and said to **Daniel**, Your **God**, Whom you serve continually, will **Himself** deliver you. 18. And a stone was brought and laid upon the mouth of the den and the king sealed it with his own signet, and with the signet of his lords, so the purpose could not be changed concerning **Daniel**.*

The earthly king could not help **Daniel** but the real **King** did come to his aid, shutting the mouths of the **Lions!**

Daniel 6:19. *Then the **king** went to his palace, and passed the night fasting, neither were instruments of music brought before him and his sleep went from him. 20. Then the **king** rose very early in the morning and went in haste to the den of **lions**. 21. And when he came to the den, he cried with a lamentable voice to **Daniel**: the **king** spoke and said to **Daniel**, O **Daniel**, servant of the **Living God**, is your **God**, Whom you serve continually, able to deliver you from the lions?*

The earthly **king** knows the power of **God**, but still is hesitant to acknowledge the **Living God** as the **Only God**.

Daniel 6:22. *Then **Daniel** said to the **king**, O **king**, live forever! 23. My* ***God** has sent His **angel** and has **shut the lions' mouths**, so they have not* *hurt me: forasmuch as innocence was found in me before Him and also before you, O **king**, I have done no hurt. 24. Then the king was exceeding glad for him and commanded that they should take **Daniel** up out of the den. So **Daniel** was taken up out of the den and no manner of hurt was found on him, because he believed in his **God**. 25. And the king commanded and they brought those **men** who had **accused Daniel** and they cast them into the **den of lions**, them, their children and their wives, and the lions had the mastery of them, and broke all their bones in pieces before they came to the bottom of the den.*

The Lions made short work of those who accused Daniel, showing that it does not pay to attack the LORD*'s anointed. Psalm 105:15. Do not touch My anointed! Do not harm My prophets! God showed what He could do to those who attack His Anointed!

The Earth was Created in the Spiritual

Genesis 1:1. ***In (the) beginning*** *God created the heavens and the earth. 2. And the earth was **totally empty** (devoid of all life) (Jer. 4:23) (both **animal and plant**); and darkness was upon the face of the deep. And the **Spirit** of God hovered, **brooded**, over the face of the waters.*

The Earth Began in the Spirit Realm! While the first verse is generally translated in The beginning, the literal is in A beginning. The expression "devoid of all life" is the translation of Hebrew synonyms meaning empty, making the Hebrew superlative, that absolutely nothing resembling life in any form was upon the Earth. The Spirit of God brooding over the face of the waters expresses a mother's concern – appropriate because the Hebrew Rua<u>h</u> for Spirit is a feminine noun! Many think of the Holy Spirit as masculine because of early English translations having been made from the Latin text, in which the Holy Spirit is masculine; never corrected in thousands of translations, the translators just continuing the error by tradition.

Genesis 1:3. *And God said, **"Light, Be!"** And there was **light**. 4. And God saw the **light**, that it was good, and God divided the **light** from the **darkness**. 5. And God called the **light Day**, and the **darkness** He called **Night**. And there was evening and there was morning, day one.*

This, too, is in the Spirit Realm. God spoke, commanding creation; and the world and the heavens were created. The Light was from the Glory of God because the sun came later! Light and Darkness were created, with Light being called Good and being separated from Darkness. Light is Good; Darkness represents Evil!

Isaiah 5:20. *Woe to those who call* bad, good *and* good, bad, *who put* darkness for light *and* light for darkness, *who put bitter for sweet and sweet for bitter!*

Isaiah 60.1. *Arise, and give* **Light***! For your* **Light** *has come, and the* **Glory of the LORD*** *has shone* **(like the sun)** *upon you. 2. For, behold, the darkness will cover the earth and gross darkness the people, but the* **LORD*** *will* **rise** **(like the sun)** *upon you, and His glory will be seen upon you. (Rev. 21:11) 3. And nations will come to your* **Light***, and kings to the brightness of your rising* **(like the sun)***.* (Rev. 21:24)

The words in parentheses, like the sun are added because the word translated Rise is only used for the Rising of the Sun!

John 3:19. *Now the judgment is this, that the* **Light** *has come into the world and people loved the* **darkness** *rather than the* **Light** *(John 1:5): for their works were evil. 20. For everyone doing wicked things hates the* **Light** *and does not come to the* **Light***, so that his deeds would not be exposed. 21. But the one who does truth comes to the* **Light***, so that his works would be revealed because they were worked through God."*

The comparison of Light for Good and Darkness for Bad or Evil is used well over one hundred times in Scripture.

The Coming of the LORD* is Spiritual:

Revelation 1:7. "Behold He is coming with the clouds," (Dan. 7:13)

"and every eye will see Him

even they who had pierced Him,

and all the tribes of the earth will mourn on account of Him."

(Zech. 12:10,12)

This is a Spiritual view; every eye on earth will see Him at the same moment, which is impossible physically, but not in the Spirit!

Zechariah 14:1. *Behold, the* **Day of the LORD*** *is coming and booty from you will be divided in your presence. 2. For I shall gather all the nations against Jerusalem in battle and the city will be taken and the houses rifled and the women ravished, and* **half the city will go into captivity** *but the* **rest of the people will not be cut off from the city***. 3. Then the* **LORD*** *will go forth and fight against those nations, like when He fought in the day of battle, 4. and* **His feet** *will stand in that* **Day** *upon the* **Mount of Olives,** *which is before Jerusalem on the east, and the **Mount of Olives** will split in the middle toward the east and toward the west and there will be a very great valley, and half of the mountain will remove toward the north and half of it toward the south.* (Acts 1:11)

His Feet in the Hebrew text refers to the LORD* Who is One with Y'shua. This means one pair of feet steps on the Mount of Olives and the two, the LORD* and Y'shua, are One. This whole operation is Spiritual, not physical. It will only be seen in the Spiritual, including the Mount of Olives splitting and removing half to the north and half to the south.

Zechariah 14:5. *And you will flee to the valley of the mountains, for the valley of the mountains will reach to **Azel**. Yes, you will flee, like you fled from before the earthquake in the days of Uzziah king of Judah and the **LORD* my God** will come and **all the saints** will be with you.*

Azel is an unknown place. An ancient scholar said it must be east of the Mount of Olives, but since this is a Spiritual exodus, it does not matter to us. What counts is that the LORD* our God will be with us. All the Saints being with us means that billions of Spiritual Beings will be there, which would be impossible in the physical.

Zechariah 14:6. *And it will be in that **Day** that there will be no bright light or thick darkness. 7. But it will be one **day** which will be known to the **LORD***, not day or night, but it will be, at **evening time** it will be **light**.* (Isa. 60:19,20, Rev. 21:23,25; 22:5)

The Jewish day begins at sundown, so this is at sundown, dusk, the beginning of a New Day; a true New Beginning!

Zechariah 14:8. *And it will be in that **Day** that **living waters** will go out, half of them toward the **eastern sea** and half of them toward the **western sea**: it will be in <u>summer and in winter</u>. (Rev. 22:1) 9. And the **LORD*** will be **King** over all the earth. In that **Day** the **LORD*** will be **One** (John 17:11) and His name **One**.* (Rev. 11:15)

The Living Waters go throughout the world, the spiritual Living Waters represent the Torah, carrying the message of God's love to the east and to the west. This is all in the Spirit, with everyone who is written in the Book of Life joining in.

Exodus 32:33. *And the LORD* said to Moses, "Whoever has sinned against Me, I shall erase him from My book.*

Psalm 69: 29. *They will be erased from the* Book of Life, *and they will* not *be written with the righteous.* (Rev. 17:8; 20:12; 21:27)

> Revelation 3:5. *The one who **conquers** will be clothed in this way, in **white garments**, and I shall **not** wipe out his name from the **Book of Life** (Exod. 32:32,33, Dan. 12:1) and **I shall confess his name before My Father and before His angels**.*

The one who Conquers has overcome the wiles of the devil and is clothed in White Garments as evidence of that righteous state. This is a Spiritual garment, which is waiting for you! All these elements are Spiritual, including the Book of Life, the Torah, and the White Garments. The Spiritual is Real, just not physical, like the army Elisha saw at Dothan and that the Assyrian army of Sennacherib heard before fleeing from Samaria.

The Disciples, Like Us, Think in Terms of a Physical World

The Disciples are thinking of a physical world for End Times so they ask Y'shua at His ascension if this is the start of His reign on Earth. In the first century as now, many are looking for the establishment of an Earthly Kingdom of God, but such is not to be. The Kingdom of God is within you and the Kingdom is Spiritual, not physical.

Acts 1:6. *Therefore indeed those who came asked Him saying, "Lord, are You restoring the* kingdom *in Israel at this time?"*

The Apostles expected Y'shua to begin His Earthly, physical reign right away!

> Acts 1:7. *But He said to them, "It is not for you to know the times or seasons which the Father set by His own authority, 8. But you will take power when the Holy Spirit comes upon you and you will be My witnesses in Jerusalem and in all Judea and Samaria and to the outermost part of the earth." 9. And after He said these things, as they were watching, **He was lifted up and a cloud bore Him up and away from their eyes. 10. And as they were looking intently into the sky at His going**, then there were **two men in white clothing** who stood by them, 11. And they said, "Men of Galilee, why have you stood looking into the sky? This **Y'shua**, Who, as He has been taken up from you into the sky, **will come back in the same way as you saw Him going into the sky**."*

The two men were angels who told how we would see His return! Those looking for the physical return of Y'shua will only see the Kingdom in the Spirit! The LORD*'s coming will be Spiritual! But His coming will be Real!

Zechariah 14:4. *"And **His (the LORD's) feet will stand in that Day upon the Mount of Olives, which is before Jerusalem on the east, and the Mount of Olives will split in the middle toward the east and toward the west and there will be a very great valley, and half of the mountain will remove toward the north and half of it toward the south.**"*

His coming is Spiritual, not physical! The earth splitting is Spiritual, not physical! The Earth may split or disintegrate, or maybe not, but the catastrophe is Spiritual! The Catastrophe is real even though it is Spiritual! All those events in the End are Real, but only in the Spirit Realm.

Babylon is Destroyed!

Revelation 14:8. *And another, a **second angel**, followed saying, "**She has fallen, she has fallen! Babylon the Great**, by whom all the heathens had been given to drink from the wine of the wrath of her **idolatry**."*

The Kingdom of the Heavens has no place for, no room for any form of idolatry. Satan has no authority nor any presence there. Satan is thrown into the second death, so he has no existence in the Kingdom of God! For all forms of idolatry, see *Harlot* in the One New Man Bible Glossary. The winecup of His fury is an idiom for dire prophecy. See Rev. 16:19, Deut. 28:15ff, and Jer. 25:15. Both the Hebrew Hamah and the Greek Thumos speak of heat, of great rage.

Isaiah 21:8. *And he cried like a lion: My lord, I stand continually upon the watchtower in the daytime, and I stand at my post whole nights 9. And, behold, here comes a chariot of men, with a couple of horsemen. And he answered and said, **Babylon is fallen. It is fallen!**"*

In the physical world, Babylon was destroyed by Cyrus in 539 BC and never rebuilt. Jeremiah refers to the destruction of Babylon on Judgment Day. Babylon represents the idolatrous physical world in which we live, the world which will be destroyed as the Saints enter Life, their ETERNAL SPIRITUAL HOME.

Jeremiah 51:6. *Flee from the midst of Babylon (Rev. 18:4) and each man deliver himself. **Do not be cut off by her iniquity, for this is the time of the LORD's*** vengeance. He will render a recompense to her. 7. **Babylon** has been a golden cup in the **LORD***'s hand that **made all the earth drunk**. The nations have drunk of her wine, therefore the nations are mad (out of their senses). 8. **Babylon** suddenly **has fallen and been destroyed**.*

Babylon's utter destruction was prophesied by Jeremiah thousands of years before Judgment Day. But physical Babylon was destroyed in 539 BC, not long after Jeremiah's death, with Cyrus coming on the scene about fifty years after Nebuchadnezzar destroyed Jerusalem. Spiritual Babylon refers to all the idolatrous entities of the world that will be destroyed on Judgment Day, the places wherever immorality, greed, human trafficking, prostitution, gambling, and selfishness dominate. They are all the modern Spiritual Babylon.

The Mark of the Beast is Spiritual.

Revelation 16:2. *Then the* first *came and poured his* vial *to the earth, and very evil sores came upon mankind, those who had the* mark of the beast, *those who bowed down to his image.*

Very Evil is the translation of a Hebrew idiom in which two words meaning evil are used to make the superlative, Very. This Mark of the Beast is Spiritual, not physical, but totally real as the Spirit of the Beast is Evil, it is deleted, erased on Judgment Day. The Saints will be marked by the man with the Inkhorn in Ezekiel 9, a Spiritual Mark.

The Spirit Enters Ezekiel

> Ezekiel 2.1. *And He said to me, Son of man, stand upon your feet and I shall speak to you. 2. And the **Spirit** entered me when **He** spoke to me and set me upon my **feet**, so I heard **Him Who spoke to me**. 3. And He said to me, **Son of man, I AM sending you to the children of Israel**, to a **rebellious nation** that has **rebelled** against **Me**. They and their **fathers** have **transgressed** against **Me**, to this very day. 4. For they are **impudent children** and stiff hearted. I AM sending you to them and you will say to them, **The word of Adonai, the LORD***. 5. And they, whether they will **hear**, or whether they will **hold back**, (for they are a **rebellious** house) will yet know that there has been a **prophet** among them.*

Ezekiel was brought in the Spirit to Jerusalem, bringing a Spiritual message, including the Third Temple, which is a Spiritual Temple! It will not be physical. Today there are politicians and celebrities in the United States and around the world Denying God, even Cursing God. They are Transgressing, deliberately sinning against the Living God; purposely wanting to anger God. They are making the same mistakes those leaders of Judah made.

> Ezekiel 3:12. *Then the **Spirit** took me up and I heard behind me a great rushing, a voice (saying), **Blessed** be the **Glory of the LORD*** from His place. 13. I also heard the noise of the wings of the **living creatures** that touched one another and the **noise** of the **wheels** over against them and a*

*noise of a great rushing. 14. So the **spirit** lifted me up and took me away and I went in **bitterness**, in the **heat** of my **spirit**, but the **hand** of the **LORD*** was **strong upon me**. 15. Then I came to those of the **captivity** at **Tel Aviv**, who lived by the river of Chebar and I sat where they sat and remained there dumbfounded among **them seven days**.*

Tel Aviv is not the modern city in Israel, but is in Babylon as Ezekiel was carried back there in the spirit to testify to the people of Jerusalem who had been taken there. It is easy to understand that such doings would make Ezekiel dumbfounded for seven days. Tel Aviv Israel was founded in 1909 AD.

Ezekiel 3:16. *And it was at the end of seven days;*

> *Then it was the **word of the LORD*** came to me saying, 17. **Son of man**, I have made you a **watchman** for the **House of Israel**, therefore **hear** the **word** from **My mouth** and give them **warning** from **Me**. 18. When I say to the **wicked**, **You will surely die** and you do **not give him warning**, nor are you speaking to **warn** the **wicked** from his **wicked** way, to **save** his **life**. The same **wicked** man will **die** in his **iniquity**, but I shall **require his blood** from your **hand**. 19. Yet if you warn the **wicked** and he does **not** turn from his **wickedness** or from his **wicked way**, he will **die** in his **iniquity**, but you have **delivered your very being**.*

There are undoubtedly Prophets on Earth today who have and are delivering a similar message. All believers should be sounding the alarm!

> Ezekiel 3:20. *Again, When a **righteous** man does **turn** from his **righteousness** and commit **injustice**, and I lay a **stumbling block** before him, he will **die** because you have **not** given him warning, he will **die** in his **sin** and his **acts of loving kindness** which he has done will **not be remembered**, but I shall require his **blood** at your hand. 21. Nevertheless if you **warn** the **righteous** man, that the **righteous** (person) should **not** sin, then he does **not** sin, he will surely **live** because he is warned. You have also **delivered your very being**.*

Our situation is now very much like the days of Ezekiel. Sound the Alarm!

> Ezekiel 3:22. *And the hand of the **LORD*** was there upon me and **He** said to me, **Get up! Go out** to the plain! **I** shall **talk** with you there. 23. Then I **got up** and **went out** to the plain and, behold, the **Glory of the LORD*** stood there, like the **glory** which I saw by the river of **Chebar** and I fell on my **face**. 24. Then the **Spirit** entered me and set me upon my feet and spoke with me and said to me, **Come!** Shut yourself within your **house**, 25. And*

*you, **son of man**, behold, ropes will be put upon you and you will **not go out** among them. 26. And I shall make your **tongue** cling to the roof of your mouth and you shall be **mute**, for there will **not** be a man to reprove them for they are a **rebellious** house. 27. But speaking with you I **will open your mouth** and you will say to them, **Thus says Adonai, the LORD*! He who listens must listen and he who refuses, let him refuse**, for they are a **rebellious** house.*

The **Spirit** will enter the ones appointed for this task! There will be no way to deny the appointment. We turn from **Ezekiel** to **Daniel** who introduced the earthly king to the **True King!**

*Daniel 6:22. Then **Daniel** said to the **king**, O **king**, live forever! 23. My God has sent His **angel** and has **shut the lions' mouths**, so they have not hurt me: forasmuch as innocence was found in me before Him and also before you, O **king**, I have done no hurt.*

The Kingdom of God is Spiritual

*Luke 17:20. And having been asked by the Pharisees when the **Kingdom of God** is coming He answered them and said, "**The Kingdom of God does not come by means of, or in company with, close observation,** 21. And will they not say, 'Behold it is here,' 'There it is,' for behold **the Kingdom of God is within you.**"*

The Kingdom of God is another phrase for Judgment Day, which is within you! That means His coming is Spiritual! It is not a natural Day but is individual and spiritual for each one of us! The LORD* setting foot on the Mount of Olives is allegorical, not natural. The Greek preposition meta in verse twenty-one can be translated either 'by means of,' 'in company with,' or just 'with.' Another way of saying it is that watching for Messiah will not bring Him any sooner. The Kingdom of God is within you or among you. Paul wrote in 1 Corinthians 15:50. "But I say this, brothers, that flesh and blood are not able to inherit the Kingdom of God.." The Kingdom is Spiritual.

The LORD will protect believers on Judgment Day

*Ezekiel 9.1. Then He cried in my ears with a loud voice saying, Cause those who have charge over the city to draw near, even every man with his destroying weapon in his hand. 2. And, behold, **six men** came from the road of the higher gate, which lies toward the north and **each man a slaughter weapon in his hand,** and **one man among them was clothed with linen, with a writer's inkhorn by his side.** And they went in and stood beside the*

63

bronze altar. 3. And the glory of the God of Israel went up from the cherub, upon which it was, to the threshold of the House. And He called to the man **clothed in linen**, *who had the* **writer's inkhorn by his side**.

The Man with the Inkhorn marks those who are Righteous!

#1 Mark the Saint

9:4. And the LORD* said to him, Go through the midst of the city, through the midst of Jerusalem, and **set a mark** *upon the foreheads of the people who sigh and who cry over all the abominations that are done in its midst. (Rev. 7:3; 9:4; 14:1; 22:4) 5. And to the others He said in my hearing,*

#2 Strike the Sinner

Go after him through the city, and **strike**! **Do not let your eye spare! Do not have pity**! *6. You (pl) will slay completely old and young, virgins, little children, and women!* **Do not come near anyone upon whom is the mark!**

#3 Begin at My Sanctuary

Begin at My Sanctuary. *Then they began with the* **elders** *who were in front of the* **House**. *7. And He said to them, Defile the House and fill the courts!* **Begin at My Sanctuary** *with the slain. Go forth! And they* **went** *forth and* **slew** *in the city. 8. And it was, while they were slaying them, and I was left, that I fell upon my face and cried and said, Ah* **Adonai, LORD***! *Will You destroy all the residue of Israel in Your pouring out of Your fury upon Jerusalem?*

Ministers and other leaders will be the first ones sought by the slayers! The Saints are protected on the Day of the LORD*. This is the beginning of Judgment Day.

Revelation 9.1. Then the **fifth** *angel* **trumpeted**: *and I saw a star that had fallen out from heaven to the earth, then the key of the pit of the abyss was given to the star 2. And it opened the pit of the abyss and smoke rose from the pit like smoke of a great furnace, (Gen. 19:28, Exod. 19:18) and the sun and the air were darkened by the smoke from the pit. 3. And* **locusts** *came out from the smoke to the earth, (Exod. 10:12,15) and* **authority** *was given to them as the* **scorpions** *have* **authority** *over the earth. 4. And it was said to them that* **they could not injure the grass of the earth nor any green thing and not any tree, only** the people who do not have the seal of God on their foreheads. *(Ezek. 9:4, Rev. 7:3; 14:1; 22:4) 5. And it was given to them that they could* **not kill** *them, but that they would be* **tormented** *for* *five months, and their **torment** will be like a **torment** of a **scorpion** when it would **sting** someone. 6. And in those days people will **seek death** but they will **not** find it, and they will **desire** to **die** but **death flees** from them. (Jer. 8:3, Hos. 10:8, Job 3:21)*

Those who have the Mark of the Man with the Inkhorn are those who have the Seal of God. This is yet another description of the stretching of the Torment on Judgment Day which will be spread out over whatever length of time the LORD* has determined for it. See the Chapter *The Book of Revelation.*

Ezekiel 18.1. And the LORD said to Aaron, "You and your sons and your father's house with you **will bear any iniquity in the Sanctuary**, and you and your sons with you will bear any iniquity of your priesthood.*

The priests, ministers, pastors are responsible that no iniquity (intentional sin) takes place in or about the holy place. There is a burden to know and to do what is right, to hold to the very highest standards; a higher standard than for other people and those in secular organizations. Included in this is any message given by a priest, so those today who are advocating relaxed Biblical commandments that may be popular today will definitely be subjected to the high standard on Judgment Day. All, whether in ministry or not, need to walk in repentance all day every day. Every believer is a priest!

*Ezekiel 1.1. Now it happened in the **thirtieth year**, in the fourth month, Tammuz, on the fifth of the month, as I was among the captives by the river Chebar, the heavens were opened (Rev. 19:11) and **I saw visions of God**. 2. On the fifth of the month, (it was the fifth year of king Jehoiachin's captivity) 3. The word of the LORD* came expressly to Ezekiel the priest, the son of Buzi, in the land of the Chaldeans by the river Chebar and the hand of the LORD* was upon him there.*

This is the thirtieth year from the last Year of Jubilee in Israel. In that year the Torah scroll was found as reported in 2 Kings 22:8-20. The finding of the scroll is considered the first sign of the coming disaster.

*Ezekiel 1:4. And I looked and, behold, a **whirlwind** came out of the north, a great cloud and a flaming fire and a brightness was around it and out of the midst of it like the color of amber, out of the midst of the fire. 5. Also out of the midst of it was the likeness of **four living creatures**. And their appearance was the likeness of a man. 6. And each one had **four faces** and each one had **four wings**. 7. And their **feet** were straight feet and the **sole** of their **feet** was like the **sole** of a **calf's foot** and they **sparkled** like the color of* *gleaming bronze. 8. And their hands were like a man's under their wings on their four sides and the four had their faces and their wings. 9. Their wings were joined one to another. They did not turn when they went, each one going straight forward. 10. As for the likeness of their faces, the four had the face of a man and the face of a lion on the right side. And the four had the face of an ox on the left side. The four also had the face of an eagle. (Rev. 4:7) 11. Thus were their faces, and their wings were stretched upward, two wings of each one were joined one to another and two covered their bodies. 12. And each one went straight forward, they went wherever the spirit was to go. They did not turn when they went. 13. As for the likeness of the living creatures, their appearance was like burning coals of fire, like the appearance of torches. (The fire) went up and down among the living creatures and the fire was bright and lightning went forth out of the fire. 14. And the living creatures ran and returned like the appearance of a flash of lightning.*

With this detailed description it is still difficult to imagine these Living Creatures, but remember they are not physical, but they are REAL When we are in our Spiritual Bodies we will see the Living Creatures and we will know that they are REAL

Ezekiel 1:15. Now as I beheld the living creatures, there was one wheel on the earth beside the living creatures, at each of their four faces. 16. The appearance of the wheels and their work was like the color of a beryl, and the four had one likeness and their appearance and their work was as it were a wheel in the middle of a wheel. 17. When they went, they went on their four sides, they did not turn when they went. 18. As for their rims, they were so high that they were awesome, and their rims were full of eyes surrounding the four of them. (Rev. 4:8) 19. And when the living creatures went, the wheels went with them and when the living creatures were lifted up from the earth, the wheels were lifted up. 20. They went wherever the spirit was to go, there their spirit was to go and the wheels were lifted up over against them, for the spirit of the living creature was in the wheels. 21. When those went, they went. And when those stood, they stood. And when those were lifted up from the earth, the wheels were lifted up over against them, for the spirit of the living creature was in the wheels.

Our future Spiritual Life will be very interesting as we find that all these Spiritual Things are REAL You will see the Living Creatures. In verse sixteen Beryl is transparent and is found in different colors, this from Tarshish. This color is now called topaz.

Ezekiel 1:22. *And the likeness of a firmament was over the heads of the living creatures, like the color of the terrible ice, stretched forth over their heads above. 23. And under the firmament their wings were straight, the one toward the other. Each one had two, which covered their bodies on this side and each one had two, which covered on that side. 24. And when they went, I heard the noise of their wings, like the sound of many waters (Rev. 14:2), like the voice of the Almighty, the noise of tumult, like the noise of an army. When they stood, they let down their wings. 25. And there was a voice from the firmament that was over their heads, when they stood and had let down their wings.*

The Firmament is the sky we see, the stars, planets, moons that are seen from Earth. The Hebrew word is Rakia, which you can read about in the One New Man Bible Glossary under Heavens.

A Rainbow

Ezekiel 1:26. *And above the firmament that was over their heads was the likeness of a throne, like the appearance of a sapphire stone (Exod. 24:10, Rev. 4:2) and upon the likeness of the throne was the likeness as the appearance of a man above it. 27. And I saw as the color of amber, like the appearance of fire all around within it, from the appearance of his loins even upward and from the appearance of his loins even downward, I saw as it were the appearance of fire and it had brightness all around. 28. Like the appearance of the bow that is in the cloud on the day of rain, so was the appearance of the brightness all around. This was the appearance of the likeness of the Glory of the LORD*. And when I saw it, I fell upon my face and I heard a voice of One Who spoke.*

You too will see the Glory of the LORD*. No wonder Ezekiel fell on his Face! It is wondrous to think that someday we too will see these Spiritual Things! No doubt we too will have reactions similar to Ezekiel's.

Daniel Makes Clear that All Who are Listed in the Book of Life are Safe

Daniel 12.1. *And at that time Michael will stand up, the great prince who stands for the children of your people (Rev. 12:7) and there will be a time of trouble, such as never was since there was a nation even to that same time and at that time <u>your people will be delivered</u>, everyone who will be found <u>written in the book</u>. (Rev. 3:5; 20:12; 21:27) 2. And many of those who sleep in the dust of the earth will awake, some to everlasting life and some to shame and everlasting contempt. (Matt. 25:31-33, Acts 24:15) 3. And* *those who are wise **shine like the brightness of the firmament**, and those who turn many to **righteousness** like the **stars forever and ever**.*

On **Judgment Day** the **People of the LORD* <u>will be delivered</u>**, shining like the sun as they are taken away from the **destruction, murder**, and **torture** about to begin.

> Malachi 3:13. *Your **words have been stout against Me**, says the **LORD***. Yet you say, What have we spoken so against You? 14. You have said, **It is vain to serve God**, and what profit is it that we have kept His ordinance and that we have walked mournfully before the LORD* of Hosts? 15. And now we are calling the arrogant happy. Yes, **those who work wickedness are set up. Yes, they even tempt God and are delivered.** 16. Then those who **revered the LORD*** spoke often one to another and the **LORD*** listened and heard it, and a **scroll of remembrance was written** before Him for those who **revered the LORD*** and who **thought on His name**. 17. And they will be, says the **LORD* of Hosts**, in that **Day** which I AM preparing **My special treasure**, and I shall **spare them** as a **man spares his own son who serves him**. 18. Then you will **return** and **discern** between the **righteous** and the **wicked**, between him who **serves God** and him who does **not serve Him**.*

The people have questioned the need to Serve the LORD*, saying "It is vain to serve God." And "What Profit is it that we have kept His Ordinance?" Why should we Serve Him? The bad people prosper more than we do. The answer points to Judgment Day and Eternal Life. Also, earthly wealth does transfer into Spiritual Blessings! The physical things of this world do not transfer into the Spiritual ETERNAL LIFE

Saints Are Marked in Revelation

> Revelation 7.1. *After this I saw four angels standing upon the four corners of the earth, holding the four winds (Jer. 49:36, Ezek. 37:9, Zech. 6:5, Dan. 7:2) of the earth so that the wind could not blow upon the earth and not upon the sea nor even upon any tree. 2. And I saw another angel going up from the east, having a seal of the Living God, and in a loud voice he cried out to the four angels to whom it was given to destroy the earth and the sea 3. Saying, "**Do not harm the earth or the sea or the trees, <u>until we could seal the servants of our God upon their foreheads</u>.** (Ezek. 9:4, Rev. 9:4; 14:1; 22:4) 4. Then I heard the number of those who had been sealed, a hundred forty-four thousand, that they had been sealed from every tribe of the children of Israel:*

The number 144 represents Perfection of Divine Government, 1,000 represents Perfect Reign. The Tribe of Dan is missing from this list in Revelation seven.

Day of the Lord

> 1 Thessalonians 5.1. *And concerning the times and the seasons, brothers, you do not need it to be written to you, 2. For you know accurately that the* **Day** *of the* **Lord** *is coming as a thief at night. 3. When unbelievers would say, "Peace and safety," (Jer. 6:14; 8:11, Ezek. 13:10) then sudden destruction is standing near just as travail would be in the womb, and they would* **not** *escape. 4. But you, brothers, are not in darkness, so that the* **Day** *would overtake you as a thief: 5. For you are all sons of light and sons of day. We are* **not of night** *and* **not of darkness**: *6. We should therefore not sleep like the rest but we should be watchful and we should be sober. 7. For those who are sleeping sleep of night, and those who get* **drunk** *get* **drunk** *at* **night**: *8. But, since we are of day, we should be sober,* <u>*putting on a* **breastplate of faith** *and of* **love** *and for a* **helmet** *the* **hope of salvation**</u>: *(Isa. 59:17) 9. Because God did not put us here to be subject to* **wrath** *but to gain* **salvation through our Lord Y'shua Messiah**, *10. The* **One Who died instead of us**, *so that whether we would be awake or we would sleep* **we will live together with Him**. *11. On this account you must continually exhort one another, and you must steadily build up one another one on one, just as you are doing.*

Judgment Day comes like a thief in the night when no one expects it! The Day will not be hastened by praying for it or calling for it. It will come in God's timing. Day speaks of light, with Dawn alluding to Redemption. Night alludes to exile, separation from God's presence. In verse seven, Drunk refers to being under the influence of any intoxicant, so as you prepare to meet the LORD* your God, be careful not to be under the influence of any intoxicant. Recreational drugs are a great hindrance to relationship with the LORD*.

WAIT FOR THE LORD*

Isaiah Waits for a Message from the LORD*:

> Isaiah 26:7. *The way of the **righteous is 'uprightness.'** You, **Upright One**,
> do weigh the path of the righteous. 8. Yes, in the Way of Your judgments,
> LORD*, **have we waited for You**. The desire of our inner beings is for
> **Your name** and for the **remembrance of You**. 9. **With my inner being
> I have desired You in the night**. Yes, with **my spirit within me I will
> eagerly seek You before dawn**, for when Your judgments are in the earth,
> the inhabitants of the world will learn righteousness. 10. Let favor be shown
> to the wicked, yet he will not learn righteousness. He, the wicked, will deal
> unjustly in the land of uprightness, and will not behold the majesty of the
> LORD*.*

Isaiah's waiting for the LORD* is a nightly practice for Isaiah. Each of us should
have the same habit, spending time with the LORD* daily to understand His
assignments for us. This requires listening more than telling the LORD* what we
want. The LORD*'s will is more important by far than your wish list.

> Isaiah 33:2. *LORD*, be gracious to us! We have waited for You. Be their arm every
> morning, our deliverance also in the time of trouble.*

Isaiah again uses the modest plural 'we' instead of the singular. In Hebrew this is
called the Majestic singular as opposed to the proud singular "I."

All who Wait for the LORD* will be Rewarded:

> Isaiah 40:29. *He gives power to the faint and to those who have no might
> He increases strength. 30. Even the youths will faint and be weary and the*

young men will utterly stumble, 31. But **they that <u>wait upon</u> the LORD*** **will renew their strength.** *They will* **mount up with wings as eagles.** *(Ps. 103:5) They will* **run and not be weary.** *They will* **walk and not grow faint.**

The Hebrew verb translated Wait upon, is Koof-Vav-Hey, showing endurance, that is just waiting a short time, but they are prepared to wait for however long it takes. They will run and not grow weary no matter how long the run. They will walk on, no matter how long the time or distance. Their strength will be renewed as they Wait! They will be ready to soar like eagles as they eagerly expect the LORD*. In English <u>Wait Upon</u> also relates to serving, so this applies to those who serve the LORD*, those who never falter, never go slack in serving the LORD* This relates to another teaching:

Isaiah 28:16 is quoted in Romans 9:33; 10:11, and 1 Peter 2:6. The last sentence of verse 16 is often translated similarly to the Greek rendering, *and the one who believes upon Him will not be put to shame.* The NIV has *..the one who trusts will never be dismayed.* The Hebrew is stronger and deeper than that. *..the one who believes will not make haste.* The word translated 'one who believes' or 'one who trusts' is ma'amin, which has a root meaning that speaks of both training and loyalty or faithfulness. There is a difference between just believing and being loyal through hard times. Jacob 2:19 says, *You believe that God is One, you do well: the demons also believe and shudder.* The demons know God and His power, but are not obedient, faithful, and committed to Him.

The two words translated <u>not make haste or dismayed</u> are more difficult, but refer to something not done quickly. In the twelfth century Rabbi Ibn Ezra wrote, "He (the faithful one) will remain steadfast in his faith however long realization may be delayed." Each of us must understand that when the LORD* has given us a vision for ministry, that the timing is His, not ours, and we need to hold strong in faith while He brings all things in His timing. If we get ahead of His timing the ministry becomes our ministry, not His. That ministry may have financial success but will not have spiritual success. When He gives any of us the vision for a ministry there may be years of preparation before we are to begin.

What to us seems to be a delay may be something the Lord is doing in us. Paul wrote in Philippians 4:11-13: *Not that I am talking on account of a great need, for I have learned to be content with what things I have. And I know how to submit myself to want, and I know how to be abundant: in everything and in all things I have learned the secret, both how to be filled and how to be needy and how to be affluent and how to suffer want: I have strength to overcome all things in the One Who strengthens me.*

71

Psalm 105:17 says, *He sent a man before them, Joseph, who was sold for a servant, 18. Whose feet they hurt with fetters: he was laid in iron 19. Until the time that his word came: the word of the LORD* purified him.* This refers to the time Joseph spent in slavery and in prison. The word translated purified comes from a root which means to refine, purify, test, or burn. The time spent waiting for the LORD's* timing has a purpose, whether to purify the minister or to prepare other elements, completely unrelated to the one waiting. Look at Genesis 37 to see why Joseph had this purging. We need to be like Paul, content in this season of lack. The lack can be money as Paul wrote about or it may be in ministry. Each of us has a ministry, with or without man's ordination. The real Ordination is from God, not man. Remember, each of us is a priest. We are a *..kingdom, priests to His God and Father..* (Rev. 1:6). It is important to be obedient; to wait contentedly, to keep the faith and grow spiritually while He works His will in us.

Jeremiah Waits Ten Days for a Word from the LORD*

> Jeremiah 42:7. *And it was **after ten days that the word of the LORD* came to Jeremiah**. 8. Then he called Johanan the son of Kareah and all the captains of the forces that were with him and all the people from the least even to the greatest 9. And said to them, Thus says the LORD*, the God of Israel, to Whom you sent me to present your supplication before Him. 10. **If you (Israel) will still live in this land, then I shall build you and not pull you down and I shall plant you and not pluck you up**, for I am grieved by the evil that I have done to you. 11. **Do not be in awe of the king of Babylon of whom you are afraid! Do not be in awe of him!** Says the LORD*, for I AM with you to save you and to deliver you from his hand. 12. And I will show compassion to you, so he will have compassion on you and cause you to return to your own land. 13. But if you say, We will not stay in this land or obey the voice of the LORD* your God 14. Saying, No! But we will go to the land of **Egypt** where we will see no war or hear the sound of the shofar or have hunger of bread, and we will live there. 15. And now therefore hear the word of the LORD*, you remnant of Judah, Thus says the LORD* of Hosts, the God of Israel, If you set your faces to enter **Egypt** and go to sojourn there, 16. Then it will be that the **sword** of which you were in awe will overtake you there in the land of **Egypt**, and the famine of which you were afraid will follow close after you there in Egypt, and there you will die. 17. So will it be with all the men who set their faces to go to Egypt to sojourn there. They will **die by the sword, by the famine, and by the pestilence** and none of them will remain or escape from the evil that I AM will bring upon them.*

In spite of that declaration that they would die if they went to Egypt – they went to Egypt.

Jeremiah 42:18. *For thus says the LORD* of Hosts, the God of Israel, As My anger and My fury has been poured upon the inhabitants of Jerusalem, so will My fury be poured upon you, when you enter* **Egypt** *and you will be denounced as evil and an astonishment and a curse and a reproach and you will see this place no more. 19. The LORD* has said concerning you, O you remnant of Judah,* **Do not go to Egypt!** *Know certainly that I have admonished you this day. 20. For you were deceitful in your hearts when you sent me to the LORD* your God saying, Pray for us to the LORD* our God and according to all that the LORD* our God will say, so declare to us and we will do it. 21. And I have this day declared to you, but you have not obeyed the voice of the LORD* your God, nor anything for which He has sent me to you. 22. Now therefore know certainly that* **you will die by the sword, by the famine, and by the pestilence in the place where you desire to go to sojourn.**

Jeremiah waited ten days for those words to the remnant in Jerusalem, who did not accept the message, but went to Egypt, taking Jeremiah with them. Some of those who went to Egypt did escape and return, so we hope Jeremiah and Baruch were among the escapees.

Daniel Waits until Night, Then is Given the Answer in a Dream

Daniel 2:17. *Then* **Daniel** *went to his house and made the thing known to his companions,* **Hananiah, Mishael,** *and* **Azariah,** *18. So they would desire compassion of the* **God of Heaven** *concerning this* **secret,** *that* **Daniel** *and his friends should not perish with the rest of the wise men of Babylon. 19. Then* **the secret was revealed to Daniel in a night vision and Daniel blessed the God of Heaven.** *20.* **Daniel** *answered and said, Blessed be the name of God forever and ever, for wisdom and might are His, 21. And He changes the times and the seasons. He removes kings and sets up kings. He gives wisdom to the wise and knowledge to those who know understanding. 22. He* **reveals** *the* **deep** *and* **secret** *things, He knows what is in the* **darkness,** *and the* **light** *dwells with Him. 23. I thank you and praise You, O You God of my fathers, Who has given me wisdom and might and has* **made known to me** *now what we desired of You, for You have now made known to us the king's matter.*

The Spirit of the LORD* gave the Secret Dream to Daniel.

Daniel Introduces the king to the One Who Reveals Secrets:

> Daniel 2:27. **Daniel** *answered in the presence of the king and said, The* **secret** *which the king has demanded no wise men, astrologers, magicians or soothsayers, can tell the king, 28. But there is a* **God in heaven Who Reveals Secrets** *and makes known to the king* **Nebuchadnezzar** *what will be in the latter days. (Rev. 1:19) Your dream and the visions of your head upon your bed are these: 29. As for you, O* **king**, *your* **thoughts** *came into your mind upon your bed, what should happen hereafter and* **He Who Reveals Secrets** *makes* **known** *to you what* **will be**. *(Rev. 22:6) 30. But as for me, this* **secret** *is not revealed to me for any* **wisdom** *that I have more than any living, but that the interpretation may be made* **known** *to the* **king** *and that you can know the* **thoughts** *of your* **heart**.

Daniel begins his Spiritual Ministry with a message that only the God in Heaven could provide!

Later, Daniel Waits Even Longer Than Jeremiah's Ten Days:

> Daniel 10:11. *And he said to me, O* **Daniel**, *the man greatly beloved, understand the words that I speak to you and stand upright, for I am now sent to you. And when he had spoken this word to me, I stood trembling. 12. Then he said to me,* **Do not be in awe, Daniel!** *For from the first day that you set your heart to understand, and to chasten yourself before your God, your words were heard and I have come because of your words. 13. But the* **prince of the kingdom of Persia withstood me for** <u>**twenty-one days**</u>, *but lo,* **Michael, one of the chief princes**, *came to help me and I remained there with the kings of Persia. (Rev. 12:7) 14. Now I have come to make you* **understand** *what will befall your* **people** *in the* **latter days**, *for yet the vision is for many days.*

Three Weeks is a long time to wait for a Word from the LORD*. It took Gabriel and Michael together to overcome the Prince over Persia. Spiritual warfare against the principalities over cities and countries is not to be engaged in lightly. That warfare is dangerous and must be coordinated by experienced warrior ministries.

Zechariah Records the Repentant Waiting for the Word!

> Zechariah 11:10. *And I took My staff,* **Pleasantness**, *and* **broke** *it, so I could* **break My covenant** *which I had* **cut** *with all the* **peoples**. *11. And it was* **broken** *that day, and so the* **poor of the flock (Repentant)** *who* **waited on Me** *knew that it was the* **word** *of the* **LORD***.

It was those who Repented who waited for the message.

David Waited!!

Psalm 40:2. *I waited patiently for the LORD*; and He inclined to me and He heard my cry.*

Simeon Waited Decades!

> Luke 2:25. *And behold a man by the name of **Simeon** was in Jerusalem and this righteous and devout man was **waiting** for the **Comforter of Israel**, and the **Holy Spirit** was upon him: 26. And it was revealed to him by the **Holy Spirit** that **he would not see death before he would see the Messiah of the Lord.***

Simeon's promise was fulfilled.

Anna (Hannah) Waited Longest of All!

> Luke 2:36. *And **Anna** was a prophetess, daughter of Phanuel, from the tribe of Asher: she had gone forward many days, living with a husband **seven years from her virginity** 37. And she was a widow until **eighty-four years**. She did not leave the Temple, while she was **serving night and day in fasting and prayer**. 38. And at this time she was standing and giving thanks to God and speaking about Him to all those who were waiting for the redemption of Jerusalem.*

Hannah (Anna) apparently waited about sixty years! Her name in both Hebrew and Greek is Hannah; Latin has Anna.

Joseph of Arimathea waited!

> Luke 23:50. *Then behold, a man named **Joseph** who was a member of the council and a good and righteous man 51. – this one was not agreeing with the resolution and with what they did – **from Arimathea**, a Jewish city, who was **waiting for the Kingdom of God**, 52. After this one came to Pilate he asked for the body of Y'shua 53. And when he took Him down he wrapped Him in fine linen and placed Him in a tomb hewn in the rock where no one had lain.*

Joseph waited patiently for the Messianic Kingdom, for which many today are still waiting!

TRANSITION

This chapter is to help each of us, including me, transition into the Spirit Realm, to understand that the Spirit Realm is Real; the Physical Realm with which we are so familiar does not exist in the Spirit Realm.

The End Times are Submerged in the Spiritual

Isaiah 11.1. *And there will come forth a shoot out of the trunk of Jesse, and a* Branch *will grow out of his roots:* (Matt. 2:23, Rev. 5:5; 22:16)

The Branch is Y'shua, God's Incarnate Body. The Hebrew word for Branch is netser and that is the root of the name of the city now called Nazareth. The Biblical name of the town is Natsrat – not Nazareth. Instead of Nazarene in reference to its citizens, the correct word is Notsri. This is important for several reasons, one being that there is no connection, which some have made, to the vow of the Nazirite. The Spirit is manifest completely in End Times because the End Time is Spiritual, rather than Physical.

> Isaiah 11:2. *and the **Spirit** of the LORD* will rest upon Him, the **Spirit** of **1 wisdom** and **2 understanding**, the **Spirit** of **3 counsel** and **4 might**, the **Spirit** of **5 knowledge** and of the **6 reverence** and **7 awe** of the LORD*. (Rev. 5:6) 3. And He will be filled with a **Spirit** of awesome **reverence** for the LORD*. He will not judge after the sight of His eyes, nor decide after the hearing of His ears, 4. but He will judge the **<u>poor</u>** with **righteousness** (Rev. 19:11) and decide with equity for the **<u>humble</u>** of the earth and He will strike the earth with the **rod** of His mouth, and with the **breath of His lips He will slay the wicked**. (Eph. 6:17)*

The Poor and the Humble are synonyms referring to those who are Repentant, having Poor and Humble together are an idiom that makes the Repentant a superlative, showing a greatly increased importance of Repentance to our God.

On the Day of the LORD* the Saints will have a Spiritual Blessing, and those who do not Repent will suffer Eternal Death, the Second Death – the Lake of Fire.

> Isaiah 11:5. *And **righteousness will be the belt around His loins**, and **faithfulness the belt around His waist**. (Eph. 6:14) 6. The wolf also will dwell with the lamb and the leopard will lie down with the kid, and the calf and the young lion and the fatling together, and a small youth will lead them. 7. And the cow and the bear will feed. Their young ones will lie down together and the lion will eat straw like the ox. 8. And the nursing child will play on the hole of the asp, and the weaned child will put his hand on the viper's den. 9. They will not hurt or destroy in all My holy mountain, for the earth will be full of the **knowledge of the LORD***, **as the waters cover the sea.***

All these wonderful reports are Spiritual, with this allegorical setting of Heaven. Without the physical body there can be no physical pain! I want to be FULL OF THE KNOWLEDGE OF THE LORD*!

> Isaiah 11:10. *And in that **Day** there will be a **root of Jesse** Who will **stand** for a sign, a **miracle**, for the peoples. To Him will the nations seek, and His resting place will be glorious. (Rom. 15:12, Rev. 5:5; 22:16)*

The Root of Jesse is the same Spiritual Body that appeared in Jerusalem and Galilee after His Resurrection.

> Isaiah 60.1. ***Arise, and give Light!** For your **Light** has come, and the **Glory of the LORD*** has shone like the sun upon you. 2. For, behold, the darkness will cover the earth and gross darkness the people, but the **LORD* will rise like the sun upon you**, and **His glory will be seen upon you**. (Rev. 21:11) 3. And nations will come to your Light, and kings to the brightness of your rising like the sun. (Rev. 21:24)*

On Judgment Day the Light will be the Glory, the Honor, of God; the LORD* of Hosts, Who is One with Y'shua!

> Isaiah 60:4. *Lift up your eyes all around and see: they all gather themselves together, they come to you. Your sons will come from afar and your daughters will be **trained at your side**. 5. Then you will see and be brightened up, and your **heart** will **tremble with joy** and be **enlarged**, because the **abundance***

***of the sea will be converted** for you, the **wealth of nations** will come to you.*

How will wealth be measured in the Hereafter? This is speaking of Spiritual Wealth, the Knowledge of the LORD* as the Waters cover the Sea. The Wealth that comes to the people will be Spiritual Knowledge of the LORD*! (Isaiah 11:9) The Spiritual Body will not have any need for money and will not have any substance resembling any of the things we associate with Earthly Wealth. Heaven is the Kingdom of God!

For the Kingdom of God *is* not food and drink, *but* righteousness *and* peace *and* joy *in (the)* Holy Spirit: Romans 14:17

Our children will be trained by royalty:

> *And **kings will be your nursing fathers and their queens your nursing mothers**. They will bow down to you with their face toward the earth and lick up the dust of your feet, and you will know that I AM the LORD*, for they will not be ashamed who wait for Me. Isaiah 49:23.*

The Wealth of the Heathens (Nations) in the Spiritual is the Honor, Praise, and Glory that now come to the rich and powerful in our society, but will instead flow to the Saints in the Hereafter. With Humility a requirement for entry to the Hereafter; the Honor, Praise, and Glory will not affect our personalities.

> Isaiah 60:6. *The multitude of camels will cover you, the dromedaries of Midian and Ephah. All those from Sheba will come. They will bring gold and incense and they will **herald the praises of the LORD***. 7. All the flocks of Kedar will be gathered together to you, the rams of **Nebaioth** will minister to you. They will come up with acceptance on My altar, and I shall **glorify** the House of My **glory**.*

Nebaioth is a nomadic tribe of Edom and Moab. The word translated **Glorify** is literally **Beautify**; the LORD* will make His **House,** His **Throne, Beautiful**.

> Isaiah 60:8. *Who are these who fly like a cloud and like the doves to their cotes? 9. Surely the **isles** will wait for Me and the ships of Tarshish first, to bring your sons from afar, their silver and their gold with them to the name of the LORD* your God and to the Holy One of Israel, because He has glorified you.*

The Isles represent all the people of the earth, showing that God desires everyone to be saved, to live in relationship with Him.

Isaiah 60:10. *And the sons of strangers will build up your walls and their kings will minister to you, for in My wrath I struck you, but in My favor I have had compassion on you. 11. Therefore your gates will be open continually. They will not be shut day or night, so men can bring the* **wealth of nations** *to you and so their kings may be led to the* **wealth of Jerusalem.** *(Rev. 21:25) 12. For the* **nation and kingdom that will not serve you will perish.** *Yes, those nations will be utterly* **wasted.**

The Wealth of the Heathens (Nations) in the Spiritual is the Honor, Praise, and Glory that now come to the rich and powerful in our society, but will flow instead to the Saints in the Hereafter. This is not man's idea of wealth, but what Y'shua referred to in Matthew 13:22.

And the one sown among the thorns, this is the one who hears the message, and the anxiety of the age and the **deceitfulness of wealth** *(Matt. 6:24) choke the message and it becomes useless. Luke 16:9. And I say to you, you must at once make friends for yourselves* **apart from unrighteous wealth,** *in order that when it would give out they would take you into the eternal dwellings.*

Only the Saints, the people who have dismissed Unrighteous Wealth, opting instead for the True Riches, will appreciate the Spiritual Wealth of the Hereafter,

Luke 16:10. *The one* **faithful** *in the* **least** *is also* **faithful** *in* **much,** *and the one* **unrighteous** *in the* **least** *is also* **unrighteous** *in* **much.** *11. If therefore you were not faithful in* **unrighteous wealth,** *who will trust the* **true (riches)** *to you?*

The True Riches are Spiritual, not measured by bank accounts, net worth, or any Physical asset!

Luke 16:12. *And if you are not faithful in that belonging to another, who will give your (property) to you? 13. And no house servant is able to serve two masters: for he will either hate the one and will love the other, or he will be devoted to the one and he will despise the other.* **You are not able to serve God and wealth.** *"* (Matt. 6:24)

The Wealth of the Heathens (Nations) in the Spiritual is the Honor, Praise, and Glory that now come to the rich and powerful in our society, but will flow instead to the Saints in the Hereafter. Only those who are apart from, separated from unrighteous wealth, are the ones who have eternal dwellings. Those looking for the physical Wealth of the Heathens to come to them will surely be disappointed.

There will be no transfer of Gold, shares of Stock, or Real Estate Portfolios, with the Real Wealth in Praise, Honor, and Glory that all belong to the LORD*! This does not mean that it is a sin to have money; this is a heart condition; It is possible to be wealthy and still not be obsessed with that wealth. It is also possible to not have wealth, but to be obsessed with wealth. Make sure your heart is right with God.

This article is from the One New Man Bible Glossary: "Wealth is neutral to our salvation. It is neither evil nor good of itself, but it is a great factor in many lives. Paul wrote to Timothy (1 Tim. 6:10) that *..love of money is a root of all the evils..* so, it is not the money itself that is evil, but loving money can certainly cause evil. Greed is the enemy. Many who are wealthy have put their faith in wealth and not in the LORD*. Many have acquired or retained inherited wealth because money was their god. You do not need to have money to love money, so there are many poor who have money as their god.

The **Kingdom of God** here on earth benefits from the **wealth** of those who are not greedy and who give generously to God's work, but not everyone is to be **wealthy**. We should all be prosperous enough to have respectable housing and the other necessities of life, but we should not expect more than that simply because we are believers. Y'shua said *You must continually see and guard yourselves from all* ***covetousness***, *because someone's life is* ***not abundant from his possessions***. (Lk. 12:15) Paul wrote to the Philippians (4:11) that he had *..****learned to be content*** *with what things I have.*

The story of the Rich Ruler in Luke 18:18-23 tells about a young man whose possessions were more important to him than the **Kingdom of God**. **Y'shua** saw that quality in him so He told the man to **sell all his possessions, give the money to the poor**, and **then follow Him**. We all have to view our **possessions**, no matter how **small** or how **great**, as less important than the **Kingdom of God**."

The Kingdom of God *is not food and drink (physical things), but* Righteousness and Peace and Joy in the Holy Spirit. Romans 14:17.

> Isaiah 60:13. *The glory of Lebanon will come to you, the fir tree, the pine tree, and the box tree together, to* ***beautify*** *the place of* ***My Sanctuary***. *And I shall make the place of* ***My feet glorious***. *14. The sons also of those who* ***afflicted you*** *will come bending to you, and all those who despised you will bow themselves down at the soles of your feet and they will call you The City of the LORD*, The Zion of the Holy One of Israel. (Rev. 3:9)*

The Spiritual Realm is even more beautiful than the Natural, Physical Realm.

Isaiah 60:15. Whereas you have been forsaken and hated, so that no man went through you, I shall make you an eternal excellency, a joy of many generations. 16. You will also suck the milk of the nations and will suck the breast of kings, and you will know that I AM the LORD* your Deliverer and your Redeemer, the Mighty One of Jacob.

To suck the Breast of kings refers to the Wealth of the Heathens being given to the Righteous. But now we know that Wealth is not in money, gold, or other possessions, but in Honor, Praise and Glory as we Worship the King of Glory!

1 Chronicles 16:29. Give unto the LORD* the glory due His name! Bring an offering! Come before Him! Worship the LORD* in the adornment of holiness!

Adornment is the proper meaning of the Hebrew word Hadrat. As we worship Him we become adorned with the Holy Spirit and can sense the Presence of the LORD*. Worship raises the spirit of the believer to a level where the worshipper senses the presence of the LORD*. Beauty is the common translation of Hadrat, but Beauty is from the Latin text and kept by tradition in many translations. (Psalm 29:2; 96:9, 2 Chronicles 20:21) Adornment is the spiritual reaction as we experience the LORD*'s anointing power.

> *2 Chronicles 20:21. And when he had consulted with the people, he appointed singers to the LORD*, who would <u>praise</u> in the **adornment of holiness** as they went out before the army and to say, Give thanks to the LORD*, for His loving kindness endures forever. 22. And when they **began to sing and to praise, the LORD* set ambushes against the children of Ammon, Moab, and Mount Seir**, who had come against **Judah**, and they were struck. 23. For the children of **Ammon** and **Moab** stood up against the inhabitants of **Mount Seir**, to utterly exterminate and destroy them: and when they had made an end of the inhabitants of **Seir**, everyone helped to destroy **another**.*

This passage in 1 Chronicles records the victory of Jehoshaphat over these armies at the Valley called Berachah, Blessing, which is a few miles southeast of Jerusalem; it is also the Battle of Joel and the location of the battle after the armies gather at Har Megiddo in Revelation

> *Isaiah 60:17. Instead of bronze I shall bring **gold**, and instead of iron I shall bring **silver**, and bronze instead of wood, and iron instead of stones. I shall also make your **officers peace**, and your **rulers acts of loving kindness**. 18. **Violence will no more be heard** in your land, **wasting** or **destruction** within your borders, but you will call your walls **Deliverance**, and your gates **Praise**.*

Before the Coming of the LORD*

This is the description of the Third Temple, which is a universal Temple, a Spiritual Temple. The purpose of this Temple is to bring the End-Time Revival, reaching every people group in the world. The Temple Institute in Jerusalem has prepared all the utensils and Instruments needed for the Third Temple, ready to begin construction when the LORD* makes the Temple Mount available, prepared for construction to begin: But the Third Temple will not be a Physical Building. It will be a Spiritual Building that will be seen during Judgment Day. Ezekiel Chapter 40 presents both approaches to the Third Temple. See the chapter The Book of Revelation in this book.

Ezekiel is Shown the Third Temple

> Ezekiel 40.1. *In the **twenty-fifth year** of our captivity, in the beginning of the year on the tenth day of the month, in the fourteenth year after the city was struck, on the selfsame day the hand of the **LORD*** was upon me and brought me there. 2. In the visions of God **He brought me to the land of Israel** and set me upon a very high mountain on which was, as it were, the frame of a city on the south. (Rev. 21:10) 3. And he brought me there and, behold, there was a **man** whose **appearance was like the appearance of bronze** with a **line** of flax in his hand and a **measuring reed**, and he stood in the gate. (Rev. 11:1)*

The twenty-fifth year of the captivity is 572 BC. At that time Ezekiel is carried in the Spirit, by the Spirit, to Israel from the river Chebar in Babylon. The word Man in verse three is Ish in Hebrew, meaning Husband, the Incarnate Body of the LORD* Whom we call Y'shua.

> Ezekiel 40:4. *And the **man** said to me, Son of man, behold with your eyes and hear with your ears and set your heart upon all that I shall show you, for you were brought here so I could show you. **Declare everything you see to the House of Israel.***

What Ezekiel sees is to be reported to the House of Israel, which is in Babylon so Ezekiel is taken to Jerusalem in the Spirit, then returned to the river Chebar in Babylon to speak to the House of Israel. In Jerusalem, in the Spirit Ezekiel saw the Third Temple.

Ezekiel is Given a Long, Complicated Vision of the Third Temple:

> Ezekiel 40:5. *And there was a wall around the outside of the **House** and in the man's hand was a **measuring reed of six cubits long** by the **cubit and***

*a **handbreadth**, so he measured the **width** of the building, **one reed**, and the **height**, **one reed**.*

One Cubit and a Handbreadth is twenty-four inches so the building is twelve feet wide and twelve feet high.

Ezekiel 40:6. *Then he came to the **gate** which looks toward the **east**, and went up the stairs and measured the threshold of the **gate**, **one reed wide**, and the other threshold of the **gate**, which was **one reed wide**. 7. And every little **chamber** was **one reed long** and **one reed wide**, and between the little chambers were **five cubits (ten feet)** and the threshold of the **gate** by the porch of the **gate** within was **one reed**. 8. He also measured the porch of the **gate** within the House, **one reed**. 9. Then he measured the **porch** of the **gate**, **eight cubits (sixteen feet)** and its **posts**, two **cubits** (four feet) and the porch of the **gate** was inward. 10. And the little chambers on the **east** of the **gate** were three on this side and three on that side, the three were of one measure and the posts had one measure on this side and on that side. 11. And he measured the width of the entry of the **gate**, ten cubits and the length of the **gate**, thirteen cubits. 12. The space before the little chambers was one cubit on this side and the space was one cubit on that side and the little chambers were six cubits on this side and six cubits on that side. 13. He then measured the **gate** from the roof of one little chamber to the roof of another: the **width** was **twenty-five cubits** (fifty feet), door against door. 14. He also made **posts** of **sixty cubits** (one hundred twenty feet) in **height**, even at the post of the court at the **gate** on around. 15. And from the face of the **gate** of the entrance to the face of the porch of the **inner gate** were **fifty cubits (one hundred feet)**. 16. And there were **closed windows** to the little chambers and to their posts around the **gate**, and likewise to the porches: and windows were around inward, and palm trees were on each post.*

The Gatekeepers have several duties, including seeing that only authorized people enter their gates and they have control over the Treasury. The closed windows are covered by lattice work.

Now Ezekiel is shown the Outer Court, which is evidence that the Third Temple will be shown before the end of the Day of the LORD*, because the Outer Court is for sinners, pagans, who cannot enter the Inner Court. At the end of Judgment Day, there will be no need for the Outer Court; all the sinners will have been sent to the Second Death and the Saints will be in Heaven.

The Third Temple is Spiritual, with Ezekiel seeing in the Spirit, not seeing a physical Temple. This Temple will never be built, but will be a Spiritual Temple during Judgment Day. When the Day of the LORD* comes, the sinners will have to respond to the testimony of the Two Witnesses to be saved. Judgment Day will not be a twenty-four hour day as know a day now; The Day will be a Spiritual Day, lasting an unknown amount of time. This is a Spiritual Temple, so it covers the whole world, being seen by those whose spiritual eyes have been opened, seen all around the world simultaneously. This Spiritual event will bring the salvation of all who commit to the LORD*. This will not be Revival because it is going to reach every person alive, especially those in areas where the love of God has never been preached! The Salvation of billions of people will be much larger than is possible without special anointing from God, because somehow God will disable all the governmental and religious laws that now inhibit evangelism by Christians and Jews.

> Ezekiel 40:17. *Then he brought me into the **outer court** and there were chambers and a pavement made around the court: thirty chambers were on the pavement. 18. And the pavement by the side of the **gates** over against the length of the **gates** was the lower pavement. 19. Then he measured the **width** from the **front of the lower gate** to the **front of the inner court** on the outside, a **hundred cubits** (two hundred feet) **eastward** and **northward**. 20. And the **gate** of the **outer court** that looked toward the **north**, he measured its **length** and its **width**. 21. And its little chambers were three on this side and three on that side and its posts and arches were the same as the measure of the first gate. Its **length was fifty cubits (one hundred feet)** and its **width twenty-five cubits (fifty feet)**. 22. And their windows and their porches and their palm trees were like the measure of the **gate** that looks toward the east and they went up to it by **seven steps** and its **porches** were in front of them. 23. And the **gate** of the **inner court** was opposite the **gate** toward the north and toward the east, and he measured a hundred cubits from **gate** to **gate**.*

The Porches are at the top of the Seven Steps. The Outer Court was one hundred feet by fifty feet. Then Ezekiel described the Inner Court:

> Ezekiel 40:24. *After that he brought me toward the south and there was a **gate** toward the south and he measured its posts and its **porches** according to these measures. 25. And there were windows in it and in its **porches** all around, like those windows. The **length** (of the **Inner Court**) **was fifty cubits (one hundred feet)** and the **width twenty-five cubits (fifty feet)**. 26. And there were **seven steps** to go up to it and its **porches** were in front of them and it had palm trees, one on this side, and another on that side, on its posts. 27. And there was a gate in the **inner court** toward the south, and he*

*measured a **hundred cubits (two hundred feet)** from gate to gate toward the south.*

Again, the Porches are at the top of the seven steps.

> *Ezekiel 40:28. Then he brought me to the **inner court** by the south **gate** and he measured the south **gate** according to these measures 29. And its little chambers and its posts and its **porches**, according to these measures and there were windows in it and in its **porches** all around. It was **fifty cubits (one hundred feet)** long and **twenty-five cubits wide (fifty feet)**. 30. And the **porches** around it were **twenty-five cubits long (fifty feet)** and **five cubits (ten feet) wide**. 31. And its **porches** were toward the **outer court** and palm trees were on its posts and the stairway to it had **eight** steps.*

The Outer Court welcomed everyone, including Heathens, but the Inner Court welcomed only those who were dealing with Sin at the Altar. The Porches now have Eight Steps. The Holy Place was only for Priests who had been sanctified.

> *Ezekiel 40:32. And he brought me into the **inner court** toward the **east** and he measured the **gate** according to these measures. 33. And its little chambers and its posts and its porches were according to these measures and there were windows in it and in its **porches** all around. It was **fifty cubits (one hundred feet) long** and **twenty-five cubits wide (fifty feet)**. 34. And its **porches** were toward the **outer court** and palm trees were on its posts, on this side and on that side and the **stairway had eight steps**.*

> *Ezekiel 40:35. Then he brought me to the north **gate** and measured it according to these measures; 36. Its little chambers, its posts and **porches** and the windows to it all around, the **length** was **fifty cubits (one hundred feet)** and the **width twenty-five cubits (fifty feet)**. 37. And its posts were toward the **outer court** and palm trees were on its posts on this side and on that side and the **stairway had eight steps**. 38. And a chamber with its entry was by the posts of the **gates**, where they washed the burnt offering. 39. And in the **porch** of the **gate** were two tables on this side and two tables on that side, on which to **slay the burnt offering**, the **sin offering**, and the **trespass offering**. 40. And at the outside, as one goes up to the entry of the north **gate**, were two tables and on the other side, which was at the **porch** of the gate, were two tables. 41. Four tables were on this side and four tables on that side, by the side of the **gate**, **eight tables** where they **slew their offerings**. 42. And the four tables were of **hewn stone** for the burnt offering, of a cubit and a half long and a cubit and a half wide and one cubit high: on which they also laid the instruments with which they **slew the burnt offering** and the*

*sacrifice. 43. And hooks a handbreadth long were fastened all around inside and the flesh of the offering was on the tables. 44. And outside the inner **gate** were the chambers of the singers in the **inner court**, which was at the side of the north **gate** and they faced toward the south, one at the side of the east **gate** facing toward the north. 45. And he said to me, This chamber that faces toward the south is for the **priests**, the keepers of the charge of the **House**. 46. And the chamber that faces toward the north is for the **priests**, the keepers of the charge of the altar, who are the sons of Zadok among the sons of Levi, the ones who come near to the **LORD*** to minister to Him.*

The Tables for slaying the offerings are made of stones because stone does not become ritually unclean.

At the time of this vision Ezekiel and all the Jewish people knew that any future Temple would a place for Burnt Offerings, Sin Offerings, Peace Offerings, and Thank Offerings: But now we know that those offerings will no longer be made, because of Y'shua's offering. The completed Temple will be Spiritual, not Physical, and will not be in New Jerusalem, so, it is a fixture only during Judgment Day. The Third Temple is an element of Transition, never actually built.

*Ezekiel 40:47. So he measured the **court**, a **hundred cubits (two hundred feet) long** and a **hundred cubits (two hundred feet) wide**, foursquare, and the **altar** that was before the **House**. 48. And he brought me to the **porch** of the **House** and measured each post of the **porch**, five cubits on this side and five cubits on that side, and the width of the **gate** was three cubits on this side and three cubits on that side. 49. The length of the **porch** was twenty cubits and the width eleven cubits, with the steps by which they went up to it and there were pillars by the posts, one on this side, and another on that side.*

Holy of Holies

*Ezekiel 41:3. Then he went inside and measured the **post** of the door, **two cubits**, and the **door, six cubits**, and the **width** of the **door, seven cubits**. 4. So he measured its **length, twenty cubits** and its **width, twenty cubits** along the **width** of the **Temple** and he said to me, This is the **Holy of Holies**.*

The Third Temple does not have a veil before the Holy of Holies, but has doors opening into it. Here the Sanctuary is called the Temple, with the Holy of Holies the same width as the Sanctuary of the Temple. The entire structure, referred to next in verse thirteen as the House was much larger than the Second Temple.

*Ezekiel 41:5. After that he measured the **wall** of the **House, six cubits (twelve feet)** and the **width** of each **side chamber, four cubits (eight feet)**,* *all around the **House** on every side. 6. And there were **thirty-three side chambers**, one over another and in order, and they were against the wall of the **House** for the side chambers all around, so they could be anchored, but they were not anchored to the wall of the **House**. 7. And the **side chambers** had greater width as they ascended, spiraling around the **House**, for the **width** of the **House** increased as it spiraled higher and higher around the **House**. Therefore, the **width** of the **House** continued upward and so one ascended from the lowest story to the highest by a staircase in the middle. 8. I also saw the **height** of the **House** all around, the foundations of the **side chambers** were a full reed of **six cubits (twelve feet)**. 9. The thickness of the wall, which was for the **outer side chambers**, was **five cubits** and that which was left was the place of the **inner side chambers**. 10. And between the **chambers** the **width** was **twenty cubits (forty feet)** around the **House** on every side. 11. And the doors of the side chambers were toward the place that was left, one door toward the north, and another door toward the south and the **width** of the place that was left was **five cubits** (ten feet) all around. 12. Now the building that was before the **Separate Place** at the end toward the west was **seventy cubits wide** and the wall of the building was five cubits thick all around and its length **ninety cubits**.*

The Third Temple is much larger than Solomon's Temple: The Third Temple will be two hundred feet long by one hundred feet wide vs. ninety feet long and thirty feet wide for the First Temple. The original Temple Mount was seventeen acres; the Third Temple Mount will encompass more than eight hundred twenty-six acres for the Third Temple Complex with a wall surrounding the entire area. The Third Temple is Spiritual – not Physical!

Ezekiel 41:13. *So he measured the **House**, a **hundred cubits (two hundred feet)** long and the **Separate Place**, and the building with its walls, a **hundred cubits long (two hundred feet)** 14. And the **width** of the face of the **House** and of the **Separate Place** toward the east, a **hundred cubits (two hundred feet)**. 15. And he measured the **length of the building** over against the **Separate Place** which was behind it and its galleries on the one side and on the other side, a **hundred cubits (two hundred feet)**, with the **inner Temple** and the porches of the court, 16. The door posts, the closed windows, and the galleries all around on their three stories, opposite the door, paneled with wood all around and from the ground up to the windows and the windows were covered 17. To that above the door, even to the **inner House**, and outside, and by all the wall around inside and outside, by measure. 18. And it was made with cherubim and palm trees, so that a palm tree was between a cherub and a cherub and each cherub had two faces 19. So that* *the face of a **man** was toward the palm tree on the one side and the face of a young lion toward the palm tree on the other side: it was made through the whole **House** all around. 20. Cherubim and palm trees were made from the ground to above the door and on the wall of the **Temple**. 21. The **posts** of the **Temple** and the **face** of the **Sanctuary** were **squared**, the appearance of the one like the appearance of the other.*

The **Separate Place** is the **House**, the **main Temple building** including the side chambers. The word for **Man** in verse nineteen is Adam, the generic word for mankind. What the galleries are is a mystery, with some scholars saying they are the chambers around the walls while others say a system of balconies, and still others say corner structures. The **Inner Temple** is the **Sanctuary**.

*Ezekiel 42:15. Now when he had made an end of measuring the **Inner House**, he brought me out toward the **gate** which faced the **east** and measured it all around. 16. He measured the east side with the measuring reed, **five hundred reeds (six thousand feet), all around with the measuring reed**. 17. He measured the **north side, five hundred reeds (six thousand feet), all around with the measuring reed**.*

*18. He measured the **south side five hundred reeds (six thousand feet), with the measuring reed**. 19. He turned about to the **west side and measured five hundred reeds (six thousand feet) with the measuring reed**. 20. He measured it by the **four sides**: it had a **wall around it, five hundred reeds (six thousand feet) long and five hundred (six thousand feet) wide**, to make a **separation between the Sanctuary** and the **profane place**.*

Five hundred reeds equal six thousand feet, making the Temple Complex to be more than a mile long on each of its four sides. The Third Temple has a wall surrounding the complex, separating the Holy from the Profane, which is everything outside the wall. The Complex is more than eight hundred twenty-six acres so the city of Jerusalem would be over-run to make room for the Third Temple, with the current rebuilding of the ancient wall around the old city holding one hundred sixty acres vs. eight hundred twenty-six acres. The size of the Third Temple Complex and the next verses indicate that this Temple is Spiritual, not physical.

*Ezekiel 43.1. Afterward he brought me to the **gate**, the **gate** that looks toward the east 2. And, behold, the **Glory of the God of Israel** came from the way of the **east** and His voice was like a sound of many waters (Rev. 14:2; 19:6) and the earth shone with **His glory**. 3. And it was according* *to the appearance of the **vision** which I saw, according to the **vision** that I saw when **I came to destroy the city** and the **visions** were like the **vision** that I saw by the river Chebar and I fell upon my face. 4. And the **Glory of the LORD*** came into the **House (Temple)** by the way of the **gate** that faces the **east**. 5. So the **spirit took me up and brought me into the inner court and, behold, the Glory of the LORD* filled the House**. 6. And I heard (Him) speaking to me out of the **House (Temple)** and a **Man** stood by me. 7. And **He** said to me, **Son of man**, the place of **My throne** and the place of the soles of **My feet**, is where **I** and **My holy name** will dwell in the midst of the **children of Israel forever**. The **House of Israel** will no longer defile, they or their kings, by their harlotry or by the carcasses of their kings in their high places. 8. In their setting of their threshold by **My thresholds** and their post by **My posts** and the wall between Me and them, they have even defiled **My holy name** by their abominations that they have committed: therefor **I have consumed them in My anger**. 9. Now they will put away their harlotry and the carcasses of their kings far from Me and **I shall dwell in their midst forever**.*

Ezekiel was taken in the Spirit to Jerusalem, to make known the Third Temple. The Man Who stood by Ezekiel in verse six is Ish in Hebrew, which also means Husband, the One Who married Israel (Jeremiah 3:14), the Incarnate Body (Y'shua) of the LORD*. This Vision sets the stage for the LORD*'s coming on Judgment Day. The Spiritual Third Temple is shown to Ezekiel in the Spirit. Everything unclean will be kept outside the wall on the Day which would mean no sinner could come into the Temple Complex. Then all who become saved will be grafted into the Domestic Olive Tree, the Jewish Tree with its Jewish Roots and they will dwell inside the Wall while the LORD* dwells throughout the city and in each person! On Judgment Day the House of Israel will be expanded to apply to the Entire World among whom the LORD* will dwell forever! See the New Jerusalem in the chapter, *The Book of Revelation*.

Ezekiel 44:15. *But the* priests, *the Levites, the sons of Zadok* who kept the charge of My Sanctuary *when the children of Israel went astray from Me, they will come near to Me to minister to Me and they will stand before Me to offer the fat and the blood to Me: the word of Adonai, the* LORD*. 16. They will enter My Sanctuary *and they will come near to* My table *to* minister to Me *and they will* keep My charge. 17. And it will be, when they enter the gates of the inner court, they will be clothed with linen garments and no wool will come upon them while they minister in the gates of the inner court and inside. 18. They will have linen turbans upon their heads and linen breeches upon their loins. They will not gird themselves with anything* *that causes sweat. 19. And when they go out to the* outer court, *to the* outer court *to the people, they will take off their garments in which they minister and lay them in the holy chambers and they will put on other garments, and* they will not sanctify the people with their garments.

Because nothing or no one defiled can enter the Temple Complex, the Outer Court no longer exists after this world-wide Salvation! So, right after this happens everyone inside the Third Temple Complex is Holy – no one defiled will be there! Everyone will be a Priest and will be in their own Spiritual bodies. No one will be married or given in marriage, but each will be a Perfected Spirit.

Ezekiel 44:20. *Neither will they shave their heads or let their locks grow long, they will only trim their heads. 21. Neither will any* priest *drink wine when they enter the* inner court. *(Lev. 10:9) 22. Neither will they take for their wives a widow, nor she who is divorced, but they will take virgins of the seed of the House of Israel, or a widow that is the widow of a priest. 23. And* they will teach My people the difference between the holy and profane *(Rom. 2:18, Heb. 5:14), and cause them to* discern between the unclean and the clean.

Teaching is the primary function of every priest, especially the priest of each home since we are a kingdom of priests! (Exod. 19:6, 1 Pet. 2:5,9, Rev. 1:6) The following rules no longer apply, with no more sin offerings. There will be no more defiling by the dead because in ETERNAL LIFE, there is no more Death.

Ezekiel 44:24. *And in conflicts they will stand in judgment and they will* judge *it according to* My judgments *and they will keep* My teachings *and* My statutes *in all* My appointed times *and they will* sanctify My Sabbaths. *25. And they will come to no dead person to defile themselves, except for father or for mother or for son or for daughter for brother or for a sister who has had no husband, they may defile themselves. 26. And after he is cleansed, they will count seven days for him. 27. And on the day that he goes into the* Sanctuary, *to the* inner court *to minister in the* Sanctuary, *he will offer his* sin offering: *the word of Adonai, the LORD*.*

After Judgment Day there will be no more Death! Therefore, the rules on being defiled by contact with the Dead will no longer be valid! We will all be in Heaven, not in the physical world!

Ezekiel 44:28. *And it will be for an* inheritance *for them.* I AM their inheritance *and <u>you will give them no possession in Israel</u>.* I AM their possession. *29. <u>They will eat the meal offering and the sin offering and</u>*

the guilt offering and every dedicated thing in Israel will be theirs. 30. And all the First Fruits *of everything and every donation, of every sort of your offerings, will be for the* priests. *You will also give to the* priest *the first of your dough so he can cause the blessing to rest in your house. 31. The* priests *will not eat of anything that is dead of itself, or torn, whether it be fowl or beast.*

In the Hereafter there will not be any offerings, no Repentance, although we will be Humble because our Spiritual bodies will be perfected forever! In Bible times the priest drew no salary, so his provision was from his share of offerings. See *First Fruits* in the One New Man Bible Glossary under *Seasons of the LORD*.*

The Spiritual Third Temple exists on earth only briefly during Judgment Day as it prepares the world for ETERNAL LIFE. "Only Briefly" may be misleading because this Spiritual Day could last thousands of years as we know years in the natural. The Third Temple covers the entire Transition from natural to Spiritual.

Water (Torah) Flows from the House.

Water represents Torah so this passage describes how the Third Temple faithful will grow Spiritually as their spiritual bodies grow in knowledge and understanding of God. Water represents Torah in Isaiah 55:1 and Exodus 14:22. As we enter the Hereafter, no matter how learned we are in Scripture, we only know a shadow of what we will eventually know.

> Ezekiel 47.1. *Afterward he again brought me to the door of the* House *and, behold, waters issued from under the threshold of the* House *eastward, for the front of the* House *faced the east and the waters came down from under the right side of the* House, *at the south side of the altar. (Rev. 22:1) 2. Then he brought me out by the way of the* gate *northward and led me around the way outside to the outer gate by the way that looks eastward and, behold,* waters *ran out on the right side.*

The coming verses indicate our growth as we truly learn the treasures hidden in our Scriptures. We begin this trip with our earthly brains, using only 10% of each brain; then gradually increase our mental capacity as we grow into our fully Spiritual Selves.

> Ezekiel 47:3. *And when the* man *who had the line in his hand went out eastward, he measured a thousand cubits and he brought me through the* waters. *The waters were to the* ankles. *4. Again he measured a thousand and brought me through the waters. The waters were to the* knees. *Again he measured a thousand and brought me through. The waters were to the*

91

loins. 5. Afterward he measured a thousand and it was a river that I could not cross, for the waters had risen, waters to swim *in, a river that could* not be *crossed. 6. And he said to me, Son of man, have you seen this? Then he brought me, and caused me to return to the bank of the river.*

As each one progresses in understanding of Scripture the deeper water represents deeper understanding of God's Word. Each one will eventually be saturated in the Word of God. That is when each will use 100% of his or her Brain, at that point each will be fully Spiritual! Transition is over!

Ezekiel 47:7. *Now when I had returned, behold, at the bank of the river were very many trees on the one side and on the other. 8. Then he said to me, These waters issue out toward the east country and go down into the desert and go into the sea. When brought out into the sea, the* waters will be healed, *9. And it will be that everything that lives, which moves, wherever the rivers will come, will live, and there will be a very great multitude of fish, because these waters will come there for they will be healed and everything will live wherever the river comes. 10. And it will be that the fishermen will stand upon it from Ein Gedi even to Ein Eglaim. There will be a place to spread nets, their fish will be according to their kinds, like the fish of the Great Sea, a great number. 11. But its miry places and its marshes will not be healed. They will be given to salt. 12. And beside the river, on its bank, on this side and on that side, will grow* all trees for food, *whose leaf will not fade, neither will it fail to produce fruit. It will bring forth new fruit according to its months, every month, because their* waters *issued out of the* Sanctuary, *and its* fruit will be for food *and its* leaf for medicine. (Rev. 22:2,14)

The Waters Being Healed are the from the pure water coming from the Temple flushing the salt wat water from the Dead Sea. The pure water replaces all the Dead Sea water. The Food we consume in the Hereafter will be the Word of God; the Spiritual Trees will be for added beauty in the Hereafter. The leaves of trees will be a balm for those who enter Eternal Life with wounds, especially emotional wounds from all abuse, mis-treatment. The Water's being healed also refers to the atmosphere of our eternal home being pure, far different from the contaminated atmosphere we know on Earth where foul spirits rule over various cities and countries, like the one that contended with an angel who was coming to instruct Daniel.

Daniel 10: 7. *And I alone,* Daniel, *saw the vision, for the men who were with me did not see the vision, but a great quaking fell upon them, so that they fled to hide themselves. 8. Therefore I was left alone and saw this great vision, and there remained no strength in me, for my comeliness was turned in me into corruption and I retained no strength. 9. Yet I heard the sound of his words and when I heard the sound of his words, then I was in a deep sleep on my face, and my face toward the ground. 10. And, behold, a hand touched me, which moved me upon my knees and the palms of my hands. 11. And he said to me, O* Daniel, *the man greatly beloved,* understand the words that I speak to you *and* stand upright, *for I am now sent to you. And when he had spoken this word to me, I stood trembling. 12. Then he said to me,* Do not be in awe, Daniel! *For from the first day that you set your heart to understand, and to chasten yourself before your God,* your words were heard *and I have come because of your words. 13. But* the prince of the kingdom of Persia withstood me for twenty-one days, *but lo,* Michael, *one of the chief princes, came to help me and I remained there with the kings of Persia. (Rev. 12:7) 14. Now* I have come to make you understand *what will befall your people in the latter days, for yet the vision is for many days.*

Heaven has no foul spirits controlling anything! There is not now and will not ever be any foul spirit ruling any part of Heaven!

This passage transforms each Saint from the Natural to the Spiritual Realm, with the Heathens witnessing the transformation. The Heathens who do not Repent do not get to experience the Acts of Loving Kindness! Those Heathens who do Repent are ushered into the Hereafter. Before that Glorious event, Believers will be subject to Persecution!

Revelation 11:7. *And when they finish their testimony, the* beast *that ascends from the abyss (Dan. 7:3) will* make war *with them, and will* overcome them *(Dan. 7:7,21) and he will* kill them. *8. And their corpses will be upon the streets of the great city, which is called spiritually Sodom and Egypt, where also their* Lord *was crucified. 9. And they from the people and tribes and languages and nations will see their corpses three and a half days and they will not allow their corpses to be placed in a tomb. 10. And those who dwell upon the earth will rejoice over them and they will be happy and they will send gifts to one another, because these* two prophets *tormented those who dwell upon the earth.*

The Heathens of the world try to kill the Two Witnesses, but get a rude awakening! The celebration of the Heathens is short-lived!

Revelation 11:11. *And after the three and a half days the breath of life from God entered them, and they stood upon their feet, (Ezek. 37:5) and great fear fell upon those who saw them. 12. Then the two heard a loud voice from* heaven saying to them, *"You must ascend to this place."* *Then they ascended into heaven (2 Ki. 2:11) in the cloud, and their enemies watched them. 13. And in that hour there was a great earthquake, and a tenth of the city fell and seven thousand named of mankind were killed in the earthquake and the rest of the people became terrified and gave glory to the God of heaven. (Ezek. 38:19,20)*

Revelation 11:15. *Then the seventh angel trumpeted: and there was a loud voice in heaven saying,*

"The kingdom of the World of our Lord

and of His Messiah has come

and He will reign forever and ever."

(Exod. 15:18; 7:14, Ob. 21, Zech. 14:9, Ps. 10:16; 22:29, Dan. 2:44)

In this Kingdom there is one throne and He will reign forever! He is both the LORD* and His Messiah, Who are One!

This is a description of New Jerusalem, the spiritual City, so these are Spiritual attributes, not physical; The Spiritual Bounty is literally beyond our imaginations!

Isaiah 60:19. *The* sun *will no longer be your* light *by day. Neither will the* moon *give* light *to you for brightness, but the* LORD* *will be an* everlasting Light *for you, and your God, your Splendor. (Rev. 21:23-25) 20. Your sun will no longer go down nor will your moon withdraw itself, for the* LORD* *will be your* everlasting Light, *and the days of your mourning will be ended. (Rev. 21:23; 22:5)*

The Glory of the LORD* permeating everything is beyond imagination, too beautiful to express! Imagine His brilliant Glow permeating everything! There will be no night, but a perpetual, brilliant Glow! There will not be night; Saints will not need sleep, but will be refreshed as they worship and praise the LORD*.

Isaiah 60:21. Your people *also will* all *be* righteous: *they will* inherit the land *forever, the branch of* My *planting, the* work *of* My hands, *so I can be* glorified. 22. *A little one will become a thousand, and a small one a numerous nation. I AM, the LORD*, will hasten it in its time.*

This is ETERNAL LIFE!

END TIMES

End Times are those that have signs noted throughout Scripture that people look for to indicate the Coming of the Lord. The problem is that there have been continuous signs of His coming, so often that every few years there has been a clamor warning of the End. But it is not yet. I remember back in the 1930s there was a picture on the cover of Life Magazine of a family of four sitting on the roof of their ranch style home, each one holding a suitcase packed for the journey. That is a poignant picture of the common misunderstanding of the Day. The following passages list some of the Scriptures leading to the false picture.

Coming Persecutions

Matthew 10:16. *"Behold I am sending you as sheep in the midst of wolves: therefore you must become as* prudent *as* serpents *and as* innocent *as* doves. *17. And you must be on guard from men: for they will give you over to* sanhedrins *and they will scourge you in their* public gatherings: *18. and you will be led before rulers and even kings because of Me, in witness to them and to the* heathens. *19. And when they would* arrest you, *do* not be anxious *how or what you would say: for* what you should say *will be* given to you *at that moment: 20. for you will not be those speaking but (it will be) the* Spirit *of your* Father, *the* One *Who* speaks through you. *21. And a* brother *will betray a* brother *into death and a* father *a* child, *and* children *will rise up in* rebellion *against* parents *and they will put them to* death. *(Mic. 7:6) 22. And you will be* hated *by all because of* My name: *but the one who has* persevered *to (the) end will be* saved. *23. And when they would pursue you in this city, you must flee to another: for truly I say to you, you would not finish the cities of* Israel *until the* Son of Man *would come.* (Mark 13:9-13, Luke 21:12-17)

Sanhedrins are the first century equivalent of local courts. Public Gatherings could be translated synagogues, but "a gathering of people" is the primary meaning and no one would be scourged in a synagogue. Luke 4:28 tells of Y'shua being driven from the city when the congregation was enraged but they could not harm Him physically in the synagogue. See *Congregation* in the One New Man Bible Glossary. The Persecution is one of the most prominent predictions of the Coming of the Lord; with so much persecution of Christians and Jews throughout the world right now. In many countries like China, families of Christians are severely persecuted, being imprisoned, tortured, even dying in prison; Moslem countries can be just as bad. In Nigeria gangs of Moslems in recent years killed dozens of Christians. Persecution in the United States is increasing; with the 2021 order granting rights to transgender boys to join girl's high school teams and use the girls' locker rooms and bathrooms; freedom of religion does not overcome the new rules, although a number of states have laws counter-manding the federal edict. With all this persecution maybe His Coming for Judgment Day is fast approaching! That Day will not be the quick twenty-four hour Day that we are used to; it will be a Spiritual Day, prolonged for a long time.

The Son of Man will Suffer

> Luke 17:23. *Then they will say to you, 'Behold there' or 'Behold here:' you should not go away and you should not pursue. 24. For just as the lightning flash lights from one place under the sky to another place under the sky, **so will be the Son of Man in His Day.** 25. But first it is necessary for Him to **suffer many things** and to be rejected by this generation. 26. And just as it was in the days of Noah, so also it will be in the days of the **Son of Man:** 27. They were eating, they were drinking, they were marrying, they were being given in marriage, until that day Noah entered the box (ark) and the flood came and killed everybody. 28. Likewise just as it happened in the days of Lot: they were eating, they were drinking, they were buying, they were selling, they were planting, they were building: 29. But on the **day Lot came out from Sodom**, it **rained fire and brimstone** from heaven and **killed them all.** 30. It will be according to these things on the day the **Son of Man** is revealed. 31. In that **Day** he who will be on the roof and his property in the house, must not go down to take it, and likewise the one in a field must not return for the things behind. 32. You must continually remember Lot's wife. 33. Whoever would seek to **keep** his **own life** safe will **lose** it, but whoever would **lose** it will **preserve it alive.** 34. I say to you, on this night two will be on one bed, the one will be taken along, and the other will be left: 35. Two women will be grinding upon this stone, the one will be **taken along**, but*

*the other will be left. 36. Two will be in the field, one will be **taken** and the other will be left." 37. And when they answered they said to Him, "Where, Lord?" And He said to them, "Where the body is, there also the eagles will be gathered."*

The Greek word Paralambano in verses thirty-five and thirty-six speaks of a bride being taken to a bridegroom. Each Saint will be taken to his or her Bridegroom.

Matthew 24:32. *"But you learned the parable from the fig tree: now when its branch would become tender and it would put forth its leaves, you know that summer is near: 33. So then you, when **you would see all these things**, you **know** that **He is near the doors**. 34. Truly I say to you that this generation would **not** pass until all these things would happen. 35. The **sky** and **Earth** will pass away, but **My words** would **never pass away**."*

The Unknown Day and Hour

Matthew 24:36. *"But no one knows about that **Day** and hour, and neither do the **angels** of the heavens nor the **Son**, except the **Father only**. 37. For just as the days of Noah, so will be the **coming of the Son of Man**. 38. For as people were among them in those days before the flood, **eating** and **drinking**, **marrying** and being **given in marriage**, until it was the day Noah came into the box (ark), 39. But they did not know until the flood came and it took up everything, **so** will the coming of the Son of Man also be. 40. Then two will be in the field, **one is <u>taken</u> to Him** and one is left: 41. Two women will be grinding in the mill, **one is <u>taken</u>** and one is left.* (Mark 13:32-37, Luke 17:26-30, 34-36)

Verse thirty-six tells us every generation is to believe He is coming any day now. We are supposed to be ready for the Day, every day to be occupied with Righteous deeds. Taken is the Greek word paralambano used in verses forty and forty-one speaking of a bride being taken to her bridegroom.

Matthew 24:42. *Therefore **you must steadily be watchful**, because you do not know what sort of day your Lord is coming. 43. But you know that if the house owner had known what sort of watch, when, the thief was coming, he would have been watchful and would not have allowed his house to be broken into. 44. Because of this then **you must always be prepared, because you must not continually think of the time the Son of Man is coming**."*

While we need to know about End Times, our focus is not to be on that but on what He would have us do now!

Matthew 24:3. *After He sat down upon the Mount of Olives the disciples came to Him privately saying, "You must now tell us when these things will be" and "What will be the sign of Your coming and the end of the age?" 4. And Y'shua said to them, "See that no one would lead you astray: 5. For many will come in My name saying, 'I am the Messiah,' and they will deceive many. 6. And you will be going to hear of **wars and reports of wars: see that you are not frightened: for it is necessary to happen, but it is not yet the end.***

While there are numerous wars now on the earth these events are going on even more violently in the Spiritual realm. The wars and rumors of wars are a sign for all believers to recognize Spiritual Warfare as a sign of the End. Hearing of wars and rumors of wars is perpetual, especially in the past seventy years because United States policies hang on endless wars. In the past one thousand five hundred years, only eight percent of the years have no war at all; that is a total of one hundred twenty years without war, so reports of war have been a perpetual sign all that time.

Matthew 24:7. *For **heathen** will rise against **heathen** and **kingdom** against **kingdom** and there will be **famines** and **earthquakes** in various regions: 8. and all these things (are the) **beginning of labor** in birthing. 9. Then **they will give you over to affliction** and they will **kill** you, and you will be **hated** by all the **heathens** because of My name. 10. And then many will be caused to fall away and they will give over others and they will hate others: 11. and many false prophets will be raised and they will lead many astray: 12. and because of the increase of lawlessness the love of many will grow cold. 13. But the **one who remains to (the) end**, this **one will be saved**. 14. Then this **Good News** of the **Kingdom** will be proclaimed in the whole inhabited world in witness to all the heathens, and then the **end will come**."*

There have also been famines and earthquakes all that time, with more earthquakes reported in recent decades because of having ever more sophisticated and sensitive detection. Christian and Jewish persecution has been increasing to the point that we now have persecution of Christians in the United States, including persecution by state and local governments.

There are famines and earthquakes in the natural, but even more so in the Spiritual Realm. Shakings are here and will get stronger. There is extraordinary hatred against Biblical teachings throughout the world both in the natural and in the Spiritual. People have been fined and even jailed for expressing Biblical truths in the United States, Canada, UK, and other countries, bringing more fierce Spiritual warfare than has been seen here since the United States became a nation. Darkness is increasing.

> *All things came through Him, and there was not one thing that came into being without His participation. What had come 4. In Him was life, and the life was the Light of mankind: 5. And the Light shines in the darkness, nevertheless the darkness has not appropriated it.* (John 1:3-5).

We see these signs of the End Times but do they mean the End is near? Many people think so, but we are far from completing our assignment to proclaim Kingdom throughout the world, especially with hatred of Biblical Christians and Jews increasing steadily all over the world.

We are to Think every day that He is coming Tonight!

JUDGMENT DAY

Judgment Day is described at length in the chapter *Revelation* but this preliminary discussion is the prelude for that.

> Isaiah 51:6. *Lift up your eyes to the heavens and look upon the earth beneath! For the **heavens will vanish** away like smoke and the **earth will wax old** like a garment and **those who live there will die like vermin**, but **My salvation will be forever** and **My acts of loving kindness** will not be abolished.*

At the End of Judgment Day the earth will cease to exist; all living creatures will cease to exist. All the Saints will have moved into the Spirit Realm – Eternal Life! Judgment Day is not one twenty-four day as we know days, but this is Spiritual Time, not natural time. The Spiritual Day will last a long time compared to the twenty-four hour day we are used to. No one knows how long the Spiritual Day will last, but to those who are in the Spirit it will not seem long because then a day will be as a thousand years and a thousand years as a day.

> Isaiah 51:7. *Listen to Me! Obey, you who know righteousness, the people in whose heart is My Torah (Teaching)! **Do not be in awe of the reproach of men! Do not be dismayed** at their **revilings***! *8. For the moth will eat them up like a garment and the worm will eat them like wool, but **My acts of loving kindness** will be forever, and **My deliverance/salvation** from generation to generation.*

Then, as often now, Heathens reviled those who worshipped the LORD* Do not be dismayed at the Reviling, but know that in the end the LORD* will bring justice and you will be vindicated.

Judgment Day in Israel

> Isaiah 11:11. *And it will be in that **Day**, the Lord will set His hand again the second time to recover the remnant of His people, which will be left from Assyria, from Egypt, from Patros, from Cush, from Elam, from Shinar, from Hamath, and from the **islands of the sea**. 12. And He will set up a sign for the nations, and will assemble the **outcasts of Israel** and gather together the **dispersed of Judah** from the four corners of the earth. 13. And the jealousy of **Ephraim** will cease, and the adversaries of **Judah** will be cut off. **Ephraim** will not envy **Judah**, and **Judah** will not torment **Ephraim**. 14. But they will fly against the Philistines toward the west. Together they will pillage those from the east. They will lay their hand upon Edom and Moab and the children of Ammon will obey them. 15. And the **LORD*** will utterly destroy the gulf of the **Egyptian Sea**, and with His mighty wind He will shake His hand over the **River**, and will strike it in the seven streams, and make people go over dryshod. (Rev. 16:12) 16. And there will be a highway for the **remnant of His people** who are left from **Assyria**, like it was to **Israel** in the day that He came up out of the land of **Egypt**.*

At the very beginning of Judgment Day the Martyrs are taken to Heaven, coming from the four corners of the earth, regions where Ephraim had been scattered and where Judah had been dispersed. The expression Islands of the Sea refers to all the peoples of the world. In this passage Ephraim refers to the Children of Israel. The Egyptian Sea is now called the Gulf of Suez; the River is the Euphrates. During Judgment Day people will be converted by the Two Witnesses, the Jewish and Christian congregations who go through the world preaching Kingdom. There will be more than one ascension of Saints to ETERNAL LIFE

The PROPHETS are fascinating to study, realizing that many of them spoke of events hundreds of years before the fact. Daniel identified Kingdoms centuries before they existed, while Isaiah and others spoke of the coming of Messiah, describing His ministry hundreds of years before His birth. Jonah knew of Nineveh's destruction centuries before the fact. They often prophesied about End Times, referring to the Day, Judgment Day, two hundred eighty-seven times in the bible. The End Times need to be understood by everyone because when those times come, Judgment comes, and it is too late to Repent. It is necessary to live every day as if He is coming tonight! When He comes, it is over, there is no tomorrow! Expect Him tonight! Be Prepared! Repent!

In the Book of Revelation we learn that Judgment Day is much longer than our twenty-four hour day on Earth. The best way to prepare for Judgment Day is by walking in Repentance all day every day. Also study and become immersed in Jewish Roots because entrance to New Jerusalem is only through Jewish Gates!

Zephaniah Prophesies the Total Destruction

> Zephaniah 1:2. *I shall utterly consume all things from off the land, says the* **LORD***. 3. **I shall consume man and beast**. *I shall consume the fowls of the sky and the fishes of the sea and the stumbling-blocks with the wicked, and I will cut man off from the land, says the* **LORD***. 4. I shall also stretch out My hand over Judah and over all the inhabitants of Jerusalem and I will* **cut off the remnant of Baal** *from this place and the name of the idolatrous priests with the priests, 5. And those who* **worship the host of heaven from the housetops**, *and those who worship, who swear by the* **LORD*** *and swear by their* **King**, *6. And those who are turned back from the* **LORD***; *and those who have* **not** *sought the* **LORD*** *or inquired for Him. 7.* **Hold your peace** *at the* **presence** *of my* **Lord, the LORD***, *for the* **Day** *of the* **LORD*** *is at hand, for the* **LORD*** *has* **prepared a sacrifice**, *He has* **bid His guests**.

Idolators will be removed. The last three words (Bid His Guests) of verse seven are the key to what is coming. The Hebrew word translated Guests literally means Sanctified, which can be either human Saints or Angels. Bid is His Invitation to the Guests who are about to do the LORD's bidding, cutting off all of the Remnant of idol worshippers.

The Call to Repent!

> Zephaniah 2.1. **Gather** *yourselves together! Yes, gather together, O nation not ashamed. 2. Before the decree brings forth, before the day passes as the chaff, before the* **fierce anger of the LORD*** *comes upon you, before the* **Day** *of the* **LORD's*** *anger comes upon you. 3.* **Seek the LORD***, *all you* **humble** *of the earth who have done His ordinance!* **Seek righteousness! Seek humility!** *It may be* **you will be hidden on the Day of the LORD's*** **anger**, *4. For Gaza will be forsaken and Ashkelon a desolation. They will drive out Ashdod at the noon day and Ekron will be rooted up.*

Gather in verse one speaks of gathering a bundle of twigs or straw for kindling a fire. The Humble are those who Repent! The Repentant will be Hidden from the angels who bring the Wrath of the LORD* to torment the sinners. The name Zephaniah means Hidden by Yah.

Rendering Double to the idol-worshipping Greeks is a picture of the LORD*'s actions on Judgment Day. The LORD* delights in doing the impossible, which

He did in the Hasmonean victory over the best Greek armies, which were not only the best armies of Greece, they were the best armies in the world at that time. See *Hanukkah* under *Seasons of the Lord* in the One New Man Bible Glossary.

Isaiah 24:21. *And it will be on that **Day**, the LORD* will **punish** the army of the high ones who are on high, and the **kings** of the earth upon the earth. 22. And they will be **gathered** together like prisoners are gathered in the pit and will be shut up in the prison and after many days they will be visited. 23. Then the **moon will be confused** and the **sun ashamed**, when the **LORD* of Hosts reigns** on **Mount Zion** and in **Jerusalem**, and **gloriously** before **His elders**.* (Rev. 4:4)

The Book of Revelation goes into great detail about the Day, so see the chapter titled *The Book of Revelation* in this book. The Day is considerably longer than our twenty-four hour day. All through that Day the Wrath of God will be poured out, but also people will be converted and more than once the Saints will be taken to ETERNAL LIFE.

The Coming of Y'shua on Judgment Day Is Reported in Zechariah 14:4:

Zechariah 14.1. *Behold, the **Day of the LORD*** is coming and booty from you will be divided in your presence. 2. For I shall **gather all the nations** against **Jerusalem** in battle and the city will be taken and the houses rifled and the women ravished, and half the city will go into captivity but the rest of the people will not be cut off from the city. 3. Then the **LORD*** will go forth and fight against those nations, like when He fought in the day of battle, 4. and **His feet** will stand in that **Day** upon the **Mount of Olives**, which is before **Jerusalem** on the east, and the **Mount of Olives** will **split** in the middle toward the east and toward the west and there will be a very great valley, and half of the mountain will remove toward the north and half of it toward the south. (Acts 1:11) 5. And you will flee to the valley of the mountains, for the valley of the mountains will reach to Azel. Yes, you will flee, like you fled from before the earthquake in the days of Uzziah king of Judah and the LORD* my God will come and all the saints will be with you.*

Judgment Day is Spiritual. The split in the Mount of Olives is in the Spirit Realm, not a physical splitting of the earth.

Coming of Messiah

Many expect our Messiah to have His own Coming, but He said "The Father and I are One." In Revelation there is one throne for both Y'shua and the LORD* to share, so we should not be looking for separate returns.

John 10:27. *My sheep hear My voice and I know them and they are following Me, 28. and I am giving them **eternal life**, and they would **not ever** die and no one is able to seize them from My hand. 29. My Father Who has given them to Me is greater than all, and no one is able to seize them from the hand of the Father. 30. **We, the Father and I, are One.**"*

John 14:6. *Y'shua said to him, "I AM the **Way** and the **Truth** and the **Life**: no one comes to the Father except through Me. 7. **If you have known Me, then you will know My Father.** And from now on you do know Him and you have been seeing Him." 8. Philip said to Him, "Lord, You must now show us the Father, and it is sufficient for us." 9. Y'shua said to him, "I have been with you for so long a time and you have not known Me, Philip? **The one who has seen Me has seen the Father: how can you say, 'You must show us the Father?'** 10. Do you not believe that **I am in the Father and the Father is in Me**? The words which I speak to you, I am not speaking from Myself, but **the Father Who lives in Me does His works**. 11. Believe in Me, that **I am in the Father and the Father is in Me**: but if not, believe because of these works.*

Verse six refers to the Way of Y'shua, which is obedience to the Father, doing only what we see the Father doing. It means walking in the Spirit of all Scripture, but not being legalistic: focus on the Father, not on the behavior of others with a critical spirit.

Isaiah 43:11. Says I AM, I AM the LORD*. *Besides Me there is no* Deliverer/Savior*!*

The word translated Deliverer/Savior is Moshia, which is Y'shua with a Mem prefix, denoting added emphasis.

John 17:20. *"I do not ask concerning them only, but also concerning those who believe in Me because of the disciples' message, 21. so that all would be one, just as **You, Father, are in Me and I in You, that they also would be in Us, so that the world would believe that You sent Me.** 22. And I have given them the glory which You have given to Me, so that they would be one just as **We are One:** 23. I in them and You in Me, so that they would have been brought into unity, so that the world would know that You sent Me and You loved them just as You loved Me. 24. Father, the One Who gave to Me, I want that where I am those would be with Me, so that they would see My glory, which You have given to Me because You loved Me before the* *foundation of the world. 25. Righteous Father, even though the world did not know You, but I did know You, and these knew that You sent Me: 26. and I made Your name known to them and I shall make known, so that the love with which You loved Me would be in them and I would be in them."*

In Zechariah 14:4 it is the LORD* Who steps down on the Mount of Olives. We see many signs that lead us to believe that Y'shua could return any day now. Look at some of Y'shua's statements about His return. Read all of Matthew 24, and then note verses 36, 42-44, which say, *36. But no one knows about that day and appointed time or hour, and neither do the angels of the heavens or the Son, except the Father only....*

42. Therefore you must steadily be watchful, because you do not know what sort of day your Lord is coming. 43. But you know it, that if the house owner had known what sort of watch when the thief was coming, he would have been watchful and would not have allowed his house to be broken into. 44. Because of this then you must always be prepared, because in this you must not continually think of the time the Son of Man is coming.

Always be Prepared is really a definitive command: we are to be about His business, feeding the hungry, caring for those less fortunate, and not to be focused on His return, but on Him.

Revelation 22:3. And there will no longer be anything there (that is) cursed. And the throne of God and of the Lamb will be in it, and His servants will serve Him 4. and they will see His face, (Ps. 17:15; 42:2) and His name (will be) upon their foreheads. (Ezek. 9:4, Rev. 7:3; 9:4; 14:1) 5. And there will no longer be night and they will not need (the) light of a lamp or (the) light of (the) sun, (Zech. 14:7) because the Lord God will give light upon them, and (those whose names are written in the Book of Life) will reign forever and ever. (Isa. 60:19,20, Dan. 7:18,27)

There is one Throne for God and the Lamb because the two are One. We all, everyone, will see the Face of the LORD* and the Lamb. All those whose names are written in the Book of Life will reign with Him as Priests - to administer the edicts of the King – One King, the rest are Priests. Hebrew Scholars say the Name on the foreheads will be Emmet, Truth.

Mark 13:32 states, But concerning that day and the hour no one knows, not even the angels in heaven and not the Son, only the Father. 33. You must watch out! You must continually be alert: for you do not know when the time is. In Luke 12:40 He says, ..the Son of Man is coming in a time you do not think He is coming. Then He talks of the coming **Kingdom of God** in Luke 17:20-37. Verse 20 includes *The **Kingdom of God** does **not come** by means of, or in company with, **close observation**.* Watching for Him will not speed up His coming. If anything can speed up His coming, it would be feeding the hungry, housing the homeless, and so on as listed in Matthew 25:35-40. This is according to Ephesians 5:27. *in order that He would present for Himself the glorious congregation, not having spot or wrinkle or any of such things, but so that His **bride** would be **holy** and **without blemish**.*

That the **Day of the LORD*** does **not** come by watching for it means that the average Christian should not be obsessed with a focus on His Coming. However, there are evangelists with very effective ministries who are called to preach on End Times and His Coming; They are being faithful to their calling, bringing millions into the fold.

Matthew 10:23 *And when they would persecute you in this city, you must flee to another: for truly I say to you, you would not finish the cities of Israel until the Son of Man would come.* Matthew 24:32 *Truly I say to you that this generation would not pass until all these things would happen.* Since these words were written in the first century each generation has had advocates that THIS is the generation that will see His coming. Paul believed He was coming soon as we can see in his remark, *And I say this, brothers, the time is short:..* talking about not getting married, 1 Corinthians 7:29.

> Matthew 24:45 *Who then is the faithful and wise servant whom the owner appointed over his household servants to give them food in due season? 46. Blessed is that servant who when his master comes will find him doing this: 47. truly I say to you that he will place him over all his possessions. 48. but if that evil servant would say in his heart, 'My lord lingers,' 49. and he would begin to beat his fellow servants, and he would eat and he would drink with the drunkards, 50. the master of that servant will come in a day in which he does not expect and in a moment that he does not know, 51. and he will punish him severely and his lot will place him with the hypocrites: there will be weeping and gnashing of teeth in that place.*

Paul expresses the attitude of the apostles in 1 Thessalonians 4:15 when he writes, *Indeed we say this to you in a word of the Lord, that we, those left behind who are living to the coming of the Lord, would not precede those who are sleeping:* a very clear statement of expecting His return in Paul's lifetime.

Clearly, we need to be taught about the end times, but just as clearly, we need to focus on the task at hand, to raise up mature believers and to evangelize, to feed the poor, and bring deliverance to the world. Each generation is to believe the time is at hand as Jacob wrote in Jacob 5:8 *You too must now be patient, you must strengthen your hearts, because the coming of the Lord has drawn near.* This does not put down those who are teaching about the soon coming of the Messiah. Those evangelists are being obedient to their call and are keeping many occupied as good servants as well as bringing many converts to the Lord. Then too, He might come tonight! Be Ready! **Judgment Day** is at hand!

KINGDOM OF GOD

Kingdom of God speaks of several things and it is also called by another name, Kingdom of the Heavens. It is difficult to put kingdom references into the neat pigeonholes with which we are so comfortable. One use of the kingdom is to refer to God Himself as in:

> *But you must continually seek first the **Kingdom of God** and His righteousness, then all these things will be provided for you.* (Matt. 6:33) and another, *But if I am casting out demons by a finger of God, then the **Kingdom of God** has come upon you.* (Lk. 11:20).

Then we have in the same vein *But if I cast out demons by the Spirit of God, then the* Kingdom of God *has come upon you,* Matthew 12:28. This means that all who have the Spirit of the Living God should expect deliverance from demonic influence, whether sickness or the evil spirits like those that oppressed the Gadarene demoniac.

Another use refers to the eternal kingdom:

> *I say to you that many will come from east and west and will recline with Abraham, Isaac, and Jacob in the **Kingdom of the Heavens**.* (Matt. 8:11) *And Y'shua said to them, 'Truly I say to you that you who follow Me in the restoration of all things, when the Son of Man would sit upon the throne of His glory, then you will be seated upon twelve thrones judging the twelve tribes of Israel.'*

This is in Matthew 19:28, also referring to the **Eternal Kingdom**.

Kingdom Now

Matthew 12:28. *But if I cast out demons by the Spirit of God, then the* **Kingdom of God** *has come upon you.* We are to bring the **Kingdom now**, in this time, by appropriating the authority given to us, healing the sick, delivering the oppressed, raising the dead – doing all the things Y'shua was doing while He walked the earth.

> John 14:10. *Do you not believe that I am in the Father and the Father is in Me? The words which I speak to you, I am not speaking from Myself, but the Father Who lives in Me does His works. 11. Believe in Me, that I am in the Father and the Father is in Me: but if not, believe because of these works. 12. Most assuredly I say to you, the* **one who believes in Me will do the works which I am doing and he will do even greater things than these, because I am going to the Father:** *13. and whatever you would ask in My name, this I shall do, so that the Father would be glorified in the Son: 14. whatever you would ask Me in My name I shall do.*

This is truly **Kingdom** living, right here, right now!

Matthew 4:17. *From then on* Y'shua *began to preach and to say, "You must continuously repent: for the* Kingdom of the Heavens *has come near."*

At the beginning of His ministry Y'shua is speaking of the powerful miracles that accompanied Him. He then chose Peter, Andrew, Jacob, and John, going around introducing the Kingdom of the Heavens to the region. The tense used in the Greek tells us to walk in repentance every day, even though we know we have been sanctified and made righteous by the blood of the Lamb. This is because we have not been perfected, but are to strive to be better today than we were yesterday, as we become more like Him. Ephesians 5:1. *Therefore you must continually be imitators of* God *as beloved children.*

Acts 1:6 has a clear reference that some were looking for, the Messianic Reign, when the King would sit on the throne, saying:

> *Therefore indeed those who came asked Him saying, "Lord, in this time are You restoring the* **kingdom** *in Israel?" 7. But He said to them, "It is not for you to know the times or seasons which the Father set by His own authority, 8. but you will take power when the Holy Spirit comes upon you and you will be* **My witnesses** *in Jerusalem and in all Judea and Samaria and to the end of the earth."*

We are His Witnesses, preaching Kingdom as we Witness.

Mark. 4:11 says, *To you has been given the mystery of the **Kingdom of God**.* The **Kingdom** means more than one thing, so each time we read it we are to meditate to discern the appropriate meaning.

The **Kingdom** speaks of **God Himself**, the **Eternal Kingdom (Heaven)**, evidence of **His Kingdom** in us, and the **Messianic Reign**.

The Lord's Prayer gives insight in Matthew 6:9 with:

> Our Father, Who is in the heavens:
>
> Your name must at once be made holy:
>
> 10. Your Kingdom *must now come:*
>
> Your will must be done right now,
>
> as in heaven also on Earth:

Y'shua is teaching us to say in the strongest terms that His Kingdom must immediately come. This is not ordering Him to bring the Kingdom, but emphasizing that we are to do all in our power to effect Kingdom living in the here and now, right where we are!

> Luke17:20. *And having been asked by the Pharisees when the **Kingdom of God** is coming He answered them and said, "The **Kingdom of God** does not come by means of, or in company with, close observation, 21. and will they not say, 'Behold it is here,' 'There it is,' for behold the **Kingdom of God** is **within you**.*

Y'shua said in Matthew 12:28. *But if I cast out demons by the* Spirit of God, *then the* Kingdom of God *has come upon you.* His commission is stated in Matthew 28:18. Then when Y'shua came He spoke to them, saying:

> **All authority** *has been given to **Me** in **heaven** and upon the **Earth**. 19. Therefore when you go, you must now make disciples of all the heathens, 20. teaching them to keep all the things that I have been commanding you: (Amos 9:12) and behold I AM with you all the days until the end of the age.*

All His disciples are to preach the Kingdom, as in Matthew 10:7:

> *And while you are going you must preach, saying that 'The **Kingdom of the Heavens** has come near.' 8. **You must continually heal sicknesses, raise the dead, cleanse lepers, cast out demons**: you took freely, you must now give freely.*

Since the Kingdom is within each of us, we are the ones; each one of us is responsible to exhibit Kingdom living in the here and now. We are the ones, each one, to do His will right now.

> Matthew 11:28. *Come to Me all those who work and are burdened, and I shall give you rest. 29. You must immediately take **My yoke** upon you and you must now learn from Me, because I am gentle and humble in My heart, and you will find rest in your lives: 30. for **My yoke** is **pleasant** and **My burden** is **insignificant.***

The LORD*'s yoke means total spiritual surrender. See Deuteronomy 6:5. *And you will* love *the* LORD* your God *with* all *your* heart, *with your very being, and with all your might.*

> Matthew 22:36. *Teacher, which is the greatest commandment in the Torah (Teaching) 37. And He said to him, **You will love the Lord your God with your whole heart** and with your **whole being** (Deut. 6:5) and with your **whole mind**: 38. this is the greatest and first commandment.*

This spiritual surrender is necessary to exhibit the Kingdom for the whole world to see. Each one of us is to live in the Spirit Realm, showing Miracles to the Heathens of the world.

Our actions and reactions sanctify His name, which each of us reciting the Lord's Prayer swears to do, in saying "Your name must at once be made holy."

> John 17:20. *I do not ask concerning them only, but also concerning those who believe in Me because of the disciples' message, 21. so that **all** would be **one**, just as You, **Father**, are in **Me** and **I** in **You**, that **they** also would be in **Us**, so that the **world** would **believe** that **You sent Me**.*

There needs to be evidence that each of us is in Him.

Although the Lord's Prayer has other meanings, the function that Y'shua taught us to pray is the Kingdom Now, making our walk with God to be so different from the world's walk, that others cannot help but see the difference.

The late Chief Rabbi of the British Empire, J. H. Hertz, wrote, "Peace is no negative concept and is not the equivalent of inactivity. Whether for the individual or for society it is that harmonious co-operation of all human forces towards ethical and spiritual ends which men call the **Kingdom of God**. The Prophets longed for a Messianic peace that would pervade the universe, and include all men, all peoples – that should include also the beasts of the field; Isaiah 11:6-10. This idyllic reign is described in those verses:

The wolf also will dwell with the lamb and the leopard will lie down with the kid, and the calf and the young lion and the fatling together, and a small youth will lead them. 7. And the cow and the bear will feed. Their young ones will lie down together and the lion will eat straw like the ox. 8. And the nursing child will play on the hole of the asp, and the weaned child will put his hand on the viper's den. 9. They will not hurt or destroy in all My holy mountain, for the earth will be full of the knowledge of the LORD*, as the waters cover the sea."

Each believer is to live in the Spirit now to show unbelievers that the Spiritual is real, that what is to come will be so much greater than what we see now in this walk.

Matthew 6:25. *"Because of this I say to you,* **stop being anxious for your life**, *what you would eat or what you would drink, or what you would put on your body. No indeed! Is life not more than food and the body more than clothing? 26. You must consider the birds of the sky that do not sow and do not harvest and do not gather into a storehouse, and your heavenly Father feeds them: are you not worth more than they? 27. And who of you if you are anxious is able to add one single hour upon his age? 28. And concerning clothing, why are you anxious? You must observe the lilies of the field, how they grow: they do not labor and they do not spin: 29. but I say to you that Solomon in all his glory did not dress himself as one of these. 30. And if God clothes the grass of the field this way, which is here today and tomorrow is cast into a furnace, will He not much more clothe you, little faiths? 31. Therefore you should not be anxious saying, 'What could we eat?' or, 'What could we drink?' or, 'What should we wear?' 32. For the* **heathens** *are striving for all these things: for indeed your heavenly Father knows that you need all these things. 33.* **But you must continually seek first the Kingdom of God and His righteousness, then all these things will be provided for you.** *34. Therefore do* **not be anxious for tomorrow**, *for tomorrow will be anxious of itself: each day's trouble is enough for that day." (Pro. 27:1)*

This reference to God is placed with the full explanation of just Who God is, that leads all believers to seek the fullness of the LORD* that all believers should have. Walk by Faith, not by sight.

Matthew 12:28. *But if I cast out* **demons** *by the* **Spirit of God**, *then the* **Kingdom of God has come upon you.** *29. Or how is someone able to enter the house of the strong one and to steal his property, unless he would first bind the strong one? And then he will thoroughly plunder his house. 30. The one* *who is not with Me is against Me, and the one who does not gather with Me is scattering. 31. Because of this I say to you, every sin and blasphemy will be forgiven to mankind, but the blasphemy of the **Spirit** will not be forgiven.*

This is Kingdom Power that each believer is to walk in right now!

Matthew 19:23. *Then Y'shua said to His disciples, "Truly I say to you that only with difficulty will a rich person enter the Kingdom of the Heavens. 24. And again I say to you, it is easier for a camel to go through the eye of a needle than a rich person to enter the **Kingdom of God**."*

Here, Kingdom of God presents the Hereafter! This passage is contrary to the teachings of the Pharisees, who said that obedience to the legalistic rules, traditions, would be rewarded with wealth in this life, parallel to the present-day faith-prosperity teachings. What we have on Earth is our qualifying round so that when a body dies, the Spirit is able to enter the Kingdom of God.

Matthew 21:28. *"And what does it seem to you? A man had two children. And having come to the first he said, 'Child, you must immediately go today and work in the vineyard.' 29. and when he answered he said, '**I do not want to**,' but later because he **repented** he went. 30. When he went to the other he said likewise. But when he answered he said, '**I shall, sir,**' but **he did not go**. 31. Who of the two did the will of the father?" They said "The first." Y'shua said to them, "Truly I say to you that the tax collectors and prostitutes are going into the **Kingdom of God** before you. 32. For **John** came to you in a way of **righteousness**, and you **did not believe him**: but the **tax collectors** and **prostitutes** did **believe in him**: and although you saw later, **you did not repent** of it to believe him."*

This is another reference to the **Hereafter**.

Matthew 21:42. *Y'shua said to them, "And then have you never read in the Scriptures,*

'A stone which the builders rejected,

> *this became a cornerstone:*

this was done by the Lord

> *and is it a wonder in our eyes.'? (Ps. 118:22,23)*

*43. Because of this I say to you that the **Kingdom of God** will be taken from you and it will be given to a people **making its fruits**. 44. And the one who falls upon this stone will be dashed to pieces: and on whomever it would fall, it will crush him."*

Mark 1:14. *And after John was arrested **Y'shua** came into Galilee proclaiming the **Good News of God** 15. and saying that "The time has been fulfilled and the **Kingdom of God** has drawn near: you must **continually repent** and **believe** in the **Good News**."*

Time after time Y'shua tells us the Kingdom has drawn near and to continually Repent.

Mark 4:10. *And when He happened to be alone, those around Him with the twelve were asking Him about the parables. 11. And He was saying to them, "To you has been given the mystery of the **Kingdom of God**: but to those outside everything is in parables, 12. so that*

'When they look they would look but they would not see,

and when they would listen they would hear but they would not understand,

*lest at any time they would **turn back (repent)** and **it would be forgiven them**.'"*

The Parable of the Mustard Seed

Mark 4:30. *And He was saying, "How would we liken the **Kingdom of God** or with whom should we stand in this parable? 31. It is like a mustard seed, which when it would be sown upon the ground, it is smaller than all the seeds on the earth, 32. and when it would be sown, it comes up and becomes greater than all the vegetables and makes large branches, so that the birds of the sky are able to dwell under its shade."*

These passages compare the Gospel of Kingdom of God to a message which sounds good, but does not reveal the Power of God. Preaching Kingdom lacks power in the message, but requires a demonstration to go with it. Too often our appeal has been to say the sinner's prayer, but not to demonstrate the Power of God – which Y'shua demonstrated continually, When the seventy-two were sent to evangelize in Luke (10:17) they returned with the report "Lord, even the demons are subject to us in Your name." The Sinner's prayer is not the ticket to Heaven, but the changed lifestyle of the one who prays is the ticket to Heaven.

Mark 9.1. *And He was saying to them, "Truly I say to you that there are some of those who stand here who would **not** in any way taste death until they would see the **Kingdom of God** when it comes in power."*

Here, Kingdom refers to the Messianic Reign.

The Messianic Reign is Mistakenly Thought to be in the Physical World

The Reign is in the Hereafter, not here on Earth. The Earth will be destroyed at the end of Judgment Day so the Messianic Reign will begin with the LORD* and Y'shua on the One Throne in Heaven.

The next reference is clearly to the Hereafter.

> Mark 9:42. *"And whoever would cause one of the least of these who believe in Me to sin, it is better for him if a **millstone** turned by a **donkey** were placed around his neck and he were cast into the sea. 43. And if your hand would cause you to sin, you must immediately cut it off: it is expedient for you to **enter life** crippled rather than, having two hands, to go into Gehenna, into the unquenchable fire (44. where their worm does not die and the fire is not put out.) 45. And if your foot would cause you to sin, you must immediately cut it off: it is better for you to **enter life** lame rather than having two feet to have been thrown into Gehenna (46. where their worm does not die and the fire is not put out.) 47. And if your eye would cause you to sin, you must immediately cast it out: it is more profitable for you to **enter** the **Kingdom of God** with one eye rather than having two eyes to have been cast into **Gehenna**, 48. where their worm does not die and the fire is not put out. (Isa. 66:24) 49. For everyone will be salted with fire. 50. Salt is good: but if the salt would become salt-less, with what will you season? You have salt in yourselves and you must continually live in peace with one another."*

Entering Life is used frequently by Y'shua referring to the Hereafter, our promotion to Heaven! Verses 44 and 46 are in parentheses because they were added to Scripture in the fifth century. Gehenna was an area outside Jerusalem that reminded people of the fires of hell. It was a valley, Ge Hinnom, where trash, garbage, dead animals and even executed criminals were burned. Fires, smoke, and worms there were constant reminders of the fires of hell. Salt is a preservative and speaks of permanence, the meaning of the Covenant of Salt, Num. 18:18,19.

> Luke 18:15. *And they were bringing infants to Him so that He could touch them: but when the disciples saw them they were rebuking them. 16. But **Y'shua** summoned them saying, "You must now permit the children to come to Me and you must not forbid them, for the **Kingdom of God** is of such as these. 17. Truly I say to you, whoever would not take the **Kingdom of God** like a child could **not** come into it."*

This means to take the Kingdom of God eagerly, take it to heart. The Kingdom is to be sought eagerly; it is not to be passively received.

Luke 19:11. *And while they were listening to these things He again told them a parable because He was near Jerusalem and they thought that the* **Kingdom of God** *was going to be revealed at once, as soon as He reached Jerusalem. 12. Therefore He said, "A certain man, a nobleman, was going to a faraway land to take a* **kingdom** *for himself, then to return.*

Just as that man was going to be aggressive in taking a Kingdom, we are to be aggressive in taking the Kingdom of God!

Matthew 11:12. *From the days of John the Immerser until now the* **Kingdom of the Heavens** *is taken by* **violence**, *and shares in the* **heavenly kingdom** *are sought for with the* **most ardent zeal** *and the* **most intense exertion** *and* **violent men are seizing it**, *each* **one claiming eagerly for himself**. (also in Luke 16:16)

Stake your claim!

Luke 21:29. *Then He told this parable to them: "You saw the fig tree and all the trees: 30. when they would now put forth their leaves, when you see them for yourselves, you know that summer is already near. 31. And so then you, when you would see these things happening, you must know that the* **Kingdom of God** *is near. (Luke 17:21) 32. Truly I say to you, that this generation would* **not** *pass by until all these things would happen. 33. The sky and the Earth will pass away, but My words will* **never** *pass away."*

Kingdom of God speaks of the Spiritual Power we are supposed to be walking in right now! Y'shua told us to Preach the Kingdom! The word translated sky in verse thirty-three could also be translated heaven, but that is misleading. God is eternal and so is His throne. The Earth and the solar system may well pass away but the heavens are eternal.

Luke 22:14. *Then when the hour came, He and the apostles with Him reclined. 15. And He said to them, "I have greatly desired with a longing to eat this Seder with you before I suffer: 16. for I say to you that I would* **not** *eat it again until this would be fulfilled in the* **Kingdom of God**." *17. Then having taken a cup, after He gave thanks, He said, "You must take this and you must immediately share it among yourselves: 18. for I say to you, that from now on I am* **not** *drinking from this product of the vine until the* **Kingdom of God** *would come." 19. Then having taken bread, after He gave thanks, He broke it and gave it to them saying, "This is My body which is being given on your behalf: you must continually do this in My remembrance." 20. Then likewise the cup after they ate, saying, "This is the* *cup of the New Covenant (Jer. 31:30-33, Hos. 2:16-22) in My blood which is being poured out on your behalf.*

Y'shua says He will not drink wine again until after the Kingdom would come, not giving any clue when that time will be.

Luke records the proper order for the cups of the Seder. There are a total of four cups, the last being the cup of Elijah. The Hebrew word translated New and the Greek word translated New have primary meanings of Renew, so instead of New Covenant, Renewed Covenant would be appropriate.

Luke 23:50. *Then behold, a man named Joseph who was a member of the council and a good and righteous man 51. – this one was not agreeing with the resolution and with what they did – from Arimathea, a Jewish city, who was waiting for the* **Kingdom of God**,

Joseph was looking for the Messianic Reign on earth.

John 3.1. *And there was a man of the Pharisees,* **Nicodemus** *was his name, a leader of the Jewish people: 2. this one came to Him at night and said to Him, "Rabbi, we know that You, a teacher, have come from God: for unless God were with Him no one is able to perform these signs that You do." 3. Y'shua answered and said to him, "Most definitely I say to you, unless someone would have been* **born from above***, he is not able to see the* **Kingdom of God***." 4.* **Nicodemus** *said to Him, "How is a man able to be born when he is in old age? Is he able to enter his mother's womb and be born a second time?" 5.* **Y'shua** *answered, "Most certainly I say to you, unless someone would have been* **born** *out of* **water** *and* **Spirit** *he is not able to enter the* **Kingdom of God***. 6. What has been* **born** *of the* **flesh** *is* **flesh***, and what has been* **born** *of the* **Spirit** *is* **spirit***.*

Being born of water speaks of both Immersion and Torah! We are born of Flesh, but need to born in the Spirit to enter the Kingdom of God.

Acts 1.1. *Indeed the first narrative I made concerning everything, O Theophilus, which* **Y'shua** *began to do and also to teach, 2. until that day He was taken up, after He gave orders to the* **apostles** *whom He had chosen by the* **Holy Spirit** *3. to whom He also presented Himself alive, by many convincing proofs, after He suffered, while* **He appeared to them for forty days** *and was saying these things about the* **Kingdom of God***: 4. and while He was staying with them, He ordered them "Do not go away from Jerusalem but* **wait** *for the* **promise** *of the* **Father** *which you heard from Me, 5. for*

John on the one hand immersed in water, but you on the other hand will be **immersed in the Holy Spirit** *after these not many days."*

The Apostles had no idea what the Immersion in the Holy Spirit would bring, but it brought Speaking in Tongues and the Power to perform miracles!

Acts 8:12. *But when they believed in Philip's preaching concerning the* Kingdom of God *and the name* Y'shua Messiah, *then both men and women were being immersed.*

Acts 14:21. *And, after they preached in that city and made many worthy disciples, they returned to Lystra and to Iconium and to Antioch 22. strengthening the lives of the disciples, encouraging them to persevere in the faith, and that it was necessary for us to enter the* **Kingdom of God** *through many troubles.*

Kingdom here has all four aspects, telling us that overcoming the world system is not without effort, persecution, and perseverance.

1 Corinthians 15:50. *"But I say this, brothers, that* flesh *and* blood *are not able to inherit the Kingdom of God.*

The Kingdom is Spiritual! Every element of Kingdom is Spiritual!

Matthew 7:21. *"***Not** *everyone who says to Me, '***Lord. Lord!***' will* **enter** *the* **Kingdom of the Heavens**, *but the* **one who does** *the* **will** *of* **My Father**, *the* **One** *in the* **heavens**. *22. Many will say to Me in that Day, '***Lord. Lord!** *Did we* **not prophesy** *in* **Your name?** *And we* **cast out demons** *in* **Your name,** *and we did many* **miracles** *in* **Your name?'** *23. And then I will declare to them that '***I never knew you***: you working without* **Torah** *(Teaching) must continually* **depart from Me.'"**

Speaking in tongues, prophesying, doing miracles are not evidence of being saved, but obedience to Torah is the evidence the LORD* is looking for.

Matthew 8:5. *And when He came into Capernaum a centurion came to Him, begging Him 6. and saying, "Lord, my child has been smitten in the house by paralysis, fearfully tormented." 7. Then He said to him, "When I come I shall heal him." 8. Then the centurion said, "Lord, I am not worthy that You should come under my roof, but You must* **only say a word**, *and* **my child will be healed**. *9. For I also am a man under* **authority**, *having soldiers under myself, and I say to this one, '***You must go**,*' and* **he goes**, *and to another, '***You must come**,*' and he* **comes**, *and to my servant, '***You must do this**,*' and he does." 10. Then when* **Y'shua** *heard He was amazed*

118

*and said to those following, "Truly I say to you, I have not before found **so much faith in Israel**. 11. I say to you that many will come from east and west and will recline with Abraham, Isaac, and Jacob in the **Kingdom of the Heavens**, 12. and the sons of the kingdom will be cast out into the outer darkness: there will be weeping and gnashing of teeth in that place." 13. Then **Y'shua** said to the centurion, "**You must now go. As you believed, it must instantly be for you.**" And his **child was healed in that hour**.*

Kingdom of the Heavens is used here to refer to Heaven itself. Heaven is always plural in Hebrew, partly because seven different words are used to speak of Heaven. See *Heavens* in One New Man Bible Glossary.

Matthew 10:5. *Y'shua sent these twelve, after He commanded them, saying, "On the way do not go to the heathens and **do not enter a Samaritan city**: 6. but you must rather **go regularly to the lost sheep of the House of Israel**. 7. And while you are going you must preach, saying that '**The Kingdom of the Heavens has come near.**' 8. You must continually **heal sicknesses, raise the dead, cleanse lepers, cast out demons**: you **took freely**, you must now **give freely**. 9. You can **acquire neither gold** nor **silver** nor **copper** in your belts, 10. nor a **knapsack** for the way nor two **tunics** nor **sandals** nor a **staff**: for the **worker** is **worthy of his food**.*

This is the Power of God bringing His Power to Earth, making His Power visible to the people of the Earth. Those ministering were to be fed for their ministry, but they were not to be enriched. They were told to go only to the Lost Sheep of the Children of Israel who were back-slidden Jewish people. After His resurrection His disciples were sent to the entire world.

Matthew 11:11. *Truly I say to you: there has not been born of women greater than **John the Immerser**: but the least in the **Kingdom of the Heavens** is greater than he. 12. From the days of **John the Immerser** until now the **Kingdom of the Heavens** is taken by **violence**, and shares in the **heavenly kingdom** are sought for with the most ardent **zeal** and the most **intense exertion** and **violent** men are **seizing it**, each one claiming eagerly for **himself**. (Luke 16:16) 13. For all the **Prophets** and the **Torah** (Teaching) **prophesied until John**: 14. and if you want to accept it, he is **Elijah**, the one who was going to come. (Mal. 3:23) 15. The one who has ears must continually listen.*

These two Kingdom of the Heavens refer to the Hereafter, gaining ETERNAL LIFE. Notice that the Least in Heaven is greater than John the Immerser because each one in Heaven is perfect! Once there, each one has use of 100% of his or her brain and has no evil influence to fight.

> Matthew 13:10. *Then when the disciples came they said to Him, "Why are You speaking to them in parables?" 11. And He said to them, "Because it has been given to you to know the **mysteries** of the **Kingdom of the Heavens**, but it has not been given to those. 12. For who has, it will be given to him and he will have **great abundance**: but who does not have, even what he does have will be taken from him. 13. I am speaking to them in parables because of this, because although they see, they do not see, and although they hear, they do not hear, and they do not understand,*

In verse eleven Mysteries of the Kingdom of the Heavens speaks of all four meanings, with the Great Abundance being Spiritual Abundance, not physical or financial abundance.

> Matthew 13:44. *"The **Kingdom of the Heavens** is **like** a **treasure box** hidden in the field, which when a man found he hid, then out of his joy, went and sold all that he had and **bought** that field." 45. "Again the **Kingdom of the Heavens** is **like** a merchant seeking good **pearls**: 46. and when he found **one very precious pearl**, he left and **sold everything** that he had and he **bought** it." 47. "Again the **Kingdom of the Heavens** is like a **fishnet** cast into the lake gathering from every kind of fish: 48. which when it was filled, after they pulled it up on the shore and sat down, they **gathered** the **good** into a vessel, but they **cast** the **bad** outside. 49. And so it will be in the **end of the age**: the **angels** will come out and they will **separate** the **evil ones** from the midst of the **righteous** 50. and they will **cast them** (**the evil ones**) into the **fiery furnace**: there will be weeping and gnashing of teeth in that place."*

These all point to desirability of the Heavenly Kingdom, that it is well worth any possible sacrifice to gain entry.

Genesis 12.1. *Now the LORD* had said to Abram, "Get yourself out of here! From your country and from your kindred and from your father's house to a land that I shall show you.*

The command for Abram to get going is simultaneously a call for Abram to put his personal desires out of the Way, out of the Way of the LORD! Getting rid of SELF is often painful, sometimes awkward, sometimes accompanied by falling and back-sliding, but a necessity for those who want God's perfect will in their lives.

The three similes in Matthew thirteen are illustrations of the need for each believer to get rid of self and give everything to God. No possession is anywhere near as valuable as the surety of ETERNAL LIFE. Each of those illustrations stresses trading the most important thing in your life for the ETERNAL KINGDOM.

> Matthew 16:16. *And Simon Peter said, "You are the **Messiah, the Son of the Living God." 17. And Y'shua** said to him, "**Blessed** are you, Simon Bar-Jonah, because, **not flesh and blood**, but **My Father**, the **One** in the **heavens**, revealed this to you. 18. And I am saying to you that you are Peter, and upon this **rock** I shall build My congregation and gates of Hades will not prevail against the congregation.*

The word for "rock" is the feminine word in Greek, meaning Rock as picture of Y'shua.

> 1 Corinthians 10:1 *For I do not want you to be ignorant, brothers, because all our fathers were under the cloud and all went through the sea 2. and all were immersed into Moses in the cloud and in the sea 3. and all ate the same spiritual food 4. and all drank the same spiritual drink: for they drank from a spiritual **Rock**, which was following them, and the **Rock** was the **Messiah**.*

Peter's name is masculine, meaning a piece of a rock; with the masculine form being used only for Peter's name in the New Testament. Peter's actual name was the Aramaic word Kefa, meaning a rock about the size of a man's hand.

> Matthew 16:19. *I shall give you the keys of the **Kingdom of the Heavens**, and whatever you would **bind** upon the Earth **will already have been bound** in the heavens (with ongoing effect) and whatever you would **loose** upon the Earth **will already have been loosed in the heavens** (with ongoing effect)." 20. Then He was commanding the disciples that they should not say that He was the **Messiah**.*

To Bind is a Hebrew idiom meaning forbid. Binding and loosing here refer specifically to the judicial applications for all the dietary, Sabbath, and other regulations, including civil law, and extend to the spiritual realm as well. Loose is a Hebrew idiom meaning permit. The words "with ongoing effect" are added to express the tense used here by the Greek text. The reference is to the **Eternal Kingdom**.

> Matthew 18.1. *In that hour the disciples came to Y'shua saying, "Who is the greatest in the **Kingdom of the Heavens?**" 2. And after He called a child to Himself, He stood him in their midst 3. and He said, "Truly I say to you, unless you would change and become like the children, you could **not** enter*

*the **Kingdom of the Heavens**. 4. Therefore whoever will **humble himself** like this child, this one is the greatest in the **Kingdom of the Heavens**. 5. And whoever would take one such child in My name, takes Me."*

Although they are synonymous the Kingdom of God is used almost twice as much in Scripture as Kingdom of the Heavens – sixty-eight times versus thirty-five times. The Kingdom of the Heavens is used primarily to refer to the Eternal Kingdom.

The Kingdom of God and Mysteries of the Kingdom of the Heavens refer:

1. **To God Himself:** Matthew 6:33. *But you must continually seek first the **Kingdom of God** and His righteousness, then all these things will be provided for you.*

2. **To the Power we are to walk in.** Matthew 12:28. *But if I cast out **demons** by the Spirit of God, then the **Kingdom of God has come upon you.***

3. **To the Hereafter.** Matthew 8:11. *I say to you that many will come from east and west and will recline with Abraham, Isaac, and Jacob in the **Kingdom of the Heavens**,*

4. **To the Messianic Reign.** Luke 19:11. *And while they were listening to these things He again told them a parable because He was near Jerusalem and they thought that the **Kingdom of God** was going to be revealed at once, as soon as He reached Jerusalem.*

POWER OF GOD

The Power of God Moves in Jerusalem as the Disciples Step Out in Ministry

Ananias Finds Out Peter's View into the Spirit Realm

> Acts 5.1. *And a certain man named **Ananias**, with his wife **Sapphirah**, sold property 2. And kept back from the payment, while his wife was also fully aware, and then he brought part and placed it beside the feet of the apostles. 3. And Peter said, "**Ananias**, by what means did Satan fill your heart, for **you to have lied to the Holy Spirit** and to have kept back from the price of the property? 4. While it remained unsold was it not remaining yours until you sold it by your authority? Why did you place this deed in your heart? **You did not lie to men but to God**." 5. And when Ananias heard these words, as **he fell down he breathed his last**, and great fear came upon all those who heard. 6. Then the young men got up, covered him and after they carried him out, buried him.*

Peter may have been caught off guard when the LORD* took Ananias so suddenly, but everyone was certainly impressed that Ananias was taken.

Sapphirah Makes the Same Discovery

> Acts 5:7. *And it was about a three hour interval when his wife came in, not knowing what had happened. 8. And **Peter** declared to her, "You must tell me, if you sold the field for so much?" And she said, "Indeed, so much." 9. And **Peter** said to her, "Why was it agreed between you to test the Spirit of the Lord? Behold the feet of those who buried your husband are at the door and they will carry you out." 10. And **she fell at once at his feet and expired**: and when the young men came in they found her dead and after they carried*

her out, they buried her beside her husband, 11. And great fear was upon the whole congregation and upon all those who heard these things.

Sapphira was taken as abruptly as Ananias when God moved.

The Deacon Philip Proclaims Y'shua

Acts 8:34. *And the eunuch said to* **Philip**, *"I beg you, concerning whom is the prophet saying this? Concerning himself or concerning some other?" 35. And* **Philip** *then opened his mouth and having begun from this Scripture he proclaimed to him the* **Good News** *about* **Y'shua**. *36. And as they were going along the way, they came upon some water, and the eunuch said, "Look! Water! What prevents me from being* **immersed**?",

Philip did Immerse the Ethiopian eunuch in the only recorded New Testament Immersion by a second person. Immersion was normally self-immersion, but when Philip Immersed, the Ethiopian, Philip held his hand on the head of the man to force him to struggle like a newborn struggles to come out of the womb.

Acts 8:38. *And he ordered the* **chariot** *to stop and* **Philip** *and the* **eunuch** *both went down into the water, and* **he immersed him**. *39. And when they came up out of the water, the* **Spirit of the Lord took Philip away and the eunuch no longer saw him**, *then the eunuch went on his way rejoicing. 40. And* **Philip was found in Ashdod**: *and he was evangelizing, coming through all the cities until he came into Caesarea.*

Philip was taken away, transported to the city of Ashdod by the Holy Spirit. The Greek name for Ashdod is Azotus.

Acts 9:32. *And it happened that* **Peter** *was going through all those cities to go down also to the saints living in Lud. 33. And he found some man there named Aeneas, who was paralyzed, lying on a pallet for eight years. 34. And* **Peter** *said to him,* **Aeneas, Y'shua Messiah is healing you: you must rise and you must immediately take care of your own pallet. And he got up at once**. *35. And all who lived in Lud and Sharon saw him and* **returned** *to the Lord.*

The people of Lud and Sharon saw Aeneas walking on the streets of those cities, knowing that was a miracle. Luke says the back-sliders returned to the Lord, to the LORD* God of Israel. These were the Jews in name only, the back-slidden of the House of Israel to whom Y'shua had sent the disciples to preach deliverance/salvation.

Gazelle Wakens From the Sleep of Death

> Acts 9:36. *And in Joppa there was a certain disciple named **Tabitha**, which when it is translated means **Gazelle**: she was rich in **good deeds** and charities that she was doing. 37. And it happened in those days, that **she became sick and died**: and when they had **washed her** they placed her in an upstairs room. 38. And because Lud was near Joppa, the **disciples, having heard that Peter was in Lud, sent two men to him** urging, "Do not delay to come to us." 39. And then **Peter** got up and went with them: after they arrived they led him up to the upstairs room and all the widows came to him crying and pointing out how many tunics and garments **Gazelle** used to make when she was with them. 40. Then after he put all those outside and **knelt, he prayed and when he turned to the body he said, "Tabitha, you must immediately get up."** And she opened her eyes, and when she saw **Peter** she sat up. 41. And then he gave her a hand and stood her up: and, after he called the saints and the widows, **he presented her alive**. 42. And it became known throughout the whole of Joppa and many believed in the Lord. 43. And it happened he stayed many days in Joppa with a certain tanner, Simon.*

The Greek word for **Gazelle** is **Dorkas**. **Good Deeds** are **Mitsvot**; see *Mitsvah* in the One New Man Bible Glossary. **Washing the body** is still the way the Jewish people prepare a body for burial.

Cornelius Has a Visitation

> Acts 10.1. *And a certain man in Caesarea named **Cornelius**, a centurion from a **cohort** called **Italian**, 2. **Devout** and **God-Revering** with all in his house, doing many charitable things for the people and praying to God for everything, 3. About the **ninth hour of the day** saw clearly in a **vision an angel of God** coming to him and saying to him, "**Cornelius**." 4. Then, after he looked intently at him, he became terrified and said, "What is it, Lord?" And he said to him, "Your prayers and your charities came up as a memorial before God. 5. And now you must send men at once to **Joppa** and summon a certain **Simon** who is called **Peter**: 6. This one is staying with a certain tanner, Simon, with whom he is in a house by the sea." 7. And as the **angel**, the one who was speaking to him, left, then he called two of the household servants and a devout soldier of those attached to him 8. And after he described everything to them he sent them to **Joppa**.*

Cornelius did not waste any time sending for **Peter**. A **Cohort** has about 600 men. **God-Reverer** was the name given to those non-Jewish believers who were attending a synagogue and learning Judaism, but were not full converts. The **Ninth Hour of the Day** is 3:00PM, the time of afternoon prayer. **Joppa** was about fifty miles south of **Caesarea**, a good distance to send for **Peter** in order to provide proof that these **God-Reverers** were welcomed by God to join the Jewish believers.

Peter is given a Revelation

> Acts 10:9. *And the next day, as those traveling were nearing the city, about the **sixth hour** Peter went up on the roof to pray. 10. And he became very hungry and was wanting to eat. And while they were preparing a meal a **trance** came over him 11. And he saw **heaven opening** and something lowering, like a **great sheet**, being let down by four corners upon the ground, 12. In which were all the **four-footed animals** and **reptiles** of the earth and **birds** of the sky. 13. And a voice came to him, "**Rise, Peter**, you must right now **kill** and **eat**." 14. But **Peter** said, "Certainly not, Lord, because I never ate anything **defiled** or **unclean**." (Ezek. 4:14) 15. And again a second time a voice said to him, "**What God has cleansed**, you must not declare unclean." 16. And this happened three times, and then the object was immediately taken up into the sky.*

The critical phrase is, **"What God has cleansed,"** not saying that all things are clean, but only **what God has cleansed**. The **converts** were **cleansed because of their yearning for more of God**, with the later evidence of their **immersion in the Holy Spirit**.

> Acts 10:27. *And conversing with him he entered and found many gathered, 28. And he said to them, "You believe that it is contrary to law and justice for a Jewish person to associate with or to approach a foreigner: but **God explained to me not to say in any way that a man is common or unclean**: 29. For this reason then I came without raising any objection when I was sent for. Therefore I ask for what reason did you send for me?"*

Peter will quickly find out why God sent for him.

> Acts 10:44. *While **Peter** was still speaking these words the **Holy Spirit fell upon all those listening to the message**. 45. And the faithful from the circumcision who came with **Peter** were amazed, because the gift of the **Holy Spirit fell even upon the heathens**: 46. For they heard them **speaking in tongues** and **glorifying God**. Then **Peter** responded, 47. "No one can deny the **water**, can they, for any of these to be **immersed**, who took the **Holy Spirit** like we did?" 48. And he ordered them to be **immersed** in the name of **Y'shua Messiah**. Then they asked him to spend some days with them.*

Seeking God presented them with the Immersion of the Holy Spirit. Peter goes quickly to Jerusalem to report about the spreading of the Immersion of the Holy Spirit. In the next passage Peter reports on this to the leaders in Jerusalem.

Acts 11:11. *And behold in that instant three men stood by the house in which we were, having been sent to me from* **Caesarea**. *12. And the* **Spirit** *said for me to accompany them and not to make a distinction. They and these six brothers came with me and we entered the man's house. 13. And he reported to us how he saw the* **angel** *standing in his house saying, 'You must immediately send to* **Joppa** *to summon* **Simon**, *the one called* **Peter**, *14. Who will speak a message to you by which you and all your house would be saved.' 15. And while I was beginning to speak, the* **Holy Spirit fell upon them just as upon us in the beginning. 16. And I remembered the word of the Lord as He was saying, 'John indeed immersed in water, but you will be immersed in the Holy Spirit.'** *17. Therefore if God gave the same gift to them, as also to us believers in the Lord Y'shua Messiah,* **who was I to be able to hinder God?"** *18. And when they heard these things they remained silent, then glorified God saying,* **"So then God also gave the heathens the repentance into life."**

That anyone not Jewish could have a deep relationship with God was a new revelation to these Jewish leaders; This was a game-changing notion, surprising the leaders, extending the full relationship of believers to non-Jews.

Acts 11:19. *Then indeed those who were* **scattered** *on account of the persecution that took place against Stephen went as far as* **Phoenicia** *and* **Cyprus** *and* **Antioch**, *but* **not speaking the Word except only to Jewish people**. *20. But some of them were men of* **Cyprus** *and* **Cyrene**, *who when they came into* **Antioch** *were speaking then to the* **Hellenists** *preaching the* **Good News of the Lord Y'shua**. *21. And the hand of the Lord was with them, and a great number who believed turned to the Lord. 22. And the report concerning them was heard in the ears of the* **congregation** *that was in* **Jerusalem** *and they sent out* **Barnabas** *to come through as far as* **Antioch**. *23. Who, when he arrived and saw the favor of God, greeted and encouraged* **all** *to continue with purpose of heart in devotion to the Lord, 24. For* **Barnabas** *was a good man and full of the* **Holy Spirit** *and* **faith**. *And a huge crowd was added to the Lord. 25. Then he came out to* **Tarsus** *to look for* **Saul**, *26. And when he found him brought him to* **Antioch**. *And he was then with them a whole* **year**, *to meet with the* **congregation** *and to* **teach** *a great number of people, and in* **Antioch** *the* **disciples** *were first called* **Christians**.

The Apostles, like the Disciples sent by Y'shua, preached only to apostate Jewish people, but after Cornelius the Apostles took the Good News to everyone. The Hellenists were nominally Jewish people who had adopted Greek ways, attending the Greek games, the Greek theater, speaking the Greek language, and they were not observant Jews. See *Hellenists* in the One New Man Bible Glossary.

> Acts 12.1. *And at that time Herod the king arrested any of those from the congregation to abuse (them). 2. And he killed* **Jacob**, *the brother of* **John**, *with a sword. 3. And because he saw that it was pleasing to the Jewish (leaders), he proceeded also to* **arrest Peter**, *and they were the days of* **Unleavened Bread** *– 4. Whom he placed in jail after he seized (him), having given (him) over to four squads of soldiers to guard him, since he wanted to bring him before the people after* **Passover**. *5. So indeed* **Peter was being kept in jail**: *but there was* **fervent prayer to God** *being made by the congregation concerning him.*

Jacob was the first of the congregational leaders to be executed, with the others being martyred over the years. Martyrdom meant an early entry into ETERNAL LIFE, with John the only Apostle to die a natural death.

Peter Delivered from Prison by an Angel

> Acts 12:6. *But when Herod was going to bring him out, that night* **Peter** *was sleeping between two soldiers, bound by two chains, and there were guards by the door, guarding the prison. 7. And behold an* **angel of the Lord stood and a light shone out in the prison**: *and as he struck* **Peter's** *side, he woke him up saying, "You must get up quickly." And* **his chains fell off from his hands**. *8. And the* **angel** *said to him, "You must immediately gird yourself and put on your sandals." And so he did. Then he said to him, "You must put on your* **cloak** *and follow me."*

The Angel came only to bring Peter out of prison, an unexpected miracle for Peter, with the very impressive power of the Angel. The Cloak of every Jewish man was his Prayer Shawl.

> Acts 12:9. *Then after they went out he was following and he was not knowing that what was happening through the* **angel** *was real: but he was* **thinking he was seeing a vision**. *10. And then they came through the first guard then a second and they came upon the* **iron gate leading** *into the* **city**, *which was* **open** *to them by* **itself** *and after they came out they went down one alley, then immediately the* **angel** *left him. 11. And when* **Peter** *came to himself he said, "Now I know truly that the* **Lord** *sent out His* **angel** *and delivered me from Herod's hand and every expectation of the Jewish leaders." 12. And when he*

*understood what was going on he went to the house of **Miriam**, the mother of* ***John**, the one called **Mark**, where many were gathering and praying. 13. And when he knocked on the door of the vestibule a maid named **Rhoda** came to open, 14. And when she recognized **Peter's voice**, on account of her joy she did not open the gate, but running in reported that **Peter** was standing at the gate. 15. But they said to her, "You are mad." But she insisted it was so. And they were saying, "It is his angel." 16. And **Peter** was continuing to **knock**: and when they **opened** they saw him and they were amazed. 17. Then after he made a sign to them with his hand that they should be silent he described to them how the **Lord** led him out from the jail and said, "Report these things to **Jacob**, the **brother of Y'shua**, and to the brothers." Then when he came out he went to a different place.*

Peter went to Miriam's house to make the believers know that God could do anything, even bring Peter out of prison.

Next, we hear from Paul, teaching the Romans about the nature of God to be impartial, not giving unusual favor to anyone.

*Romans 2:4. Do you despise the riches of His kindness and His forbearance and His patience, being ignorant that the kindness of God leads you into repentance? 5. According to your hardness and your unrepentant heart you are storing up for yourself wrath on the Day of wrath and the revelation of God's righteous judgment 6. Who will **reward each according to his works**: 7. On the one hand according to the **steadfast endurance of good work, glory and honor and immortality to those who seek eternal life**, 8. But on the other hand to those who are persuaded out of a **desire to put themselves forward, and not allowing themselves to be persuaded in the truth, then they will be in the wrath and fury for their unrighteousness. 9. Trouble and affliction upon every person's life, the one who performs evil**, and **first for a Jewish person**, then a **Greek**: 10. But **glory and honor and peace to everyone who does what is good, and first for a Jewish person**, then a **Greek**: 11. For there is **no partiality** before God. (Deut. 10:17)*

Every "you" in this passage is singular, just for you! It is required for each one of us to have works attesting to the repentance of each one, showing Godly behavior. This is a reference to the responsibility once someone has been taught Scripture. Jewish children were taught Scripture from the age of three to five years old on up, beginning with Leviticus. See *Memorization* in the One New Man Bible Glossary. This indicates that those who have studied Scripture longer have greater benefit, with God's presence and peace. The more mature believer should have a greater measure of God's gifts, especially peace. Salvation is based on repentance, but someone's Reward in Heaven is based on Deeds; what you do counts.

OUR SOVEREIGN GOD

Our God created the Earth, the Sky, the Atmosphere, the Sun, and Everything on the Earth by simply commanding those things to be! Those were sovereign moves by Him, our Creator.

Genesis 1.1. *In the beginning* God *created the heavens and the earth.* 2. *And the earth was totally empty (devoid of all life) (Jer. 4:23) (both animal and plant) and darkness was upon the face of the deep. And the Spirit of God hovered, brooded, over the face of the waters.*

God creates the Earth out of nothing, just the spoken Word! The Hebrew text uses two words meaning desolate, empty, with no reference to form or shape. This emphasizes the emptiness, that there were no living things, plant or animal on earth. Then He speaks everything else into Creation. The Holy Spirit is introduced to us with the Hebrew word Ruah, meaning Spirit, which is feminine. So, in the second verse we learn that the world is totally empty, with Latin is the source of saying the earth is without form and void. In that verse we also learn that the Holy Spirit is feminine. English readers believe the Holy Spirit is masculine because the first English Bibles were translated from Latin and the Latin word Spiritus is masculine, so the myth has remained in modern texts to this day because of Tradition.

God Has Only Begun to Command!

Genesis 1:3. *And* **God** *said, "Light, Be!" And there was* **light**. *4. And* **God** *saw the* **light**, *that it was* **good**, *and* **God** *divided the* **light** *from the* **darkness**. *5. And* **God** *called the* **light Day**, *and the* **darkness** *He called* **Night**. *And there was evening and there was morning,* **day one**.

The **light** was the **aura of God** until He created the sun in verses fourteen to nineteen.

> Genesis 1:6. *And God said,* ***"Firmament, Be in the midst of the waters!*** ***Divide the waters from the waters!"*** *7. And* ***God*** *made the* ***firmament*** *and* ***divided the waters*** *which were under the* ***firmament*** *from the* ***waters*** *which were above the* ***firmament****: and it was so. 8. And* ***God*** *called the* ***firmament*** *the* ***Heavens****. And there was evening and there was morning,* *the* ***second day****.*

Firmament is Literally Expanse, referring to the **atmosphere** and the **heavenly bodies** we can see from earth, what we call the **heavens**. The **firmament** contains the **clouds**, separating the **water** in them from that on the ground. See *Heavens* in the One New Man Bible Glossary, showing that there are seven Hebrew words translated **Heaven**, each bringing a different aspect.

> Genesis 1:9. *And God said,* ***"Waters under the heavens, Be gathered*** ***together to one place! Dry land, Appear!"*** *And it was so. 10. And God called the dry land* ***Earth****, and He called the gathering together of the waters the* ***Seas****. And God saw that it was* ***good****. 11. And God said,* ***"Earth, Bring*** ***forth grass, the herb yielding seed, and the fruit tree yielding fruit*** ***after its kind, whose seed is in itself, upon the earth!"*** *And it was so. 12. And the* ***earth*** *brought forth (grass and)* ***herb*** *yielding seed after its kind, and the* ***tree*** *yielding* ***fruit****, whose seed was in itself, after its kind. And God saw that it was* ***good****. 13. And there was evening and there was morning, the* ***third day****.*

Creation is really taking shape now, all the vegetation now made, He continues creating.

> Genesis 1:14. *And God said,* ***"Lights, Be in the firmament of the heavens,*** ***to divide the day from the night! Be for signs and for appointed times*** ***and for days and years! 15. Lights, Be in the firmament of the heavens*** ***to give light upon the earth!"*** *And it was so. 16. And God made two great lights, the greater light to rule the* ***day*** *and the lesser light to rule the* ***night****. He made the stars also. 17. And God set them in the firmament of the heavens to give light upon the earth, 18. and to rule over the* ***day*** *and over the* ***night****, and to divide the light from the darkness. And God saw that it was good. 19. And there was evening and there was morning, the* ***fourth day****.*

The signs are miracles, the appointed times are for God's appearances and for the Seasons of the LORD*. See *Seasons* in One New Man Bible Glossary. Only now, the fourth day, has God defined the word Day by creating the Sun! The first three Days were Spiritual, with no time limit.

Genesis 1:20. *And God said,* **"Waters, Teem abundantly with the living creature that has life, and fowl to fly above the earth in the open firmament of heaven!"** *21. And God created the great* **whales** *and* **every living creature that moves,** *with which the* **waters teemed abundantly,** *after their kind and every* **winged fowl** *after its kind. And* **God** *saw that it was* **good.** *22. And* **God blessed them** *saying,* **"Be fruitful! Multiply and fill the waters in the seas, and fowl, multiply on the earth!"** *23. And there was evening and there was morning, the* **fifth day.**

Now we know the grasses and the trees are here to feed the animals which were created to teem abundantly and to reproduce.

Genesis 1:24. *And God said,* **"Earth, Bring forth the living creature after its kind, cattle and creeping thing and beast of the earth after its kind!"** *And it was so. 25. And God made the* **beast** *of the earth after its kind and* **cattle** *after their kind and everything that creeps upon the earth after its kind. And God saw that it was* **good.**

Now the Earth is Ready for Mankind!

Genesis 1:26. *Then God said,* **"We will make mankind in our image, after our likeness and have dominion over the fish of the sea, over the fowl of the air, over the cattle, over all the earth, and over every creeping thing that creeps upon the earth."** *27. So* **God** *created* **mankind** *in* **His own image;** *He* **created him in the image** *of* **God.** *He created them* **male** *and* **female.** *(Matt. 19:4) 28. And God blessed them and God said to them,* **"Be fruitful! Multiply! Fill the earth! Subdue it and have dominion over the fish of the sea and over the fowl of the air and over every living thing that moves upon the earth!"**

When God said "We" He was using the Majestic plural rather than use the singular "I". This is true because the verb "will make" is singular.. The word adam used here means man or mankind, the same way that man in English can refer to one person or to all mankind. That He made both male and female indicates that He was speaking of all mankind. Being made in God's image means three things: The first image is the spiritual resemblance, second is the physical resemblance to God, as we see with Y'shua, the third is the love, the feelings and emotions of God. God's first command to mankind is to "Be Fruitful! Multiply!" Then He tells Mankind to take dominion, to be in charge of everything on the Earth.

Genesis 1:29. *And God said, "Behold, **I have given you every herb bearing seed** which is upon the face of all the earth, and **every tree** in which is the **fruit** of a tree yielding seed; it will be **food for you**. 30. And to every **beast** of the earth, to every **fowl** of the air, and to everything that **creeps** upon the earth, in which there is **life**, (I have given) every **green herb** for food." And it was so.*

Genesis 1:31. *And* God *saw everything that He had made and, behold, it was* very good. *And there was evening and there was morning, the* sixth day.

After all that work of creation, a day of rest!

Genesis 2.1. *Thus the heavens and the earth and the entire host of them were finished. 2. And on the **seventh day God ended His work** which He had made, and **He rested** on the **seventh day** from all His work which He had made. (Heb. 4:4) 3. And **God blessed** the **seventh day** and **sanctified** it, because in it **He had rested** from all His work which God created and made.*

This closes the most impressive Sovereign Move of our Creator when He created the world as we know it, with all the Life forms as we know them, and the surroundings that we see from Earth and from our space ships that have travelled outside our gravity. The next Sovereign Move listed here brings Him to earth to oversee the scattering of the Globalists, with the breaking up of the monolithic society that men wanted to create.

Tower of Babel

Genesis 11.1. *And the whole earth was of **one language** and of **few words**. 2. And it was, as they journeyed from the east, that they found a plain in the land of Shinar and they stayed there. 3. And they said one to another, "**Come, let us make bricks** and burn them thoroughly." And they had brick for stone and they had slime for mortar. 4. And they said, "Come, **we will build a city and a tower for ourselves**, whose top may reach to the heavens and we will make a name for ourselves, lest we be scattered abroad upon the face of the whole earth." 5. And the **LORD*** came down to see the city and the tower, which the children of men built. 6. And the **LORD*** said, "Behold, the people are one, and they all have one language. And they begin to do this and now nothing will be restrained from them, which they have imagined to do. 7. Come, let Us go down and there **confuse** their language, so they will not understand one another's speech."*

Babel is from the Root, Bet-Vet-Lamed, meaning to mix, to confuse. Few Words means there was one language for all, although originally they had been divided by language, Genesis 10:5. *By these were the isles of the nations divided in their lands, each one by his language, by their families, in their nations.*

The builders were the first Globalists but this did not please God since He appreciates the differences of one person to another and from one group to another group, with each group having a personality of its own. We are to be individuals, each one building a relationship with the LORD*. God does not want a group of automatons, with not any personality; He has made us to be individuals, each having a dream and a separate relationship with the LORD*. Today there are Globalists who want the obedient automatons to obliterate national personalities and individual achievement. The Globalists brought us the Free Trade movement, which was a good sounding phrase, but not true – NAFTA brought us not free trade, but anti-US practices that put a 273% customs duty on US dairy products going to Canada! The treaty also sent US jobs to other countries, devastating the middle class in the US.

> Genesis 11:8. *So the **LORD*** *scattered them abroad from there over the face of the **entire earth** and they stopped building the city. 9. That is why the name of it is called **Babel**, because there the **LORD*** **confounded the language** of all the earth. And from there the **LORD*** **scattered them** abroad upon the face of all the earth.*

The Entire Earth refers to the first command of God to mankind.

Next, we look at another Sovereign Move of the LORD*, when His Incarnate Body comes; The LORD* comes in person to dwell among us and to teach us His Ways and the correct interpretation of Scripture.

The Birth of John the Immerser Foretold:

Luke 1:5. *In the days of King Herod of Judea there was a certain priest named Zechariah from the division* Abijah*, and his wife was of the* daughters of Aaron *and her name was* Elizabeth.

Abijah was one of twenty-four divisions of the Aaronic priesthood, with each division serving at least twice each year and two divisions serving a third time. See *Division of Abijah* in One New Man Bible Glossary.

> Luke 1:6. *And they both were righteous before God, going blameless in all the commandments and requirements of the Lord. 7. But there **was not a child for them because Elizabeth was barren, and both were advanced***

*in their days. 8. And he was in the office of the priest in the succession of his division before God, 9. according to the custom of the service, appointed to burn incense when he entered the **Sanctuary** of the Lord,*

The Greek word Naos is commonly translated Temple, but it is only used in the New Testament for its primary meaning of Sanctuary. The incense altar was in the Holy Place except on Yom Kippur when the High Priest moved it into the Holy of Holies.

Luke 1:10. *and all the multitude of people was outside, praying at the hour of the incense.*

The hour of incense refers to the two times each day that incense was burned in the Holy Place. Exodus 30:7 & 8 order the burning of the incense in the morning when the priest dresses the lamps and afternoon when he lights the lamps.

Luke 1:11. *And an **angel** of the Lord appeared to him, standing by the right of the **altar of incense**. 12. And when **Zechariah** saw him he was disturbed and fear fell upon him. 13. And the **angel** said to him, "Do not fear, **Zechariah**, because your entreaty has been listened to and your wife **Elizabeth** will bear a **son** to you and you will call his name **John**. 14. And for you there will be joy and gladness and many will rejoice over his birth. 15. For he will be great before the Lord, and he should **not** drink wine or strong drink, and he will be **filled with the Holy Spirit** while he is still in his mother's womb, 16. and he will return many of the children of Israel to the Lord their God. 17. And he will go before **Him** in the **spirit and power of Elijah**, he will cause the **hearts of fathers to return to their children** and (the) **disobedient** to an understanding of righteousness, to prepare a people being made ready by the Lord." (Mal. 3:23,24) 18. Then **Zechariah** said to the **angel**, "How will I know this? For I am an old man and my wife is advanced in her days." 19. And the **angel** said to him, "I am **Gabriel**, the one who stands before **God**, and I was sent to speak to you and to give you this good news: 20. now behold, you will be silent and not able to speak until the day these things happen because you did not believe my words, which will be fulfilled in their time."*

Like the Patriarch Isaac, Zechariah prayed for his wife Elizabeth to bear a child! The First Step in Y'shua's coming in the flesh is to arrange for the birth of the one who is to announce His Coming, which is announced in the following passage:

Luke 1:26. *And in the sixth month (of **Elizabeth's** pregnancy) the **angel Gabriel** was sent down from **God** to a city of Galilee by the name of*

*Nazareth, 27. to a **virgin** betrothed to a man by the name of **Joseph** out of the house of David, and the name of the **virgin** (was) **Miriam**. 28. And when he came to her he said, "Hail, highly favored (one), the Lord is with you." 29. But she was confused over the message and was wondering what sort of greeting this might be. 30. And the **angel** said to her, "Do not be afraid, **Miriam**, for you have found favor with **God**. 31. And behold **you will conceive in (your) womb** and you will bear a **Son** and will call **His** name Y'shua. 32. This One will be great and **He** will be called **Son of the Most High**, and the **Lord God** will give Him the throne of **David** His father, 33. and He will reign over the **house of Jacob** forever, and **His kingdom** will not end." 34. And **Miriam** said to the **angel**, "How will this be, since I have not had intimacy with a husband?" 35. Then the **angel** said to her, "(The) **Holy Spirit** will come upon you and power of the **Most High** will cover you: for this reason then the **Holy One Who is birthed** will be called (the) **Son of God**. 36. And behold your kin **Elizabeth** has also conceived a son in her old age and this is her sixth month (from) her being called barren: 37. because with **God nothing is impossible**." (Gen. 18:14, Jer. 32:17,27, Job 42:2) 38. And **Miriam** said, "Behold the servant of the Lord: may it be according to your word." Then the **angel** left from her.*

All is Ready for His Incarnate Body to come live with us and teach us His Ways!

*Luke 2.1. And it happened in those days there came out a decree from Caesar Augustus to register all the inhabited world. 2. This first census was while Quirinius was governing Syria. 3. And all were going to be registered, each to his own city. 4. And **Joseph** went up from Galilee from the city of Nazareth to Judea to a city of David, which is called Bethlehem, because he was out of the house and clan of David, 5. to be registered with **Miriam**, who was big with child, to whom he had become betrothed. 6. And it happened while they were there the days were completed for her to bear the child. 7. And she **delivered her son**, the **Firstborn**, and she wrapped Him and she laid Him in a manger, because there was not a place for them in the inn.*

The Holy One, the Messiah, was born in a cave near the Tower of the Flock. Migdal Eder in Hebrew, refers to the Tower in fields near Bethlehem which sheltered the Shepherds and from which they watched over the Lambs. There the Lambs were cared for that were to become the Lambs offered in the Temple, kept by Levitical Priests. The Aaronite priests offered two Lambs every day, one in the morning and one in the evening. Each Lamb had to be unblemished, prefect. Each Lamb was offered to take away the sins of the people, so, it is no wonder that this is the place the LORD* chose for the birth of His Incarnate Body.

John the Immerser announces His appearance.

> John 1:29. *The next day he saw **Y'shua** coming toward him and he said,* **"Behold the <u>Lamb of God</u>, the One Who takes away the sin of the world.** *30. This is concerning Whom I said, 'A man is coming after me Who was before me, because He is more prominent than I.' 31. And I had not known Him, but, so that He would be revealed to Israel through this, I came immersing in water." 32. And John testified, saying that "I had seen the Spirit descending from heaven as a dove and it was staying on Him. 33. And I would not have known Him, but the One Who sent me to immerse in water, that One said to me **'Upon whomever you would see the Spirit descending and remaining upon Him, He is the One Who immerses in the Holy Spirit.' 34.** And I saw and I had borne witness that this **One** is the **Son of God.***"

Y'shua is still immersing believers into the Holy Spirit today!

Luke 2:21. *And when the eight days were completed to circumcise Him (Lev. 12:2,3) His name was called* Y'shua, *being called that by the angel to the one who conceived Him in her womb.*

God Incarnate is Jewish!

The Presentation of Y'shua in the Temple

> Luke 2:22. *And when the days of their **purification** were completed according to the Torah (Teaching) of Moses, they brought Him up to **Jerusalem** to present Him to the **Lord**, 23. just as it has been written in the Torah (Teaching) of the **Lord** that "Every male opening the womb will be called **holy** to the **Lord**," (Exod. 13:2) 24. and to give an offering according to that which was said in the Torah (Teaching) of the **Lord**, "A pair of turtledoves, or two young doves."*

The required Purification is from Leviticus 12:3 & 4. Verse three sets a full seven-day period and verse four sets a thirty-three day period for a total of forty days. The LORD* moved Sovereignly to bring Y'shua to His people.

The Boy Y'shua in the Temple

> Luke 2:41. *And His parents were going to Jerusalem from year to year to the Feast of Passover. 42. And when He was **twelve years (old)** they went up for the feast according to their custom (and for His Bar Mitzvah) 43. and when the days were completed, on their return the child **Y'shua** remained*

*in Jerusalem, but His parents did not know that. 44. And thinking He was in the caravan they came a day (on the way) and they were searching (for) Him among their relatives and acquaintances, 45. but when they did not find Him they returned to Jerusalem looking for Him. 46. Then it happened after three days they found Him in the **Temple**, sitting in the **middle of the teachers** and **listening** to them and **questioning** them: 47. and all those who heard Him were amazed over His understanding and answers. 48. And when they saw Him they were amazed, and His mother said to Him, "Child, why did You do this to us? Look, Your father and I were suffering while we were searching for You." 49. Then He said to them, "Why were you seeking Me? Had you not known that it was **necessary for Me to be among these of My Father?**" 50. And they did not understand the answer that He spoke to them. 51. Then He went down with them and came into Nazareth and was subject to them. And His mother was keeping all the words in her heart. 52. And **Y'shua** was progressing in wisdom and stature and favor before God and men.*

Bar Mitzvah refers to the service, a custom which had been kept for hundreds of years by Y'shua's time, at which a Jewish boy assumes the religious responsibilities of an adult, although, in the first century the ceremony had not yet been called Bar Mitzvah. When traveling long distances, the women and children walked in the center of the group, while the men split, with half walking in front of the women and half behind them for protection. On the way to Jerusalem He walked with the women and children, but on the return, after His admission to adulthood, He would have walked with the men, so Joseph had assumed He was with the other group of men. In the ceremony at the Temple many of His answers could have been in the form of questions, still a common form for Torah study.

When the LORD* brought His Incarnate Body to Earth He was thoroughly Jewish! He still is:

Malachi 3:6. *For I AM the LORD*! I* do not change!

Psalm 102:28. *But* You are the same *and Your years will have no end.*

Hebrews 13:8. Y'shua Messiah *is the* same yesterday and today and forever.

Y'shua was born Jewish, raised Jewish and is still Jewish. He and the Father are ONE! Our Heavenly Father is Jewish!

God Sovereignly Moves

> 1 Kings 22:29. *So the **king of Israel** and **Jehoshaphat** the **king of Judah** went up to Ramot Gilead. 30. And the **king of Israel** said to **Jehoshaphat**,*

I shall disguise myself and enter the battle, but you put on your robes. And the **king of Israel** *disguised himself and went into the battle. 31. But the king of Syria commanded his thirty-two captains that had rule over his chariots saying, Fight neither with small nor great, save only with the* **king of Israel**. *32. And it was, when the captains of the chariots saw* **Jehoshaphat** *that they said, Surely it is the* **king of Israel**. *And they turned aside to fight against him, and* **Jehoshaphat** *cried out. 33. And it was, when the captains of the chariots perceived that it was* **not** *the* **king of Israel** *that they* **turned back** *from pursuing him.*

Ahab was trying to escape detection, but God had him in His sights.

1 Kings 22:34. *And a* **certain man drew a bow by chance and struck the king of Israel** *between the joints of his armor. Therefore he said to the driver of his chariot, Turn your hand and carry me out of the battle, for I am wounded. 35. And the battle increased that day and the* **king** *was propped up in his chariot against the Syrians and* **died** *at evening, and the blood ran out of the wound in the midst of the chariot. 36. And a proclamation went throughout the camp about the going down of the sun saying, Every man to his city and every man to his own country. 37. So the* **king** *(Ahab) died and was brought to Samaria, and they buried the* **king** *in Samaria.*

Another Sovereign Move:

1 Kings 22:48. *There was then no king in Edom, a deputy was king. 49.* **Jehoshaphat** *made ships of Tarshish to go to Ophir for gold, but he did not go, for the ships were broken at Ezion Gaver. 50. Then* **Ahaziah** *the son of* **Ahab** *said to* **Jehoshaphat**, *Let my servants go with your servants in the ships. But* **Jehoshaphat** *would not.*

The LORD* Does it Again!

2 Kings 7:1. *Then* Elisha *said, Listen to the word of the LORD*! *Thus says the LORD*, *Tomorrow about this time a* seah *of fine flour will be sold for a* shekel *and* two seahs *of barley for a shekel in the gate of Samaria.*

One Seah is seven quarts.

2 Kings 7:2. *Then the* **captain** *on whose hand the king leaned answered the man of God and said, Behold, if the LORD* *would make windows in heaven, might this thing be? And he said, Behold,* **you will see it with your eyes, but you will not eat of it**.

That Prophetic Word comes True!

> 2 Kings 7:3. *And there were **four men** with **leprosy** at the entrance of the gate and they said to one another, Why are we sitting here until we die? 4. If we say, We will enter the city, then the famine is in the city and we will die there. And if we sit still here, we will also **die**. Now therefore come and let us fall to the army of the Syrians. If they save us alive, we will live and if **they kill** us, we will but **die**.*

The Lepers Tell Samaria!

> 2 Kings 7:5. *And they rose up in the twilight to go to the camp of the **Syrians**, and when they had come to the outermost part of the camp of Syria, behold, no one was there. 6. For the **Lord had made the army of the Syrians to hear a noise of chariots and a noise of horses, the noise of a great army, and they said to one another, Look, the king of Israel has hired against us the kings of the Hittites and the kings of the Egyptians to come against us.** 7. Therefore they got up in the twilight and **left their tents and their horses and their donkeys, even the camp as it was, and fled for their lives.***

In His Sovereignty the LORD* created the Sound that made the Syrians go home, leaving all their loot, their weapons, even the animals they rode on! That action by the lepers apparently healed them because in the next chapter Gehazi, who had to be Sovereignly healed of his leprosy, speaks to the king!

Two Witnesses will be sent by God.

> Revelation 11.1. *And a reed like a rod was given to me, the **angel** saying, "You must rise and you must measure the **Sanctuary** of God and the **altar** and count those who worship at it." (Ezek. 40:3, Zech. 2:5) 2. And you must **exclude the court outside the Sanctuary** and do **not** measure this outside, because it has been given to the heathens, and they will tread upon the holy city forty-two months. (Isa. 63:18, Ps. 79:1)*

The Outer Court welcomed heathens and others who had not dealt with sin. The Sanctuary is only for Priests, and only Priests who had already dealt with sin.

Revelation 11:3. *And I shall give My two witnesses (power) and they will prophesy one thousand two hundred sixty days clothed in sackcloth.*

Zechariah 4:14 refers to the "two anointed ones" who are Joshua and Zerubbabel in the literal, restored second Temple. It is commonly accepted today that the two anointed ones are the spirits of Moses and Elijah but they will not be the Two Witnesses of Revelation; the Congregations of the Jews and Christians who go throughout the World, bringing Heathens to the LORD*. Their Power is awesome.

> Revelation 11:4. *These are the **two olive trees** and the **two menorahs** that are standing before the **Lord of the Earth**. (Zech. 4:3,11-14) 5. If anyone determines to injure them **fire** goes out from their mouth and **devours their enemies**: (yes), if someone would **purpose to injure them**, it is necessary for him to be **killed** in this way. (2 Sam. 22:9, 2 Ki. 1:10, Jer. 5:14, Ps. 97:3) 6. These have the authority to close the sky so that rain would not fall the days of their prophecy, (1 Ki. 17:1) and they have authority upon the waters to turn them into blood, (Exod. 7:17,19,20) and to **strike the earth** with **every plague** (1 Sam. 4:8) as often as they would want.*

The Two Witnesses, the Congregations of Kingdom Preaching Christians and Jews, have great authority so they can burn to death anyone who attempts to injure them, cause a drought, or turn water into blood.

This is the Message the Two Witnesses will Preach

> Isaiah 61.1. *The **Spirit** of **Adonai**, the **LORD***, is upon me, because the **LORD*** has **anointed me** to **preach Good News** to the **humble**. (Matt. 5:3) He has sent me to bind up the broken-hearted, to proclaim liberty to the captives, and **opening of eyes** (Isa. 42:7) for those who are bound, 2. to proclaim the **acceptable year of the LORD***, (Luke 4:18-20) and the **day of vengeance** of our God; to **comfort** all who mourn, (Matt. 5:4) 3. to **appoint** to those who mourn in Zion, to give to them **beauty** instead of **ashes**, the **oil of joy** instead of **mourning**, the **garment of praise**, (prayer shawl), **instead** of the spirit of **infirmity**, so they could be called **oaks of righteousness**, the planting of the **LORD***, so **He** would be **glorified**.*

Another name for this message is **Kingdom Preaching. Humble** refers to the **Repentant,** to those who have **Entered Life. Opening** refers to opening of both **eyes** and **ears** in both the **physical** and **Spiritual**! It was **physical** in **Isaiah's** day and in **Y'shua's** ministry, but will be brought to full **fruition** in the **Hereafter,** the **Spirit Realm! Infirmity** is the translation of **Kehah**, literally meaning to be pale or dim and it is used as an expression for feeling **weak, sickly.** They are called **oaks** as the opposite of **weak, sickly.**

> Isaiah 61:4. *And they will build the old **wastes**, they will raise up the former **desolations**, and they will **repair** the **waste** cities, the desolations of many*

*generations. 5. And **strangers** will stand and feed your flocks, and the sons of the alien will be your plowmen and your vine dressers. 6. But you will be named the **Priests of the LORD***: they will call you the **Ministers of our God**: you will **eat the riches of the nations**, and you yourselves will boast in their **glory**. (Rev. 5:10)*

Those who Enter Life will be a Priest of LORD*, feeding on the Honor, Praise, and Glory as they worship the King! Worship restores their strength, giving them the power to resume their duties in the Hereafter! They Worship in the Adornment of Holiness. The Adornment of Holiness is the Spirit Realm that is palpable!

Isaiah 61:7. *You will have double because of your shame and instead of confusion* they *will rejoice in their portion. Therefore in their land they will possess the* double portion: everlasting joy *will be for them. 8. For I AM the* LORD*. I love justice. I hate robbery with burnt offering and I shall direct their work in truth, and I shall cut an everlasting covenant with them. 9. And their seed will be known among the nations and their offspring among the peoples. All who see them will acknowledge them, that they are the seed which the* LORD* *has* blessed.

They, in verse seven, are the nations to which Israel had been exiled. The Saints will have a Double Portion in the Hereafter! That is when the Perfect Rule will reign, according to Revelation Chapter Seven!

Isaiah 61:10. *I shall **greatly rejoice** in the **LORD***! My soul will be **enthusiastically joyful in my God**, for He has clothed me with the **garments** of **deliverance**, He has covered me with the **robe of acts of loving kindness**, like a bridegroom covers himself with ornaments and like a bride adorns herself with her jewels. (Rev. 19:8) 11. For as the earth brings out her bud and as the garden causes the seeds that are sown in it to spring forth, so **Adonai**, the **LORD*** will cause **acts of loving kindness** and **praise** to spring forth before all the nations (Heathens).*

Revelation 11:16. *Then the **twenty-four elders** who were sitting upon their thrones fell upon their faces before the **throne** of God and they paid homage to God 17. saying,*

> *"We give thanks to You, **Lord God of Hosts**,*
>
> *Who is and Who was,*
>
> *Because You have taken Your great power*
>
> *and You have come to reign.*
>
> *18. And the heathens were enraged, (Ps. 2:1; 46:7)*

and now Your wrath has come

*and the **appointed time of the dead to be judged***

*and to give the **reward to Your servants the prophets***

(Amos 3:7, Zech. 1:6, Dan. 9:6,10)

*and to the **saints and to those who revere Your name**,*

both the small and the great, (Ps. 115:13)

*and to **destroy those who destroy the earth**."*

The Twenty-four Elders are the Leaders of the Twelve Tribes of Israel and the Twelve Apostles.

> Revelation 11:19. *Then the **Sanctuary** of God, the **One** in heaven, opened and the **Ark of His covenant** (1 Ki. 8:1,6, 2 Chr. 5:7) was seen in **His Sanctuary**, and there were lightnings and voices and thunders and an earthquake (Exod. 19:18, Ezek. 1:13) and a violent hailstorm.*

This passage dictated by Y'shua includes the Oneness of God, Judgment Day, with the dead being judged and the Saints being given their rewards!

The series of passages dealing with God moving sovereignly brings two special books: Ezra and Esther, each one not stating the presence of God shows a sovereign move. The LORD* gave the Word to Jeremiah, which he spoke:

Mandate to Rebuild the House of the LORD* is a Sovereign move of God.

> Ezra 1.1. *Now in the **first year** of **Cyrus** king of Persia, **to fulfill the word of the LORD* by the mouth of Jeremiah**, the **LORD* stirred up the spirit of Cyrus king of Persia**, so he made a proclamation throughout all his kingdom, and also put it in writing saying, 2. Thus says **Cyrus** king of Persia, the **LORD* God of Heaven** has given me all the kingdoms of the earth, and He has charged me to build a **House** for Him in **Jerusalem**, which is in **Judah**. 3. Who is there among you of all His people? His God will be with him, and let him go up to **Jerusalem**, which is in **Judah**, and build the **House** of the **LORD*** God of Israel. He is the **God** that is in **Jerusalem**. 4. And whoever remains in any place where he sojourns, let the men of his place help him with silver and with gold and with goods and with beasts, besides the freewill offering for the House of God that is in **Jerusalem**.*

The first year is 539 BC, the year of Cyrus' conquering Babylon.

The LORD* Has Jeremiah Prophesy about Cyrus

Jeremiah 51:20 *You, (Cyrus), are My battle-axe (Ps. 35:2), weapons of war, for with you I shall break in pieces the nations and with you I shall destroy kingdoms, 21. and with you I shall break in pieces the horse and its rider and with you I shall break in pieces the chariot and its rider.*

Two hundred years before Cyrus conquered Babylon Isaiah Named Cyrus

Isaiah 45.1. *Thus says the LORD* to His anointed, to Cyrus, whose right hand I have held, to subdue nations before him. And I shall loose the loins of kings to open the doors before him and the gates will not be shut.*

Notice the tense of the verb that the LORD* uses, "I have held" 200 years before it happened. That is common with prophecy.

Isaiah 45:2. *I shall go before you and make the crooked places straight. I shall break in pieces the gates of bronze and cut asunder the bars of iron 3. and I shall give you the treasures of darkness and hidden riches of secret places, so that you can know that **I AM the LORD***, the **God of Israel**, Who calls you by your name. 4. For Jacob My servant's sake and Israel My elect, I have even called you by your name. I have surnamed you, though you have not known Me. 5. **I AM the LORD***, and there is no one else, there is no God besides Me. I girded you, though you have not known Me 6. so they will know from the rising of the sun and from the west, that there is no one besides Me. **I AM the LORD***, and there is no other. 7. I form the light and create darkness. I make peace and create chaos. **I AM the LORD*** Who does all these things. 5. Then the heads of families of Judah and Benjamin and the priests and the Levites, with all those whose **spirit God had raised, rose up to go up to build the House of the LORD*** which is in Jerusalem.*

The LORD* planned this all along, setting everything in order in His timing. He has the ultimate decision and the timing! Verse 7: *"I make peace and create chaos."* is difficult to translate into English because the Hebrew words are Shalom and ra. Shalom is much more than peace and ra, which is usually incorrectly translated evil, is the opposite of Shalom. See *Shalom* in One New Man Bible Glossary.

The Book of Esther is an example of the LORD* moving sovereignly to bring His will to fruition. The first step was to remove Vashti as queen. The Steps are numbered to show that Each Step is essential for the completion of God's plan.

#1 Esther 1:16. *And Memucan said before the king and the princes, **Vashti** the queen has not done wrong to the king only, but also to all the princes* *and to all the peoples who are in all the provinces of the king **Ahasuerus**. 17. For this deed of the queen, when it is reported, will come abroad to all women, so that they will despise their husbands in their eyes. King Ahasuerus commanded **Vashti** the queen to be brought in before him, but **she did not come**. 18. Also will the ladies of Persia and Media, who have heard of the deed of the queen, say the same this day to all the king's princes? Thus there will arise too much contempt and wrath. 19. **If it pleases the king, let there go a royal commandment from him and let it be written among the laws of the Persians and the Medes, so it cannot be altered, that Vashti may come no more before king Ahasuerus and let the king give her royal estate to another who is better than she.** 20. And when the king's decree which he makes will be published throughout all his empire, (for it is great) all the wives will give honor to their husbands, both to great and small.*

Except among the Jews and in matriarchal societies, women were chattels, property of their husbands. Only Jewish society held that women and men were equals. It required real courage and fortitude for Vashti to resist the call to appear, but this was a necessary first Step.

Now the problem becomes finding a new queen for the king.

Esther 2:2. *Then the king's servants who ministered to him said, Let there be fair young virgins sought for the king 3. and let the king appoint officers in all the provinces of his kingdoms, so they can gather together **all the fair young virgins to the Shushan palace**, to the house of the women, to the custody of Hegai the king's chamberlain, keeper of the women and let their ointments be given to them 4. and let **the maiden that pleases the king be queen** instead of Vashti. And the thing pleased the king and he did so.*

Two major characters, Mordecai and Hadassah, are introduced in the next passage. Among the hundreds of contestants for the position of Queen was a lone Jew, Hadassah, with her name changed to Esther. Mordecai was well respected, sitting in the king's gate made him known throughout the city.

#2 Esther 2:5. *Now in the Shushan palace there was a certain Jew, whose name was **Mordecai**, the son of Jair the son of Shimei the son of Kish, a Benjamite, 6. who had been carried away from Jerusalem with the captivity which had been carried away with Jeconiah king of Judah, whom Nebuchadnezzar the king of Babylon had carried away. 7. And he brought up **Hadassah, that is Esther, his uncle's daughter**, for she had neither father nor mother and the maid was **pleasing and beautiful**, whom Mordecai when her father and mother were dead, took for his own daughter.*

Certainly, nearly every girl in this contest was pleasing and beautiful, But Esther stood out against all odds, being looked upon with favor by Hegai, another important Step..

#3 Esther 2:8. *So it was, when the king's commandment and his desire was heard, and when many maidens were gathered together in the Shushan palace, in the custody of **Hegai**, that Esther was also brought to the king's house in the custody of **Hegai**, keeper of the women. 9. And the **maiden pleased him** and she **obtained kindness** from him and he speedily gave to her her things for purification, with such things as belonged to her, and seven maidens who were appropriate to be given to her out of the king's house, and he moved her and her maids to the best place of the house of the women.*

Esther stood out over hundreds of others. Cousin Mordecai kept close watch over the entire operation of choosing the new queen. Their being Jewish was kept quiet, another significant Step.

#4 Esther 2:10. ***Esther** had not made known her people or her kindred, for **Mordecai** had charged her that she should not make it known. 11. And **Mordecai** walked every day before the court of the women's house, to know how **Esther** did and what would become of her.*

Little did **Mordecai** know just how important this appointment would be; Only God knew what was at stake. Favor with **Hegai** is the next important Step.

#5 Esther 2:12. *Now when every maid's turn had come to go in to king Ahasuerus, after she had been there twelve months, according to the manner of women, for so were the days of their purifications accomplished, to wit, six months with oil of myrrh and six months with sweet odors, and with other things for the purifying of the women 13. then when each maiden came to the king, whatever she desired was given her to go with her out of the house of the women to the king's house. 14. She went in the evening and on the next day she returned to the second house of the women, to the custody of Shaashgaz, the king's chamberlain, who kept the concubines: she no longer came in to the king unless the king delighted in her and she was called by name. 15. Now when **Esther's turn**, the daughter of Abihail the uncle of **Mordecai** who had taken her for his daughter, came to go in to the king she required nothing but what **Hegai** the king's chamberlain, the keeper of the women, appointed. And **Esther** obtained favor in the sight of all those who looked upon her.*

So far so good! Esther's chances look very good, but this process is not nearly over;

the final competition is just beginning. Be sure that God is in control, just as He is today! The greatest Step so far is next!

> **#6** Esther 2:16. *So **Esther** was taken to king **Ahasuerus** in his royal house in the tenth month, which is the month Tevet, in the seventh year of his reign. 17. And the king loved **Esther** above all the women and she obtained grace and favor in his sight more than all the virgins, so that **he set the royal crown upon her head** and made her **queen** instead of **Vashti**. 18. Then the king made a great feast for all his princes and his servants, **Esther's** feast, and he made a release to the provinces and gave gifts, according to the state of the king.*

Esther's becoming Queen Esther is not the end of God's plan, but the beginning! The LORD* moves mightily in the coming times to complete the story of His power. Chapter Three brings the Evil Force to the fore!

#7 Esther 3.1. *After these things king Ahasuerus promoted* Haman *the son of Hammedatha the* Agagite *and advanced him, and set his seat above all the princes who were with him.*

Haman is introduced, set to be the villain in this book. Haman was a descendant of Agag, whom Saul had refused to kill in 1 Samuel 15:9. Although Samuel killed Agag, members of the family escaped because of Saul's disobedience, making the plot in the Book of Esther sinister – except God intervened!

> **#8** Esther 3:2. *And all the king's servants who were in the king's gate bowed and paid homage to **Haman**, for the king had so commanded concerning him. But **Mordecai** did **not** bow, **nor** did he pay homage to him. 3. Then the king's servants who were in the king's gate said to **Mordecai**, Why are you disobeying the king's commandment? 4. Now it was, when they spoke daily to him and he did not obey them, that they told **Haman**, to see whether **Mordecai's** matters would stand, for he had told them that he was a **Jew**. 5. And when **Haman** saw that **Mordecai** did not bow or pay homage to him, then **Haman** was full of wrath. 6. And he thought it disgraceful to lay hands on **Mordecai** alone, for they had made known to him that it was **Mordecai's** people, therefore **Haman** sought to destroy all the **Jews**, the people of **Mordecai** that were throughout the whole kingdom of Ahasuerus.*

Mordecai was an inspiration for the Apostle John who was sentenced to death by Domitian, the Roman emperor in 93 AD. John refused to worship Domitian on LORD's Day, the first day of each month, so John was taken to Rome to be tried for the offence. He was convicted and thrown into a vat of boiling oil, but came out untouched by the hot oil; then months later John was sentenced to Patmos, the island where he transcribed the Book of Revelation. Mordecai had earlier done something that saved him and the Jews! The LORD* also led Mordecai to tell Esther not to reveal that she was Jewish, which will soon be a major development.

#9 Esther 2:19. *And when the virgins were gathered together the second time, then **Mordecai** sat in the king's gate. 20. **Esther** had not made known her kindred or her people as **Mordecai** had charged her, for **Esther** did the commandment of **Mordecai** like when she was brought to him earlier. 21. In those days, while **Mordecai** sat in the king's gate, two of the king's officers, Bigthan and Teresh, of those who kept the door were angry and sought to lay hands on king Ahasuerus. 22. And the thing was known to **Mordecai**, who told **Esther** the queen and **Esther** notified the king in **Mordecai's** name. 23. And the matter was inquired into, and it was found out and they were both hanged on a tree and it was written in the book of the chronicles before the king.*

Years later this good deed had slipped from the king's mind. Then Haman's evil bent surfaces.

#10 Esther 3:8. *And **Haman** said to king **Ahasuerus**, There is a **certain people** scattered abroad and dispersed among the peoples in all the provinces of your kingdom and their laws are different from those of every people, neither do they keep the king's laws. Therefore it is not for the king's profit to permit them. 9. If it please the king, let it be written that **they may be destroyed** and I shall weigh ten thousand talents of silver into the hands of those that have the charge of the business, to bring it into the king's treasuries. 10. And the king took his ring from his hand and gave it to **Haman** the son of Hammedatha the Agagite, the **Jew's enemy**. 11. And the king said to **Haman**, The silver is given to you, the people also, to do with them as it seems good to you.*

Haman is about to kill all the Jews in the Persian Empire!

#11 Esther 3:13. *And the letters were sent by couriers to **all the king's provinces**, to **destroy**, to **kill**, and to **cause all the Jews to perish**, both young and old, little children and women, in one day on the **thirteenth** of the **twelfth month**, which is the month **Adar** and to take their spoil for a prey. 14. The copy of the writing for a decree to be given in every province was published for all the peoples, so they would be ready for that day.*

Haman's plan is set to eliminate all the Jews! But Mordecai knows about the plan and God gives Mordecai a plan.

#12 Esther 4.1. *When **Mordecai** perceived all that was done, **Mordecai** tore his clothes and put on sackcloth with ashes and went out into the midst of the city and cried with a loud and a bitter cry 2. and came before the king's gate, for no one could enter the king's gate clothed with sackcloth. 3. And in every province, wherever the king's commandment and his decree came, there was **great mourning** among the **Jews**, and fasting and weeping and wailing and many lay in sackcloth and ashes.*

The end was in sight for every Jew! The LORD* prompted Mordecai to appeal to Esther.

#13 Esther 4:4. *So **Esther's** maids and her chamberlains came and told her. Then the queen was exceedingly grieved and she sent garments to clothe **Mordecai** and to take away his **sackcloth** from him, but he did not accept it. 5. Then **Esther** called for **Hatach**, one of the king's chamberlains, whom he had appointed to attend to her, and gave him a commandment to **Mordecai**, to know what it was and why it was. 6. So **Hatach** went out to **Mordecai** in the street of the city, which was before the king's gate. 7. And **Mordecai** told him of all that had happened to him and of the sum of the money that **Haman** had promised to pay to the king's treasuries for the **Jews**, to **destroy** them. 8. Also he gave him the **copy of the writing of the decree** that was given at Shushan to destroy them, to show it to **Esther** and to declare it to her and to charge her that she should **go in to the king**, to make **supplication** to him and to make a request before him for her people.*

The LORD* put caution in Esther and gave her a plan of action.

#14 Esther 4:9. *And **Hatach** came and told **Esther** the words of **Mordecai**. 10. Again **Esther** spoke to **Hatach** and gave him a commandment for **Mordecai**, 11. All the king's servants and the people of the king's provinces do know that whoever, whether man or woman, will come to the king in the inner court, who is not called, there is one law of his to put him to death, except such to whom the king will hold out the golden scepter so he may live, but I have not been called to come in to the king these thirty days. 12. And they told **Esther's** words to **Mordecai**. 13. Then **Mordecai** commanded to answer **Esther**, **Do not think that with yourself you will escape in the king's house, more than all the Jews!** 14. For if you altogether hold your peace at this time, then enlargement and deliverance will arise for the **Jews***

*from another place, but you and your father's house will be destroyed and who knows whether **you have come to the kingdom for such a time as this**?*

God's plan is taking effect; God has prepared the king's heart for Esther's next move.

#15 Esther 4:15. *Then **Esther** bade them return **Mordecai** this answer, 16. Go! **Gather** together all the **Jews** that are present in Shushan and **fast for me** and neither eat nor drink **three days**, night or day. Also my maidens and I shall likewise **fast** and so I shall go in to the king, which is not according to the law. **If I perish, I perish!** 17. So **Mordecai** went his way and did according to all that **Esther** had commanded him.*

Fasting worked! Prayer is not mentioned in the Scripture but God knew their hearts so He started this move and He will carry it out!

#16 Esther 5.1. *Now it was on the **third day** that **Esther** put on her royal apparel and stood in the inner court of the king's house, opposite the king's house, and the king sat upon his royal throne in the royal house, opposite the gate of the house. 2. And it was so, when the king saw **Esther** the queen standing in the court, she obtained favor in his sight and the king held out to **Esther** the golden scepter that was in his hand. So **Esther** drew near and touched the top of the scepter.*

God's plan will now be revealed.

#17 Esther 5:3. *Then the king said to her, What is it, queen **Esther**? And what is your request? It will be given to you even to half the kingdom 4. and **Esther** answered, If it seems good to the **king**, let the **king** and **Haman** come this day to the **banquet** that I have prepared for him. 5. Then the **king** said, Cause **Haman** to hurry, so he can do as **Esther** has said. So the **king** and **Haman** came to the **banquet** that **Esther** had prepared. 6. And the **king** said to **Esther** at the **banquet** of wine, What is your petition? And it will be granted you, and what is your request? Even to the half of the kingdom it will be performed. 7. Then **Esther** answered and said, My petition and my request are, 8. If I have found favor in the sight of the **king**, and if it please the **king** to grant my petition and to perform my request, let the **king** and **Haman** come to the **banquet** that I shall prepare for them and I shall do tomorrow as the **king** has said.*

Why not just tell the king? Why have Haman come to the private gathering! God has a plan and Esther follows it!

#18 Esther 5:9. *Then **Haman** went out that day joyful and with a glad heart, but when **Haman** saw **Mordecai** in the king's gate, that he did not stand up or move for him, he was full of indignation against **Mordecai**. 10. Nevertheless **Haman** restrained himself and when he came home, he sent and called for his friends and Zeresh his wife.*

Haman has no clue to what lies ahead! What a difference a day makes! The LORD*'s plan begins to unfold.

#19 Esther 6.1. *On that night the **king** could not sleep and he commanded to bring the book of records of the chronicles and they were read before the **king**. 2. And it was found written that **Mordecai** had told of Bigthana and Teresh, two of the **king's** officers, the keepers of the door, who sought to lay hands on the king **Ahasuerus**. 3. And the **king** said, What honor and dignity has been done to **Mordecai** for this? Then the **king's** servants that ministered to him said, **Nothing** was done for him. 4. And the **king** said, Who is in the court? Now **Haman** had come into the outer court of the **king's** house, to speak to the **king** to hang **Mordecai** on the gallows that he had prepared for him. 5. And the **king's** servants said to him, Behold, **Haman** stands in the court. And the **king** said, Let him come in. 6. So **Haman** came in. And the **king** said to him, What will be done for the man whom the king delights to honor? Now **Haman** thought in his heart, To whom would the **king** delight to do honor more than to myself? 7. And **Haman** answered the **king**, For the man whom the **king** delights to honor, 8. Let the royal apparel be brought which the **king** uses to wear, and the horse that the **king** rode upon when the royal crown was set on his head 9. and let this apparel and horse be delivered to the hand of one of the **king's** most noble princes, that they may array the man whom the **king** delights to honor and cause him to ride on horseback through the streets of the city and proclaim before him, Thus will it be done for the man whom the **king** delights to honor.*

The **LORD*** caused **Haman** to be in the court so he would be invited to come to the king. Suggesting what to do for the one the **king** wants to honor sounds great to **Haman** who thinks he is the one the **king** wants to honor.

#20 Esther 6:10. *Then the **king** said to **Haman**, Make haste, take the apparel and the horse, as you have said, and do so for **Mordecai the Jew**, who sits at the **king's** gate. Let nothing fail of all that you have spoken. 11. Then **Haman** took the apparel and the horse and clothed **Mordecai** and caused him to ride on horseback through the streets of the city, and proclaimed before him, Thus will it be done for the man whom the **king** delights to honor!*

Haman now knows trouble is coming! God's plan is not over. Now we have the reason for Esther's having the second banquet.

#21 Esther 7.1. *So the **king** and **Haman** came to the **banquet** with **Esther** the queen. 2. And the **king** said again to **Esther** on the **second** day at the **banquet** of wine, What is your petition, queen **Esther**? It will be granted for you. What is your request? And it will be performed, to the half of the kingdom. 3. Then **Esther** the queen answered and said, If I have found favor in your sight, O **king**, and if it please the **king**, **let my life be given me at my petition**, and **my people at my request**, 4. for we are sold, **my people and I**, to be **destroyed**, to be **slain** and to **perish**. And if we had been sold for bondmen and bondwomen, I would have held my tongue, but the adversary could not compensate for the **king's** damage. 5. Then the **king**, **Ahasuerus**, answered and said to **Esther** the queen,*

Who is he and where is he who dared presume in his heart to do so? 6. And *Esther said, The adversary and enemy is this wicked **Haman**. Then **Haman** was afraid before the **king** and the **queen**. 7. And the **king**, rising in his wrath from the **banquet** of wine went into the palace garden and **Haman** stood up to make a request for his life to **Esther** the queen, for he saw that there was evil determined against him by the **king**. 8. Then the **king** returned from the palace garden into the place of the **banquet** of wine and **Haman** was fallen upon the couch where **Esther** was. Then the **king** said, Will he force the queen before me in the house? As the word went out of the **king's** mouth, they covered **Haman's** face.*

God's plan is working, but it is not over! As in Israel, the people recline at the table.

#22 Esther 7:9. *And Harbonah, one of the officers, said before the **king**, Also there is the gallows fifty cubits high, which **Haman** had made for **Mordecai**, who had spoken good for the **king**, stands at **Haman's** house. Then the **king** said, **Hang him there**! 10. So they hanged **Haman** on the gallows that he had prepared for **Mordecai**. Then the **king's** wrath was pacified.*

It is not over yet! **Mordecai** replaces **Haman**.

#23 Esther 8.1. *On that day king **Ahasuerus** gave the house of **Haman**, the Jews' enemy, to **Esther** the queen. And **Mordecai** came before the **king**, for **Esther** had told what he was to her. 2. And the **king** took off his ring, which he had taken from **Haman** and gave it to **Mordecai**. And **Esther** set **Mordecai** over the house of **Haman**.*

The letters to the provinces ordering the killing of the Jews are now counter-manded, with Jews now in favor!

#24 Esther 8:3. *And **Esther** spoke yet again before the **king** and fell down at his feet and besought him with tears to put away the evil of **Haman** the Agagite, and his device that he had devised against the **Jews**. 4. Then the king held out the golden scepter toward **Esther**. So **Esther** rose and stood before the **king** 5. and said, If it please the **king**, and if I have found favor in his sight, and the thing seems right before the **king**, and I am pleasing in his eyes, let it be written to **recall the letters** devised by **Haman** the son of Hammedatha the Agagite, which he wrote to destroy the **Jews** who are in all the king's provinces, 6. for how can I endure to see the evil that will come to my people? Or how can I endure to see the destruction of my kindred?*

The evil is now undone!

#25 Esther 8:7. *Then the **king Ahasuerus** said to **Esther** the **queen** and to **Mordecai** the **Jew**, Behold, I have given **Esther** the house of **Haman** and they have hanged him upon the gallows because he laid his hand upon the **Jews**. 8. Write also for the **Jews** as you like, in the **king's** name, and seal it with the **king's** ring, for the writing which is written in the **king's** name and sealed with the **king's** ring, no man may recall.*

The Order is Given, the command goes out!

#26 Esther 8:9. *Then the* king's *scribes were called at that time in the third month, that is, the month* Sivan, *on the twenty-third day; and it was written according to all that* Mordecai *commanded the* Jews, *and to the lieutenants, and the governors and rulers of the provinces which are from India to Cush, a hundred twenty-seven provinces, to every province according to its writing, and to every people after their language, and to the* Jews *according to their writing and according to their language. 10. And he wrote in king* Ahasuerus' *name and sealed it with the* king's *ring, and sent letters by couriers on horseback, riders on royal steeds bred of the royal mares, 11. where the* king *granted the* Jews *who were in every city to* gather *themselves together and to stand for their life, to* destroy, *to* slay, *and to cause to* perish *all the power of the people and province that would* assault *them, little ones and women, and to take their spoil for a prey 12. on one day in all the provinces of king* Ahasuerus, *upon the thirteenth of the twelfth month, which is the month* Adar. *13. The copy of the writing for a decree to be given in every province was published for all the peoples and that the* Jews *should be ready against that day to* avenge themselves *on their enemies. 14. So the couriers who rode upon royal steeds went out, being hastened and pressed on by the king's commandment. And the decree was given at the Shushan palace.*

The task was not complete until the Anti-Semites were eliminated! Each of these twenty-six steps was planned by God, executed by Humans, the people of Shushan. The LORD* Took Vengeance upon the Anti-Semites! As the End Times approach the LORD* will be bringing His plans into action, advancing His people as He did with Esther and Mordecai. All who are grafted into the Domestic, Jewish, Olive Tree will be blessed, the Anti-Semites will be Blasted! Sivan is May or June. Each one of the twenty-six steps is vital for the progression to work! Our Sovereign God Reigns.

Romans 11:17. *But if some of the branches were broken off, and **you**, since **you** are a wild olive, were **yourself** grafted into them, then **you** would be a participant for **yourself** of the richness of the root of the olive tree.*

Every "you" in this paragraph, verses 17-24, is singular, so each one of us is individually grafted into the cultivated, Jewish olive tree. See Isaiah 44:5. Richness literally means to grow fat, rich in your relationship with the Lord.

Roman 11:18. *Stop boasting of the branches: but, if you do boast, **you do not support the root**, but the **root supports you**. 19. Therefore you will say, "Branches were broken off so that I could be grafted in." 20. Just so: they were broken off by unbelief, but you have stood by faith. **Do not be proud**, but **you must continually fear for yourself**: 21. for if God did not spare the natural branches, **neither** will He in any way spare you. 22. You must now see the **goodness** and **severity** of **God**: on the one hand **severity** upon those who fell, but on the other hand **goodness of God** upon **you, if you would remain in the goodness, otherwise you would be cut off**. 23. And even these, if they would not remain in unbelief, they will be **grafted** in: for **God is able to graft them in again**. 24. For if you were cut off from the naturally **wild olive tree** and contrary to nature you were **grafted into the cultivated olive tree**, how much more will these **natural (branches)** be **grafted** into **their own (cultivated) olive tree**.*

This is the same olive tree into which Christians have been grafted, making One New Man, Ephesians 2:15. Celebrate your Jewishness!

Y'SHUA

Y'shua's physical body took the sins of all mankind in a very painful death, then brought the possibility of **ETERNAL LIFE** to all mankind with the resurrection of His **Spirit**. After His Resurrection, His Spiritual body then walked the Earth, being witnessed by thousands of people who miraculously saw into the Spirit Realm. The first **Glimpse** into **Y'shua's** personal **Spirit** is at his **Immersion**.

> Matthew 3:13. *Then **Y'shua** came from Galilee across the Jordan to John to be **immersed** by him. 14. But John was going to prevent Him saying, "I need to be immersed by You, so would You come to me?" 15. And when **Y'shua** answered He said to him, "You must allow it now, for so it is fitting for us to fulfill all righteousness." Then he permitted Him. 16. And after **Y'shua** was **immersed** He immediately rose from the water: and behold the **heavens opened up to Him**, and he saw the **Spirit of God descending like a dove** and coming upon Him: 17. and there was a voice from the heavens saying, "**This is My beloved Son, with Whom I am well pleased**."*

The Second Glimpse into His Spirit is at His Temptation:

> Matthew 4.1. *Then **Y'shua** was led into the wilderness by the **Spirit** to be tested by the **devil**. 2. And <u>after He fasted forty days and forty nights, He was then hungry</u>. 3. And when the one who was testing, (the devil), came, he said to Him, "If You are the Son of God, You must now say that these stones would become bread." 4. But when He answered, (**Y'shua**) said, "It has been written,*
>
> > *'Man will not live on bread alone,*
> >
> > *but upon every **word** going out*

156

through (the) mouth of God.'" (Deut. 8:3)

5. *Then the devil took Him to the holy city and placed Him on the pinnacle of the Temple 6. and said to Him, "If You are the Son of God, You must throw Yourself down at once for it has been written that*

'He will give orders to His angels concerning you

   and they will take you up in (the palms) of their hands,

so that you would not strike your foot against a stone.'" (Ps. 91:11,12)

7. ***Y'shua*** *said to him, "Again it has been written, 'You will not test (the) Lord your God.'" (Deut. 6:16) 8. Again the devil took Him to an exceedingly high mountain and showed Him all the kingdoms of the world and their glory 9. and said to Him, "I shall give all these things to You, if after You fall on Your knees You would pay homage to me." 10. Then **Y'shua** said to him, "You must immediately go back where you came from, **Satan**: for it has been written,*

*'You will **worship the Lord your God***

   *and you will **serve only** Him.'" (Deut. 6:13)*

11. *Then the **devil** left Him, and behold angels came and were ministering to Him.* (Mark 1:12,13, Luke 4:1-13)

Satan aka Devil: The Hebrew language has two spellings for Satan, "seen-tet-nun," and "samech-tet-nun." The former is the one used in Scripture, in Numbers 22:22,32, 1 Samuel 29:4, 2 Samuel 19:22, 1 Kings 5:4; 11:14,23,25, Zechariah 3:1,2, Psalm 109:6, Job 1:6,7,8,9,12; 2:1,2,3,4,6,7, and 1 Chronicles 21:1. The latter spelling, samech-tet-nun, which does not appear in Scripture, means slander, slanderer, accuser. The former means adversary, archenemy, foe, devil, the Evil One, and hinderer, accuser. The word translated Accuser refers specifically to bringing formal charges in a court of law.

The verb form means to **hate, denounce, condemn, speak against** and is used several times in Scripture. The difference between these words is not great, but it is significant that Scripture uses the stronger word because it includes, but is not limited to, accusing, but goes far beyond that in actively pursuing evil ends.

Now with the **Third Glimpse** into His Spirit we have His First Miracle of making a fine wine from ordinary, pure water!

John 2.1. *And on* Tuesday *there was a wedding* feast *in Cana of Galilee, and* Y'shua's *mother was there.*

Tuesday is the translation of "the third day" which is the Hebrew expression for Tuesday. Tuesday was the ideal day for a wedding to begin since some of those invited had to travel a good distance, and they could not travel on the Sabbath; Tuesday gave them time to get to the place of the wedding. The Wedding Feast lasted a full week so check *Wedding* in the One New Man Bible Glossary.

> John 2:2. *And **Y'shua** and His disciples were also invited to the feast. 3. And when the wine ran out the mother of **Y'shua** said to Him, "They do not have wine." 4. And **Y'shua** said to her, "Why should that concern Me, ma'am? My appointed time is not yet come." 5. His mother said to the servants, "Whatever He would say to you, you must do right away."*

Y'shua's good Jewish mother paid no attention to His reluctance to act but went right on as if He had not spoken.

John 2:6. *And lying there were six stone water pots stored for the rite of purification of the Jewish people, holding up to two or three measures.*

Stone was used for the water of purification because stone does not become ritually unclean. The rite of purification is Immersion, which we call baptism. Normally, only a synagogue would have a ritual bath, so this wedding was apparently at a synagogue, which were mostly home synagogues in Y'shua's day. The water for purification had to be running water, such as from a stream, a spring, or rainwater caught in a cistern. See *Immerse* in the One New Man Bible Glossary.

> John 2:7. ***Y'shua*** *said to them, "You must right away fill the jars with water." And they filled them to the brim. 8. And He said to them, "You must draw some now, then bring it to the wedding manager:" and they brought it. 9. As the manager tasted the water made into wine, only he did not know how it was made, but the servants, those who drew the water knew, the manager called the bridegroom 10. and said to him, "Every man first puts the good wine and then, when they would be drunk, the inferior: you have kept the good wine until now." 11.* ***Y'shua*** *did this* ***first of His signs*** *in Cana of Galilee and He revealed His* ***glory***, *and His disciples believed in Him.*

> This is our third **Glimpse into Y'shua's Spiritual Realm**, the first of many as He continually revealed His true Spiritual nature; this is the first of His many miracles.

Y'shua Commands a Demon Spirit to Come Out of a Man

> Luke 4:31. *And He came down to Capernaum, a city of Galilee: and He was teaching them regularly on the Sabbaths: 32. and they were amazed at His*

*teaching, because His message was with authority. 33. And a man having an unclean **demon spirit** was in the synagogue and (the demon) cried out in a loud voice, 34. "Ah ha! What has this to do with You, **Y'shua** of Nazareth? Did You come to destroy us? I know Who You are, the **Holy One of God.**" 35. Then **Y'shua** commanded it saying, "**You must be quiet** and **you must immediately come out from him**," Then, after the demon threw (the man) down in the middle (of them), it came out from him and did not hurt him at all. 36. And there was amazement upon all and they were discussing with one another saying, "What is this talk that He orders the **unclean spirits** with authority and power and they come out?" 37. And (the) report concerning Him was going out into every place in the region.*

That is His first reported Deliverance, one of many to come. Next, He heals Peter's mother-in-law, then goes on the heal others and deliver still more!

*Luke 4:38. And after He got up from the synagogue He entered Simon's house. And Simon's **mother-in-law** was having a high **fever** and they were asking Him about her. 39. Then as He stood before her, He **commanded the fever** and it **left her**: and then she immediately got up and was serving them. 40. And **after** the **sun set (ending the Sabbath)** they led to Him as many as were having **sickness** with various **diseases**, and as He laid hands on each one of them He was **healing** them. 41. And then **demons** came out from many, crying out and saying, "You are the Son of God." But while He was rebuking (them) He was not allowing them to speak, because they had known He was the **Messiah**.*

His next step is to name His Disciples, showing His knowledge by the Spirit where the fish are!

*Luke 5.1. And it happened while He was standing by **Lake Gennesaret** the crowd pressed in to Him to hear the Word of God 2. and He saw two boats standing to the side of the lake: and the **fishermen** from them, (who) had gotten out, were washing their **nets**. 3. And when He got in one of the boats, which was Simon's, He asked him to put out a little way from the shore, and after He sat on the boat He was teaching the crowds. 4. And as He stopped speaking, He said to **Simon**, "You must now go out into the deep (water) and you must cast your nets at once for a catch." 5. And **Simon** said, "Master, while working through (the) whole night we took nothing: but upon Your word I shall lower the nets." 6. Then when they did this they enclosed (the nets) full of many fish, and their nets were being torn. 7. Then they signaled by a nod to their partners in the other boat, who came to help them: and they*

came and they filled both boats so as to (almost) sink them. 8. And when
***Simon Peter** saw he fell down to his knees before Y'shua saying, "You must*
now go from me because I am a sinful man, Lord." 9. For astonishment
seized him and all those with him over the catch of the fish, which they took,
*10. and likewise also **Jacob** and **John**, sons of Zebedee, who were **partners***
*with **Simon**. And **Y'shua** said to **Simon**, "You must not fear: from now on*
you will be capturing men." 11. Then after they drew the boats up on the
shore, leaving everything, they followed Him.

Y'shua knew where the fish were, a tribute to His walking continuously in touch
with the Holy Spirit. The Nets they were washing were the small, personal nets,
not the commercial nets normally used at night. Though called small, they were
twenty feet in diameter so they held quite a haul and Peter needed help. The
name Jacob is the correct transliteration of the Greek and Latin texts' spelling
of the name: Iakob. The Traditional Name James is a late invention that does
not relate to any first century language. John and Simon (Peter) are the standard
transliterations.

Y'shua Reads Minds to Expose Observers to the Holy Spirit!

Matthew 9.1. Then after He got in the boat He crossed over and came into
His own city. 2. And behold they were bringing Him a paralytic who was
*lying on a stretcher. And when **Y'shua** saw their faith He said to the paralytic,*
"You must be courageous, child, your sins are forgiven." 3. And behold some
*of the scribes said among themselves "**This One is blaspheming**." 4. Then*
*since **Y'shua** knew **their thoughts** He said, "Why are you thinking evil in*
your hearts?

God knows your thoughts too! You cannot hide anything from Him.

Matthew 12:22. Then a blind and deaf demonized man was brought to
Him, and He healed him, so that the deaf one spoke and saw. 23. And all the
crowds were amazed and were saying, "Is this not the Son of David?" 24. And
*when the **Pharisees** heard they said, "**This One does not cast out demons***
except by Beelzebub, leader of the demons.**" 25. And because **He knew
***their thoughts** He said to them, "Every kingdom divided against itself is*
made desolate and not one city or house divided against itself will stand. 26.
And if Satan casts out Satan, he is divided against himself: therefore how will
his kingdom stand?

Y'shua, God, Knows Every Thought!

*Luke 9:46. And a **thought came among them**, whoever might be greatest of them. 47. But since **Y'shua saw the thought of their hearts**, after He took hold of a child, He stood him beside Himself 48. and said to them, "Whoever would take this child in My name, takes Me: and whoever will take Me, is taking the One Who sent Me: for the one who is least among you all, this one is great."*

Each of the words "take" and "taking" in verse forty-eight means to take by the hand. We are really to take hold of, to grab onto the things of God! (Matthew 11:12) That time Y'shua saw the Thoughts of His disciples. Later Paul tells us to take captive every thought!

*2 Corinthians 10:3. For though we walk in the flesh we are not serving as soldiers according to the flesh, 4. for the weapons of our warfare are not fleshly but powerful in God for the tearing down of strongholds, tearing down reasonings 5. even every high thing being lifted up against the knowledge of God, and **taking captive every thought** in obedience to Messiah, 6. and being ready to punish every disobedience, when your obedience would be achieved.*

Jeremiah 6:19. "*Listen, O earth! Behold, I AM will bring evil upon this people, the fruit of their thoughts, because they have not heeded My words or My Torah (Teaching), but rejected it.*" Every thought is Spiritual; the reason every thought is known to God. Be sure you take captive every thought! David understood those things:

Psalm 19:15. The words of my mouth and the meditation of my heart will be acceptable in Your sight, LORD*, my Rock and my Redeemer.

David was as determined, as each of us should be, to be certain that the meditation of his heart was acceptable to the LORD*.

The Cleansing of a Leper

*Luke 5:12. And it happened He was in one of the cities and there was a man full of **leprosy**: and after he saw **Y'shua**, falling on his face he begged of Him saying, "Lord, if You are willing You are able to **cleanse me**." 13. And stretching out His hand **He touched him** saying, "I am willing, **you must immediately be cleansed**:" and the **leprosy** left him at once. 14. Then He commanded him to tell no one, "But when you leave you must immediately show yourself to the priest and you must make an offering concerning your cleansing just as Moses commanded, in witness to them." (Lev. 14:2-32) 15.*

*And the word was going out more concerning Him, and many crowds were gathering to listen and to **be healed** from their **sicknesses**: 16. but He was withdrawing to the wilderness (places) and praying.* (Matt. 8:1-4, Mark 1:40-45)

Touching a leper would have made anyone else unclean, but Y'shua's touch cleansed the leper, Leviticus 6:20 says that whatever touches the flesh of the Sin Offering will be Holy. The leprosy has to go! And the Leper has been cleansed. See *Cleanse* in the One New Man Bible Glossary.

The Healing of a Paralytic

Luke 5:17. *Then it happened on one of the days that He was teaching, and Pharisees and teachers of Torah (Teaching) were sitting (listening). They were coming from every region of Galilee and Judea and Jerusalem: and (the) **power of (the) Lord** was in Him to **heal**.*

Y'shua was normally prepared to enter the Spirit Realm. The only place where He is referred to as not having the power is in Nazareth where there was a lack of Faith. See Matthew 13:58 and Mark 6:5.

Luke 5:18. *And there were men bringing a man who was paralyzed. (He was) on a stretcher and they were seeking to bring him in and to place him before Him. 19. Then not finding by what way they could bring him in because of the crowd, after they went up on the roof they let him and his pallet down through the tiles into the middle in front of **Y'shua**. 20. And **when He saw their faith** He said, "Man, **your sins have been forgiven you**."*

The common belief was that sickness and physical problems were caused by sin. It is interesting that Y'shua says He has authority to forgive sins, yet His statement to the paralytic is "Your sins are forgiven," something we can say to any repentant person.

Luke 5:21. *Then the scribes and the Pharisees began to discuss saying, "Who is this Who is speaking blasphemy? Who is able to forgive sin except only God?" 22. But **Y'shua**, well knowing their discussion, said to them, "What are you discussing in your hearts? 23. What is easier, to say 'Your sins are forgiven to you,' or to say, 'You must rise and you must walk?' 24. But so that you would know that the Son of Man has authority upon the Earth to forgive sins" – He said to the paralyzed one, "To you I say, you must rise, and when you take up your pallet you must go into your house right away." 25. Then quickly getting up in front of them, after he took up what he was reclining on,* *he went to his house glorifying God. 26. Then amazement took all and they were glorifying God and they were filled with awe saying, "(What) we have seen today is wonderful."* (Matt. 9:1-8, Mark 2:1-12)

The Man with the Withered Hand

Luke 6:6. *And it happened on another Sabbath He entered the synagogue and taught. And a man was there whose **right hand was withered**. 7. And the scribes and Pharisees were watching Him closely with evil intent, (to see) if He **healed** on the **Sabbath**, so that they would find (something) to accuse Him. 8. But He **had known** their thoughts, and He said to the man who had the **withered hand**, "You must rise and now stand in the middle:" then after he rose he stood (there). 9. And Y'shua said to them, "**I ask you if it is proper on the Sabbath to do good or to do evil, to save** or to **destroy** life?" 10. Then as He **looked around at them all** He said to him, "**You must immediately** stretch out your **hand**." And he did and his **hand was restored**. 11. But they **were filled with fury** and were discussing with one another whatever they might do to **Y'shua**.* (Matt. 12:9-14, Mark 3:1-6)

Y'shua did not shirk from Healing because religious people were looking to condemn Him, but He had the man stand in the middle of the room so all eyes would be on both the man and Y'shua. He knew what His critics were thinking and spoke directly to their thoughts; Y'shua commanded the man to stretch out his hand which was immediately healed.

Ministering to a Great Multitude

Luke 6:17. *Then, when He went down with them, He stood on a flat place, and a great crowd of His disciples, and a great multitude of people, from all of Judea and Jerusalem and the coast of Tyre and Sidon 18. came to hear Him and to be healed from their diseases: and those who were troubled by **unclean spirits were being healed**, 19. and the whole crowd was seeking to touch Him, because power was coming out from Him and He **was healing all**.* (Matt. 4:23-25)

Notice that Y'shua went down from the hill, that this is a different time and place for this teaching and not another description of the Sermon on the Mount, Matthew 5:1-7:28. The word used for Healed in verse eighteen is Therapeuo, (with the primary meaning to serve) nearly always translated to heal, strengthening the connection between deliverance and healing. Evil was Healed. At this time He Healed everyone who needed Healing, while in John 5:1-9 He picked just one person to be Healed.

The Healing at the Pool

John 5.1. *After these things there was a feast of the Jewish people and Y'shua went up to Jerusalem. 2. And He was among the people of Jerusalem at the Sheep Gate pool, the one called in Hebrew **Beit-Zata**, which had five porches. 3. Among those who were lying down were a great number of sick, of blind, of lame, of withered. 4. (For from time to time an angel of the Lord washed in the pool and agitated the water, then the first going down after the disturbance of the water was made well from whatever he was held by.)*

Beit Zata means House of Olives, but this pool was also called Beit H̲esed meaning House of Loving Kindness. John 5:4 was added in the fourth century.

John 5:5. *And some man was there thirty-eight years because he had this sickness: 6. when **Y'shua** saw this (man) lying down, knowing that he had already been there a long time, He said to him, "Do you want to become well?" 7. The sick one answered Him, "Lord, I do not have a man so that when the water would be disturbed he could put me into the pool: but while I am coming, another gets down before me." 8. **Y'shua** said to him, "**You must immediately get up**, **you must at once take your pallet** and **you must continually walk.**" 9. And immediately the man became well and he took his pallet and he was walking.*

This passage gives a pattern for taking a divine healing: taking it immediately, and then walking continually with it. Do not permit the evil to return. Some healings take time, but the confession and attitude must be of being healed. Walk by faith, not by sight, 2 Corinthians 5:7.

The Healing of a Centurion's Servant,

Luke 7.1. *After He finished all His **words** in the hearing of the people, He entered **Capernaum**. 2. And a certain **servant** of a centurion, who was dear to (the centurion), having **evil**, was going to die. 3. And when he heard about **Y'shua** he sent elders of the Jewish people to Him asking Him that if He came would He cure his **servant**. 4. And those who came to Y'shua were urging Him earnestly, saying that "This one is worthy for whom You should offer this: 5. for he loves our nation and he built the **synagogue** for us."* (Matthew 8:5-13, John 4:43-54)

Most likely this Synagogue was not an elaborate building. See *Synagogues* in the One New Man Bible Glossary.

Luke 7:6. *And **Y'shua** was going with them. But now when He was not far distant from the house, the centurion sent friends who said to Him, "Lord, You must not be bothered, for I am not worthy that You should come under my roof: 7. on this account I was not worthy to come to You myself: but You must say a **word**, and my **child** must be healed. 8. For I am also a man under authority, (and in authority) as I have soldiers under me, and I say to this one, when I order, 'You must now go,' and he goes, and to another, 'You must come,' and he comes, and to my servant, 'You must now do this,' and he does." 9. And when He heard these things **Y'shua** was amazed at him and after He turned to the crowd that was following Him He said, "I say to you, not in Israel have I found so much strong faith." 10. Then when they returned to the house, those who were sent found the **servant** in good health.*

Capernaum is the Latin spelling of the Hebrew name Kafer Na<u>h</u>um. Kafer means town or village and Na<u>h</u>um means comfort, consolation. The **Servant** was apparently a young male indentured servant because here in verse seven, and in Matthew and John he is called a **child**. Having **evil** was a synonym for being sick

The Raising of a Widow's Son at Nain

Luke 7:11. *Then it happened on the next (day) He was going into a city called Nain, and His disciples and a great crowd were going together with Him. 12. And as He approached the gate of the city, then behold an **only son** of his mother, (who) **died**, was being carried out, and she was herself a widow, and a crowd of that city was with her. 13. And when He saw her, the Lord had pity upon her and said to her, "Stop crying!" 14. Then when He went over He touched the **bier**, and those bearing (it) stood still, and He said, "Young man, I say to you, **you must rise immediately!**" 15. Then the **dead (boy)** sat up and began to speak, and He gave him to his mother. 16. And reverence took all and they were glorifying God saying that "A great prophet has risen among us" and that "God cared for His people." 17. And this message about Him went out in all Judea and in every neighboring region.*

The **Bier** was a pallet on which the body was placed, then the body was slid from the **Bier** into the grave.

The Death of Lazarus

John 11.1. *And someone was sick, Lazarus from **Bethany**, from the town of **Miriam** and her sister **Martha**. 2. And **Miriam** was the one who anointed the Lord with ointment and wiped His feet with her hair, (John 12:3) her brother **Lazarus** was sick. 3. Therefore the sisters sent to Him saying, "Lord,* *behold whom You **love** is **sick**." 4. When **Y'shua** heard (this) He said, "This* *sickness is not to death but for the **glory of God**, so that the **Son of God*** *would be **glorified** through this (sickness)." 5. And Y'shua **loved Martha*** *and her **sister** and **Lazarus**. 6. Therefore as He heard that he was **sick**, at* *that time He was indeed staying in that place (where) He was **two days**, 7.* *immediately after this He said to the disciples, "We should go to Judea again."* *8. The disciples said to Him, "Rabbi, the Jewish (leaders) were just now* *seeking to stone You, and are You going there again?" 9. **Y'shua** answered,* *"Are there not twelve hours of **daylight**? If someone would walk in the **day**,* *he does not stumble, because he sees the **light** of this world: 10. but if someone* *would walk in the **night**, he stumbles, because the **light** is not in (the* *world)." 11. He said these things, and after this He said to them, "Our friend* ***Lazarus** has fallen asleep: but I am going so that I could awaken him." 12.* *Then the disciples said to Him, "Lord, if he would be **sleeping** he will be* *saved." 13. But **Y'shua** had spoken about his **death**, only they thought that* *He was talking about the **sleep** of **slumber**. 14. Therefore **Y'shua** then said* *plainly to them, "**Lazarus died**, 15. and I rejoice for you that I was not* *there so that you would believe: but let us go to him." 16. Then Thomas, the* *one called Twin, said to his fellow disciples, "Let us also go so that we could* *die with him."*

Bethany is the Greek spelling of Beit-Anyah, meaning House of Sighing. In verse three the verb **phileo** is used for **Love**. In verse five the verb is **Agapao**, showing that the verbs are synonyms. See the One New Man Bible Glossary article *Agapao*. **Day** speaks of **light**, while **dawn alludes to redemption**. **Night alludes to exile, separation from God's presence**. Sleep is a Hebrew idiom for Death.

The Calming of a Storm,

Luke 8:22. And it happened on one of the days that He and His disciples *embarked in a boat and He said to them, "Let us go over to the other side of* *the lake," and they set out. 23. And He fell asleep while they were sailing.* *Then a **strong gust of wind came down upon the lake and they were*** ***being swamped and endangered**. 24. And when they went to Him they* *woke Him saying "Master. Master! **We are being destroyed**." Then after He* *got up He **rebuked the wind and the wave of the water**: then it **stopped*** *and it was **calm**. 25. And He said to them, "**Where is your faith?**" But* *being afraid, they were amazed, saying to one another, "Who then is this* *that even **commands the winds and the water**, and they **obey Him?**"* (Matthew 8:23-27, Mark 4:35-41)

Where is my **Faith**? Can command the **Weather** and the **Waves** but rarely try?

The Healing of the Gerasene Demoniac,

> Luke 8:26. *Then they sailed to the region of the Gerasenes, which is across the (lake of) Galilee. 27. And when He came out on the shore a man from the city, (who) had demons, met (Him). For a long time he had not worn a garment or (stayed) in a house, but was staying in the **tombs**. 28. And when he saw **Y'shua**, as he cried out, he fell down before Him and said in a loud voice, "What do You have to do with me, **Y'shua**, Son of the Most High God? I beg You, do not torment me." 29. For He **commanded** the **unclean spirit** to come out from the man. For many times it seized him and although he was guarded and bound in chains and fetters, he **broke** the **chains**, being driven by the **demon** into the wilderness areas. 30. And **Y'shua** asked **him (the Demon)**, "What is your name?" And he said. "**Legion**," because many **demons** went into him. 31. And they were begging Him not to command them to go into the abyss.* (Matthew 8:28-34, Mark 5:1-20)

The Tombs were in caves. In the first century a Roman Legion had 6,826 men, an incredible number of Demons in this case.

> Luke 8:32. *And there was a **herd** of **many pigs** there feeding on the mountain: and they begged Him to allow them to enter those: and He allowed (the **demons** to enter the **pigs**). 33. And when the **demons** came out from the **man** they entered the **pigs**, then the herd set out down the slope into the lake and was **drowned**. 34. And when those who were tending saw what happened they fled and reported (that) in the city and in the fields. 35. And they came out to see what happened and they came to **Y'shua** and they found the **man** from whom the **demons** came out, sitting by the feet of **Y'shua**, dressed and of sound mind, and they were afraid. 36. And those who saw reported to them how the one who was **demon** possessed was delivered. 37. Then all the multitude of the region of the Gerasene asked Him to leave from them, because they were being distressed with great fear: then He returned, having embarked in a boat. 38. And the **man** from whom the **demons** had come out was begging Him to be with Him: but He released him saying, 39. "You must return to your house and **you must continually tell what God did for you**." Then he left, proclaiming throughout the whole city what **Y'shua** did for him.*

Y'shua ordered the **Man** to tell others about the **Miracle Deliverance!**

Jairus' Daughter and The Woman Who Touched His Prayer Shawl.

> Luke 8:40. *And on **Y'shua's** return the crowd welcomed Him: for they were all looking for Him. 41. And behold a man named Jairus came and this one*

*was a **leader of the synagogue**, and he fell at the feet of **Y'shua**, begging Him to come to his house, 42. because his only daughter was about twelve years old and she was about to die.*

*And while He was going the throngs were crowding together around Him. 43. And a **woman** (who) was in a flow of blood for twelve years, who having spent (her) whole living on doctors was not able to be healed by anyone, 44. when she came up behind **she touched the fringe** of His **prayer shawl** and immediately her **flow of blood stopped**. 45. Then **Y'shua** said, "Who is the one who **touched** Me?" But when all denied, Peter said, "Master, the crowds are choking You and pressing in." 46. And **Y'shua** said, "Someone **touched** Me. For I know power has come out from Me." 47. And when the woman saw that she did not escape notice, she came trembling and as she fell before Him she **reported** before all the people (what) the reason was she touched Him and as (she spoke) she was **healed** immediately. 48. And He said to her, "Daughter, your **faith** has saved you. You must continually go in peace."* (Matthew 9:18-26, Mark 5:21-43)

The Prayer Shawl was the common outer garment of the Jewish men, with the fringe, called Tsit-tsit in Hebrew, representing all the commands and promises of God. That is why the woman in verse forty-four reached out to touch the fringe – and was delivered!

Luke 8:49. *While He was still speaking someone came from (the home) of the synagogue **leader** saying that "**Your daughter has died**: you must no longer trouble the **teacher**." 50. But since **Y'shua** heard He answered him, "Stop being fearful! **You must only believe, and she will be rescued**." 51. Then after He came into the house He did **not** permit any to enter with Him except **Peter** and **John** and **Jacob** and the **father** and the **mother** of the **child**. 52. But all (the mourners) were crying and mourning her. And He said, "Stop crying! For she **did not die** but she is **sleeping**." 53. Then they were laughing scornfully at Him because they knew that she had **died**. 54. But He, taking hold of her hand, spoke to her saying, "**Child, you must rise**." 55. Then her spirit returned and **she stood up immediately** and He ordered (something) to be given for her to eat. 56. And her parents were astonished: but **He ordered them not to tell what had happened**.*

Faith is required for receiving Spiritual Blessings, and is why only those He named could accompany Him when He raised the girl. This is His second raising of a dead person, the first being the son of the widow in Nain. It is odd that He ordered those in the room with Him not to tell because all the guests knew what had happened when they saw her alive. Lazarus was the third person He raised from the dead.

Y'shua the Resurrection and the Life

John 11:17. *Then when **Y'shua** came He found (that) he had now (been) in the tomb four days. 18. And Bethany was near Jerusalem, about **fifteen stadia**. 19. And many of the Jewish people had come to **Martha** and **Miriam** so that they could console them concerning their brother. 20. Then as **Martha** heard that **Y'shua** was coming she went to meet Him: and **Miriam** was sitting in the house. 21. Therefore **Martha** said to **Y'shua**, "Lord, if You had been here my brother would not have died: 22. but now I also know that **God will give You whatever You would ask.**" 23. **Y'shua** said to her, "**Your brother will rise.**" 24. **Martha** said to Him, "I know that he will rise on the last **Day** in the **resurrection**." 25. **Y'shua** said to her, "**I AM the Resurrection and the Life**: the one who believes in Me, even if he would die, he will **live**, 26. and everyone who **lives** and **believes in Me** would **not ever die**. Do you believe this?" 27. She said to Him, "Certainly Lord, I have believed that You are the **Messiah**, the Son of God, the One Who was to come into the world."*

Fifteen Stadia is about two miles. The Last Day is a Spiritual Day not our twenty-four hour natural Day! How long Judgment Day will last is anybody's guess, but it will be a very long Day. That is when the Final Resurrection takes place; the Resurrection will not be to physical bodies, but to Spiritual Bodies!

Lazarus Brought to Life

John 11:38. *Y'shua then again, being deeply moved within Himself, came to the tomb: and it was a cave and a stone was lying upon it. 39. **Y'shua** said, "You must remove the stone." **Martha**, the sister of the one who had died, said to Him, "Lord, he already has an odor, for it has been four days." 40. **Y'shua** said to her, "Did I not say that if you would believe you would see the **glory of God**?" 41. Then they removed the stone. And **Y'shua** looked up and said, "Father, I give You thanks because **You heard Me**.*

Y'shua had already prayed and knew the outcome ahead of time.

John 11:42. *And I have known that You always hear Me, but I spoke because of the crowd that was standing around, so that they would believe that You sent Me." 43. And after He said these things He cried out in a loud voice, "**Lazarus, come outside**." 44. The one who **died** came out, although his feet* *and hands had been bound with strips of cloth and his face was bound with a face cloth. Y'shua said to them, "You must **loose** him at once and you must **allow** him to go."*

Loose and **Allow** are a Hebrew poetic parallelism for emphasis, with **loose** an idiom meaning to **permit, allow**. That completes Lazarus' **Resurrection** of his **physical body**, which did eventually die. After his final death **Lazarus** was given his **Spiritual Body**. All those recorded in the Bible as being raised from the dead, except **Y'shua**, returned to their natural bodies which later did die.

The Feeding of the Five Thousand,

> Luke 9:10. *And when the apostles returned they reported to Him what they did. And then He took them and went back (with them) by themselves to a city called **Bethsaida**. 11. But when the crowds knew they followed Him: and welcoming them, He was speaking to them about the **Kingdom of God**, and those who had need of **healing** were being **healed**. 12. And the day began to draw to a close: and after the twelve came they said to Him, "You must release the crowd now, so that when they go into the villages and fields around they would find lodging and they could find provision, because we are here in a **desolate place**." 13. But He said to them, "You must now give them (something) to eat." And they said, "There are not more than **five loaves** and **two fish** with us, unless we go to buy food for all these people." 14. For there were about **five thousand men**. But He said to His disciples, "You must make them sit down in groups of about fifty or more." 15. And they did so and they all reclined. 16. And when He took the **five loaves** and the **two fish**, as He looked up into heaven He praised God for them, then He broke (them) in pieces and He was giving (them) to the disciples to set before the crowd. 17. And they ate and they all were satisfied, and the leftovers, twelve **baskets** of pieces, were taken up by them.* (2 Ki. 4:42-44 Matthew 14:13-21, Mark 6:30-44, John 6:1-14)

Bethsaida is the Greek spelling of Beit-Tside, which means House or Place of Fishing (literally hunting). The Feeding of the Five Thousand is identified in Luke 9:10 as being near Beit-Tsaida (Bethsaida). There are two towns by that name, one between Capernaum and Tiberias, on the west side of the lake. The other Beit-Tsaida was across the lake, at the northeast corner, about seven miles north and east from Capernaum, but nearly diagonally across the lake from Tiberias.

Rowing from east to west, going to Capernaum from the northeast Beit-Tsaida would be against the strong winds as described in the Gospels, as Y'shua walked on the water (Mark 6:48ff, John 6:19) to catch up to the disciples. Those strong winds blew them off course so they landed at Gennesaret (Mark 6:53) instead of the western Bethsaida (Mark 6:45). Gennesaret is a plain of good farmland northeast of Capernaum.

Numbers 1:3 teaches to count only men between the ages of twenty and fifty. So old men, women and children were not counted. These Baskets were smaller than the Hampers used for cleaning up after the Feeding of the Four Thousand.

The Feeding of the Four Thousand

> Matthew 15:32. *And after* **Y'shua** *summoned His disciples He said, "I feel sorry for the crowd, because they have already been staying with Me three days and they do not have anything they could eat: and I do not want to release them hungry lest they would become weary on the way." 33. Then the disciples said to Him, "From where in a wilderness can we get so much food so as to feed so great a crowd?" 34. And* **Y'shua** *said to them, "How much food do you have?" And they said, "**Seven loaves and a few fish.**" 35. Then after He instructed the crowd to recline on the ground 36. He took the **seven loaves and the fish** and after He gave **thanks** He broke (them) and was giving (them) to the disciples, and the disciples gave (them) to the crowds. 37. Then they all ate and were satisfied. And they took up the leftovers, **seven hampers** full of the pieces. (2 Ki. 4:42-44) 38. And those who ate were **four thousand men** not counting women and children. 39. And after He dismissed the crowds He embarked in the boat and came to the region of Magadan.* (Mark 8:1-10)

The **hamper** was large, being used in Acts 9:25 to describe Paul's being lowered through the Damascus city wall. See Matthew 16:10, Mark 8:8,20.

The Healing of a Blind Man at Bethsaida

> Mark 8:22. *And they came into Bethsaida. And they brought to Him a blind (man) and begged Him that He would touch him. 23. Then taking the hand of the blind (man), He led him outside the village and having **spit** in his **eyes**, after He placed His hands on him, He was asking him, "Do you see anything?" 24. And when he looked up he was saying, "I see men that (are) as trees I see walking." 25. Then He again laid hands upon his eyes, and he stared straight ahead and he was restored and he was looking at everything clearly. And He sent him to his house saying, "And do not enter the village."*

The **spittle** of a man who was the firstborn son of his father was believed to have healing power. The word translated **eyes** is **omma**, which means both **natural** and **spiritual** eyes, used only here and in Matthew 20:34.

Payment of the Temple Tax

Matthew 17:24. *And after they came into Capernaum those who were collecting the* two drachma *then said to Peter, "Does not your Teacher pay the* two drachmas?" *(Exod. 30:13, 38:26) 25. He said, "Indeed." And, after he came into the house, Y'shua spoke first to him saying, "What do you think, Simon? From whom are the kings of the Earth taking a tax or head tax? From their sons or from the others?" 26. And then he said, "From the others," Y'shua said to him, "Consequently the sons are indeed free. 27. But so that we would not offend them, on going to (the) lake, you must right away cast a hook and take the first fish coming up, and when you open its mouth you will find a coin: taking that you must at once give (it) to them for Me and you."*

The Two Drachmas is the half-shekel temple tax from Exodus 30:13; 38:26.

The Transfiguration of Y'shua

Luke 9:28. *And it was about eight days after these messages, and taking* Peter *and* John *and* Jacob *He went up to the mountain to* pray *(for Himself)*.

The mood of the verb indicates that Y'shua prayed for His own needs, confirmed by Moses and Elijah in verses thirty and thirty-one. The three Apostles saw clearly into the Spirit Realm.

> Luke 9:29. *And it happened while He was praying, the appearance of His face (was) different and His cloak (Prayer Shawl was) white, gleaming like lightning. 30. And behold two men were speaking with Him, who were* **Moses** *and* **Elijah**, *31. while those who had been seen in glory were speaking about His death, which He was going to fulfill in Jerusalem. 32. And* **Peter** *and those with him were burdened in sleep: but as they kept awake they saw His* **glory** *and the* **two men** *who had stood with Him. 33. Then it happened while they were being separated from Him,* **Peter** *said to* **Y'shua**, *"Master, it is good for us to be here, now let us make three booths, one for You and one for* **Moses** *and one for* **Elijah**," *although he had not understood what he was saying. 34. But while he was saying these things a cloud came and covered them: and they were afraid while they entered the cloud. 35. Then a voice came from the cloud saying, "This is My Son, the One Who has been chosen,* **you must continually listen to Him**." *36. And, after the voice came,* **Y'shua** *was found alone. And they kept silent and no one reported in those days anything that they had seen.* (Matthew 17:1-8, Mark 9:2-8)

This is an amazing view into the Spirit Realm for the three apostles who accompanied Y'shua. It tells us that Moses, who died, and Elijah, who had not died, were both in their Spiritual Bodies, meaning that since Moses had an earthly visit in his Spiritual body we can envision possible assignments on earth for our Spiritual bodies in time to come. Notice also the command from the LORD* to continually Listen to Y'shua.

The Healing of a Boy with an Unclean Spirit,

> Luke 9:37. *And it happened the next day when they came down from the mountain a huge crowd met Him. 38. And behold a man from the crowd called out saying, "Teacher, I beg You to look at my son, because he is my only (child), 39. and behold a spirit takes him and suddenly it cries out and* **convulses** *him with* **foaming at the mouth** *and it goes away from him with difficulty, wearing him out. 40. And I urged Your* **disciples** *to cast it out, but they were* **not able.*** *41. And* **Y'shua** *said, "O unbelieving and perverted generation,* **how long will I be with you and will I endure you?** *You must bring your son here at once." 42. But while he was coming the demon threw him down and* **convulsed** *(him): but* **Y'shua rebuked** *the* **unclean spirit** *and* **healed** *the child and gave him to his father. 43. And all were amazed at the majesty of God.* (Matthew 17:14-18, Mark 9:14-27)

This was a routine Healing to Y'shua but His Disciples had not realized their potential power; the Modern Church still rarely preaches Kingdom which is why it does not move in Power. Y'shua was exasperated for their unbelief and is undoubtedly exasperated with us for the same reason. His command was to: Preach Kingdom!

The Healing of a Man Born Blind

> John 9.1. *And when He was passing by He saw a* **man blind from birth.** *2. And His disciples asked Him saying, "Rabbi,* **who sinned,** *this one or his parents, that he would have been born blind?" 3. Y'shua answered, "****Neither** *he nor his parents* **sinned,** *but so that the* **works of God would be revealed in him.** *4. It is necessary for us to perform the works of the One Who sent Me while it is* **day: night** *is coming when no one is able to perform. 5. While I would be in the world, I am (the)* **Light** *of the world." 6. After He said these things He* **spit** *on the ground and He made* **clay** *from the* **spittle** *and He placed this clay upon his eyes 7. and He said to him, "You must go wash in the Pool of Siloam," the one interpreted "having been sent." Then he went and washed and came away* **seeing.** *8. Therefore the neighbors and those who saw him earlier, because he was a* **beggar,** *were saying, "Is this not the one who sits and begs?" 9. Some were saying that "This is he," (but) others were saying, "No, but he is like him." That one was saying, "I am (he)." 10. Therefore*

*they were saying to him, "How then were your eyes opened?" 11. That one answered, "The man called **Y'shua** made **clay** and spread (it) on my **eyes** and He said to me that 'You must go to **Siloam** and wash:' then when I went, after I **washed** I **recovered** my **sight**." 12. And they said to him, "Where is that One?" He said, "I do not know."*

To beg, someone had to get an official **Beggar's Cloak** from a priest, which is how all those people recognized him after he was healed and no longer wore his **Beggar's Cloak. Day** speaks of **light**, while **dawn alludes to redemption. Night alludes to exile, separation from God's presence.** People believed the **spittle** of the firstborn son of the father was **anointed for healing.** The Hebrew name of the pool is **Shilo̲h** (Sent), not **Siloam,** located near the Temple mount at the end of Hezekiah's tunnel. It was the source of the water that was used with the ashes of the red heifer for purification. This pool was discovered early in the 21ˢᵗ century. How can someone **born blind recover sight**? Could it be his eyes were perfectly formed in the womb, but by the time of his birth he was blind?

Y'shua and Beelzebub

Luke 11:14. *Then He was casting out a **demon** and this one was **deaf and mute**: and it happened, after the demon came out, the **mute** person **spoke** and the crowds were amazed. 15. But some of them said "He is casting out the **demons** by means of **Beelzebub** the leader of the demons:" 16. but others, testing, were seeking a sign from heaven from Him. 17. And because **He knew their thoughts** He said to them, "Every kingdom that is divided against itself is laid waste and a house (divided) against a house falls. 18. And if in fact **Satan** is divided against himself, how will his kingdom stand? (Yet) you say that I cast out **demons** by **Beelzebub**. 19. But if I am casting out demons by **Beelzebub**, by whom are your sons casting (them) out? Because of this they will be your judges. 20. But if I am casting out **demons** by a finger of God, then the **Kingdom of God** has come upon you. 21. 'When the strong one, since he was equipped, would guard his house, his possessions (would) be in peace: 22. but when one stronger than he attacked he would overcome him. He takes his armor from him in which he placed his confidence and they would distribute his booty.' 23. The one who is not with Me is against Me, and the one who does not gather with Me is scattering."* (Matthew 12:22-30, Mark 3:20-27)

Casting out the Deaf and Mute Demon was routine for Y'shua, then He read the minds of His critics, answering their unspoken question. Beelzebub is the Greek spelling of the Hebrew Baal Zevuv, Master or god of Flies. Preaching Kingdom includes both driving out Demons and bringing Healings.

The Healing of a Crippled Woman on the Sabbath

> Luke 13:10. *And He was (regularly) teaching in one of the synagogues on the Sabbaths. 11. And behold (there was) a woman who had a **spirit of sickness** eighteen years and she was bent over and not able to stand fully erect. 12. And when **Y'shua** saw her He called out and said to her, "Ma'am, **you have been set free from your sickness**," 13. and He placed His hands on her: and she was immediately **straightened up** and was **glorifying God**. 14. But, angered that **Y'shua** healed on the **Sabbath**, the synagogue leader was saying to the crowd that "There are six days in which it is necessary to work: therefore you must be healed (by) coming on those (days) and not on the Sabbath day." 15. And when He answered, the Lord then said, "Hypocrites! Does not each of you on the Sabbath loose his cow or donkey from the stall and lead it out (to) give (it) to drink? 16. But this one, (who) is a daughter of Abraham, whom **Satan bound eighteen** long years, is it not necessary to loose her from this bondage even on the Sabbath day?" 17. Then, while He was saying these things, all those **opposed** to Him were **put to shame**, but the whole **crowd** was **rejoicing** over all the splendid things taking place under Him.*

The Woman had a Spirit of Sickness, showing the need for us as well to take charge over any Spirit of Sickness; this is more Kingdom Preaching! After being Healed the Woman Glorified God! He gets the Glory for every Healing! Satan caused the crippling condition, so he gets the blame.

The Healing of the Man with Dropsy

> Luke 14.1. *And it happened, while He went to a house of a certain one of the leaders of the Pharisees on a Sabbath to eat a meal, that they were watching Him closely. 2. And behold a man who was suffering with **dropsy** (was) in front of Him. 3. And **Y'shua** spoke to the Torah scholars and Pharisees saying, "Is it or is it not permitted to heal on the Sabbath?" 4. But they were silent. Then after He took hold (of him) He healed him and set (him) free. 5. Then He said to them, "A son or ox of any of you will fall into a well, and will any (of you) not immediately pull him up on a Sabbath day?" 6. And they were not able to dispute these things.*

Dropsy was a swelling or tumor. Like experienced politicians, the scholars and Pharisees did not respond to a potentially embarrassing question; again, religious people criticize for healing on a Sabbath. Our Heavenly Father does not like Religion. He wants Relationship with you not obedience to some code written by Religious leaders.

Colossians 2:20. *If you died with Messiah away from the elemental spirits of the world, why are you submitting to **rules and regulations** as if you were living in (the) world? 21. You should not touch and you should not taste and you should not handle, 22. which are all things that are meant for destruction, because (they are) the **precepts** and **teachings** of **men**, 23. which (**rules and regulations**) are things indeed which have a reputation of wisdom in **self-made religion** and in having an affected and ostentatious (and) humble opinion of one's self and unsparing severity of (the) body, not in any honor (to God), but for the indulgence of the flesh.*

The reason there are so many denominations is because well-meaning people think they are helping when they write explanations of the meanings of different Scriptures so that we end up with endless accounts that make differences so apparent, dividing the congregation of the LORD*.

The Cleansing of Ten Lepers

Luke 17:11. *Then it happened, while He was going to Jerusalem, that He was crossing the border between Samaria and Galilee. 12. And when He came into a certain village ten **leprous** men met Him. They stood at a distance 13. and they raised (their) voices saying, "**Y'shua**, Master, You must immediately have **mercy** on us." 14. And when He saw (them) He said to them, "When you go you must show yourselves at once to the priests." (Lev. 14:2,3) And it happened while they were going they were cleansed. 15. And one of them, when he saw that he was healed, returned, glorifying God with a loud voice, 16. and he fell on (his) face at His feet, giving thanks to Him: and this one was a Samaritan. 17. And Y'shua said, "Were not ten cleansed? Then where are the nine? 18. Were there not found (any) returning to give glory to God except this foreigner?" 19. Then He said to him, "After you rise you must immediately go: your faith has delivered you."*

The ten lepers were together because they were ostracized by society, not able to go into any walled city or any group of people. What is called Leprosy today is not the Leprosy of the Bible which was very contagious; today's Leprosy is treated on an outpatient basis. See *Leprosy* in the One New Man Bible Glossary. Pleading for Mercy is asking for forgiveness, believing that sin caused the evil. Another asks forgiveness, this time for blindness.

The Healing of a Blind Beggar near Jericho

Luke 18:35. *And it happened while they were approaching Jericho, a certain **blind** man was sitting by the road, begging. 36. And when he heard the crowd* *passing through he asked what this might be. 37. And they were reporting to him that "**Y'shua** of Nazareth is coming by." 38. Then he shouted saying, "**Y'shua, Son of David**, You **must** right now have **mercy** on me!" 39. Then those who were going before (Him) were ordering him to be quiet, but he cried out much more, "**Son of David**, You **must** right now have **mercy** on me!" 40. And when He stopped, **Y'shua** ordered him to be led to Him. And when he came near He asked him, 41. "What do you want Me to do for you?" And he said, "Lord, that I shall recover my sight." 42. Then **Y'shua** said to him, "Look up! **Your faith has delivered you.**" 43. And he immediately **recovered his sight** and he was following Him, glorifying God. And when all the people saw (the miracle) they gave praise to God.* (Matthew 20:29-34, Mark 10:46-52)

The blind man's plea to have Mercy on me is asking for Forgiveness because he thought sin was the cause of his blindness. Mark 10:50 tells us the beggar was wearing an official cloak, meaning that a priest had issued the cloak for him to wear to show he was approved to beg for support. When he threw off that cloak he showed the crowd that he was confident that he would regain his sight. Y'shua took note of that attitude, declaring "Your faith has delivered you!" The now seeing, formerly blind man then joined the crowd to show off his miraculous healing. See *Son of David/Son of Joseph* in the One New Man Bible Glossary.

The Resurrection of Y'shua

Luke 23:23. *But, since it was the Sabbath, they rested according to the commandment. Luke 24.1. And on the* First Day of the Week, *they came to the tomb very early, bringing the spices which they prepared.*

First Day of the Week is the Hebrew expression for Sunday, which began at sundown Saturday. They were a few of the Women who came to the tomb, then told the Apostles about His disappearance.

Luke 24:2. *And they found (that) the stone had been rolled away from the tomb, 3. but when they entered they did not find the body of the Lord **Y'shua**. 4. And it happened; while they were at a loss concerning this, then behold two men in radiant clothing stood by them. 5. And because the women had been thrown into fear and they were bowing (their) faces to the ground, (the men) said to them, "Why are you seeking the living with the dead: 6. He is **not here** but **He has risen**. You must remember when He spoke to you while He was in Galilee 7. saying 'It is necessary for the Son of Man to be given over into the hands of sinful men and to be crucified and to be raised on the third day.'" 8. Then they remembered His words. 9. And after they returned from*

the tomb they reported all these things to the eleven and to all the rest. 10.
*And they were **Miriam Magdalene** and **Joanna** and **Miriam** (mother) **of***
***Jacob** and the rest (of the women) with them. They were telling these things*
*to the **apostles**, 11. but these words seemed in their sight as nonsense and they*
*did not believe them. 12. But **Peter**, when he got up, ran to the tomb and*
when he stooped he saw only the cloth, and he left, wondering to himself what
had happened. (Matthew 28:1-10, Mark 16:1-8, John 20:1-10)

Although the Disciples had all been told several times about His death and
Resurrection it still had not registered with them that He would die and would
then be Resurrected.

Matthew 28.1. *And after* Sabbaths, *on the* First Day of the Week *at* dawn, Miriam
Magdalene *and the other* Miriam *came to see the tomb.*

Sabbaths is plural because it denotes both a weekly Sabbath and a feast day, the
first day of Unleavened Bread. See Leviticus 23:7. This day had begun at sundown
on what we consider the day before. It takes some adjusting for us westerners
to appreciate each twenty-four-hour day beginning at sundown and ending at
sundown the following day.

Matthew 28:2. *And behold there was a great **earthquake**: for (there was)*
*an **angel** of the Lord, (who) descended from heaven, and after he came he*
rolled the stone away and was sitting upon it. 3. And his appearance was like
*lightning and his **clothing white as snow**. 4. And those who were guarding*
*trembled from fear of him and became as dead. 5. And the **angel** said to*
*the **women**, "You must not be afraid, for I know that you are seeking the*
***crucified Y'shua**: 6. **He is not here**, for He has **risen** just as He said.*
*Come! See the place where He was laid. 7. And go quickly, **you must tell His***
disciples**, 'He has **risen** from the **dead**, and behold He is going **before you
***into Galilee**, for you will see Him there: behold I told you." 8. Then they left*
quickly from the tomb with fear and great joy, and were running to report to
*His disciples. 9. And behold **Y'shua** met (the women) saying, "Greetings."*
And they, who had approached (Him), took hold of His feet and they paid
*homage to Him. 10. Then **Y'shua** said to them, "You must not be afraid: you*
must go, report to My brothers so they would go into Galilee, they will see Me
there." (Mark 16:1-8, John 20:1-10

This Earthquake in verse two was a spiritual sign of His Death and the Resurrection
miracle to come.

The Appearance of Y'shua to Miriam Magdalene

John 20:11. *And **Miriam** stood outside at the tomb weeping. Then as she was weeping, she bent over into the tomb 12. and saw **two angels** in white, sitting, one at the head and one at the feet, where the body of **Y'shua** had been lying. 13. And those (**angels**) said to her, "Ma'am, **why** are you weeping?" She said to them that "They took my Lord, and I do not know where they put Him." 14. After she said these things she turned to those behind and saw **Y'shua** standing but had **not recognized** that it was **Y'shua**. 15. **Y'shua** said to her, "Ma'am, why are you crying? Whom are you seeking?" Because she thought that He was the gardener she said to Him, "Sir, if you removed Him, you must tell me where you carried Him and I shall take Him." 16. **Y'shua** said to her, "**Miriam**." After she turned to that One she said to Him in Hebrew, "**Rabbi**," which means **Teacher**. 17. **Y'shua** said to her "Stop touching Me, for I have not yet ascended to the **Father**: you must go to My brothers and you must say to them, 'I am ascending to **My Father** and **your Father** and **My God** and **your God**.'" 18. **Miriam Magdalene** came and then announced to the disciples that "**I have seen the Lord**," and (that) He said these things to her.*

Y'shua's Spiritual body could be invisible or could change appearance. Later, His Spiritual Body goes through a wall, yet has the appearance of His Physical Body. See *Resurrected Body* in the One New Man Bible Glossary.

The Appearance of Y'shua to the Disciples

John 20:19. *Then when it was late on that day, on the **First Day of the Week**, and after the doors were shut where the disciples were because of fear of the Jewish (leaders), Y'shua came and stood in their midst and said to them, "Peace be with you." ("Shalom aleichem.") 20. And after He said this He showed them His hands and His side. Then the disciples rejoiced, because they had seen the Lord. 21. Then **Y'shua** said to them again "Peace be with you: just as the Father sent Me, so I am sending you." 22. And after He said this He breathed upon (them) and said to them, "**You must immediately take the Holy Spirit**: 23. whomever you would **forgive**, their **sins have been forgiven for them**, whomever you would retain (their sins) have been retained."* (Matthew 28:16-20, Luke 24:36-49)

The **First Day of the Week** is the Hebrew expression for Sunday, which began at sundown on Saturday, which we consider the day before. The **disciples** included **ten of the eleven apostles**, but could also have included others. We are ordered to **take** the **Holy Spirit**, so we have to truly **seek** the **baptism of the Holy Spirit**. See

Take/Receive in the One New Man Bible Glossary. It is not a question of a modern disciple saying "**I forgive you.**" When a disciple discerns that someone has **truly repented**, then any disciple can say as **Y'shua** did, "**Your sins are forgiven.**"

Y'shua and Thomas

> John 20:24. *And **Thomas**, one of the twelve, called Twin, was not with them when **Y'shua** came. 25. Therefore the other disciples were telling him, "We have seen the Lord." But he said to them, "**Unless I could see the mark of the nails in His hands and I could put my finger into the mark of the nails and I could put my hand into His side, I will <u>not</u> believe.**" 26. And after **eight days** His disciples were again inside and Thomas (was) with them. After the doors were closed, Y'shua came and He was in the middle (of the room) and said, "**Peace to you.**" ("**Shalom aleichem.**") 27. Then He said to **Thomas**, "Put your **finger** here and see **My hands** and you must reach out your **hand** and you must put it into My **side**, and **stop being faithless** but (have) **faith.**" 28. **Thomas** answered and said to Him, "**My Lord and my God.**" 29. **Y'shua** said to him, "Because you have seen Me have you believed? **Blessed** (are) those who have **not seen** and yet **have believed.**"*

Y'shua knew what Thomas had said, with no need for anyone to tell Him about Thomas' statements. It is easy to think that after His resurrection Y'shua was with the disciples continuously, but He was not. Eight days would have been a long time for them to go without seeing Him.

The Walk to Emmaus when the Resurrected Y'shua joined with Peter and Cleopas for the journey.

Luke 24:13. *Then behold this day two of them were going to a distant village; it was named* Emmaus, *sixty stadia from Jerusalem.*

Sixty Stadia is about seven miles from Jerusalem. Cleopas is the Latin spelling of Kleopas, the Greek spelling, which is feminine, fostering speculation that Kleopas is Peter's wife.

> Luke 24:14. *And they were speaking with one another about all these happenings. 15. And it was, while they were speaking and discussing (these things) that **Y'shua** Himself, having approached, was going with them 16. but **their eyes were being hindered (so) they did not recognize Him.***

Why do we not commonly see the Spiritual Realm? Are our eyes being hindered?

Luke 24:17. *And He said to them, "What are these accounts which you are exchanging with one another while you are walking?" And they stood still, (being) sad and gloomy. 18. And one named* **Cleopas** *said to Him, "Are You the only one living in Jerusalem and not knowing what happened in her during these days?" 19. And He said to them, "Of what sort?" And they said to Him, "The things about* **Y'shua** *of Nazareth, Who was a man, a prophet powerful in work and in word, in the presence of God and of all the people, 20. how our high priests and our leaders gave Him over in judgment of death and they crucified Him. 21. But* **we were hoping that He was the One Who was going to redeem Israel:***

The Disciples were expecting the Messianic Reign to begin immediately.

Luke 24:21b. *but even with all these things, this third day has passed since these things happened. 22. And even some of our women amazed us, since they came to the tomb early in the morning, 23. and when they did not find His body, they came saying then that in a vision they saw angels, who were saying 'He is alive.' 24. Then some of those with us left for the tomb and also found thus just as the women said, but they did not see Him." 25. But He said to them,* **"O foolish and slow in heart to believe all that the prophets were saying:** *26. for was it not necessary for the* **Messiah** *to* **suffer** *these things, then to enter* **His glory?"** *27. And beginning with Moses and with all the Prophets* **He explained to them** *with all the writings concerning Himself.*

It is odd to see that Peter was just acting human when he failed to understand what Y'shua was explaining. Humans have trouble entering the Spirit Realm.

Y'shua had to once more explain what was going on.

Luke 24:28. *Then they approached the village to which they were going, and He pretended to go farther on. 29. But they urged Him saying, "You must now stay with us because it is toward evening and the day is already over." And He came in to stay with them. 30. And it happened while He reclined with them, when He took the bread He praised God and after He broke (it) He gave (it) to them, 31. and* **their eyes were opened** *and* **they recognized Him:** *then He* **became invisible** *for them.*

The Spiritual Body can change appearance and even disappear, becoming invisible. This must be true for every Spiritual Body.

Luke 24:32. *And they said to one another, (Peter and Kleopas) "Was not our heart burning in us as He was speaking to us on the way, as He was explaining the Scriptures to us?" 33. Then after they got up they* **returned** *to* **Jerusalem** *the same hour and found the eleven and those gathered with them, 34. saying that truly the Lord had risen and was seen by Simon. 35. And they were recounting the things (discussed by* **Y'shua***) on the way and as He was recognized by them while He was breaking the bread.*

They were used to walking long distances; that the fourteen-mile round trip from Jerusalem to Emmaus and back did not make them too tired to talk to the Disciples.

The Greek spelling of Cleopas is Kleopas, while the spelling of Clopas, John 19:25, is Klopa. The "O" in Klopa is an Omega, while the "O" in Kleopas is an Omicron. Both words are in the genitive case, with Klopa masculine, Kleopas feminine. See note for verse thirty-four. This identifies Simon, clarified by Paul in 1 Corinthians 15:5 as Peter, not Simon the Zealot, as one of the disciples walking with Him to Emmaus. Verse eighteen names Cleopas as the other disciple. While most people assume Cleopas is a man, the Greek spelling has a feminine genitive (possessive) ending, so some scholars speculate that this could have been Peter's wife on the road to Emmaus with him. The transliteration of her name Kleopas with our spelling as Cleopas is evidence the transliteration was made from the Latin text, not the Greek. Greek and Hebrew have no letter C so it could not have been transliterated from either of those languages. Every name with the letter "C" in our Bibles is evidence of the first English translations being made from the Latin text, with the names never being corrected by the translators.

The Appearance of Y'shua to the Seven Disciples

John 21.1. *After these things* **Y'shua** *revealed Himself again to the disciples at the* **lake of Tiberias***: and He revealed (Himself) like this. 2.* **Simon Peter** *and* **Thomas***, the one called Twin, and* **Nathaniel***, the one from Cana of Galilee, and the* **(sons) of Zebedee** *and* **two others** *of His disciples were together. 3.* **Simon Peter** *said to them, "I am* **going to fish (from now on).***" They said to him, "We are coming and we (are) with you." They left and they embarked in the boat, and during that night they caught nothing. 4. And after dawn came* **Y'shua** *already stood on the shore, though the disciples did not yet know that it was* **Y'shua***. 5. Then* **Y'shua** *said to them, "Children, do you have any fish?" They answered Him, "No." 6. And He said to them, "You must cast the net to the right side of the boat, and you will find (fish)." Then they cast, and they no longer (had the) ability to haul (it) on account of the great number of the fish. 7. Then that disciple whom* **Y'shua** *loved said to* **Peter***, "It is the Lord." Then after* **Simon Peter** *heard that it was the Lord* *he gird around his **outer garment**, for he was without his **outer garment**, and he threw himself into the lake, 8. but the other disciples came in the little boat, for they were not far off from the shore, only about **two hundred cubits**, dragging the net of fish. 9. Then as they got off on the shore they saw coals lying (there) with fish and bread being laid on (them). 10. **Y'shua** said to them, "You must now bring (some) of the fish which you just caught." 11. Then Simon Peter went up and hauled the net to the shore, full of a hundred fifty-three big fish: even when there were so many the net was not torn. 12. **Y'shua** said to them, "Come, you must eat breakfast." And not one of (the) disciples was bold enough to ask Him, "Who are You?" since they knew that it was the Lord. 13. **Y'shua** came and took the bread and gave (it) to them, and likewise the roasted fish. 14. This (was) now the third time **Y'shua** was revealed to the disciples after He rose from (the) dead.*

The Greek word translated **Going** in verse three is **hupago**, meaning to go back where he came from, back to being a **fisherman**. This continuing action is a characteristic of the Greek present tense. This meant that they were going back to secular jobs, even while the resurrected **Y'shua** was on the Earth. Paul lists three times **Y'shua** was seen by at least all the apostles in 1 Corinthians 15:5-7. The construction in verse five indicates He anticipates a negative answer to His question. It had been some time since His last appearance and the disciples did not know His plan. In verse seven Peter's outer garment was his prayer shawl, taken off to work. In verse eight the boat was about **Two Hundred Cubits** (one hundred yards) from shore.

The Ascension of Y'shua in Luke:

*Luke 24:50. And He led them outside as far as **Bethany**, then as He raised His hands He blessed them. 51. And it happened while He was blessing them, **He went away from them, and He was being brought up into the sky**. 52. And after they paid homage to Him they returned to **Jerusalem** with great joy 53. and they were constantly in the Temple **praising God**.*

Bethany is the Greek spelling of Beit-Anyah, meaning House of Sighing.

The Ascension of Y'shua in Acts:

*Acts 1:6. Therefore indeed those who came asked Him saying, "Lord, are You **restoring the kingdom in Israel at this time?**" 7. But He said to them, "It is not for you to know the times or seasons which the Father set by His own authority, 8. but you will take power when the Holy Spirit comes upon you and you will be My witnesses in Jerusalem and in all Judea and Samaria and to (the) outermost (part) of the earth."*

Y'shua's followers were expecting the Messianic Reign to begin immediately. Many today are expecting the Messianic Reign in the physical world.

> Acts 1:9. *And after He said these things, as they were watching, He was lifted up and a cloud bore Him up and away from their eyes. 10. And as they were looking intently into the sky at His going, then there were two men in white clothing who stood by them, 11. and they said, "Men of Galilee, why have you stood looking into the sky? This **Y'shua**, Who, as He has been taken up from you into the sky,* **will come back** *in the same way as you saw Him going into the sky."*

That last statement has many looking for His Physical return, but the return will be **Spiritual**, not physical. His **Spiritual Return** will be visible over the entire world. White garments represent being in a state of spiritual preparedness, from Ecclesiastes 9:8, "Let your garments be always white; and let your head lack no ointment." Then in verse eleven:

> *And His (the LORD's) feet will stand in that Day upon the Mount of Olives, which is before Jerusalem on the east, and the Mount of Olives will split in the middle toward the east and toward the west and there will be a very great valley, and half of the mountain will remove toward the north and half of it toward the south.* (Zech. 14:4)

DISCIPLES EXPERIENCE THE SPIRIT REALM

The Coming of the Holy Spirit

Acts 2.1. *And when the day of **Shavuot** had come they were all in one place together. 2. And a sound came suddenly out of heaven as bringing a violent wind and it filled the whole **House** where they were sitting 3. and dividing tongues like fire were seen by them and the (flames) sat upon each one of them, 4. and all were filled by the Holy Spirit and began to **speak in other languages** just as the **Spirit** was giving them to speak out boldly.*

Shavuot is the Feast of Weeks, often called by the Greek name Pentecost. The Disciples were sitting on the south steps of the Temple where groups were welcome to assemble. The Temple was frequently referred to as the House by the Jewish people in Jerusalem, with Luke calling it the House in Luke 11:51. Since the steps to the South Entrance of the Temple were very wide and there were many steps, there was plenty of room for more than one hundred Disciples to gather and to listen to the leaders. There was also room for many others to observe what was going on.

Acts 2:5. *And there were **Jewish** people staying in **Jerusalem**, devout people from all the nations under heaven. 6. And when this sound was made a **multitude gathered** and was amazed, because while they were speaking, they all were hearing in their own languages. 7. And they were astounded and amazed saying, "Look, are not all those who are **speaking from Galilee**? 8. Then how do we each hear in **our own language** with which we were born? 9. **Parthians** and **Medes** and **Elamites** and those who dwell in **Mesopotamia**, **Judea**, and even **Cappadocia**, **Pontus**, and **Asia**, 10. **Phrygia**, and also **Pamphylia**, **Egypt** and the parts of **Libya** around **Cyrene**, and the visiting*

Romans, 11. Cretes and Arabs, both Jewish people and proselytes. We hear them speaking the greatness of God in our languages." 12. And all were amazed and perplexed, saying to one another, "What does this mean?" 13. But others, mocking, were saying, "They are drunk because they have been filled with sweet new wine."

Cappadocia, an inland region of Asia Minor, is referred to as Gamadim in Ezekiel 27:11 The countries named include the known world in the first century, so the earliest description of the Immersion of the Holy Spirit, also called Speaking in Tongues, includes languages that were spoken on earth at that time, while today those speaking in tongues may or may not speak known languages.

The Lame Man Healed at the Gate of the Temple

Acts 3.1. And Peter and John were going up to the Temple at the ninth hour for prayer. 2. And a certain man, (who) was lame from his mother's womb, was carried, whom they placed every day beside the door of the Temple called Beautiful Gate to ask for alms from those going into the Temple: 3. who, when he saw Peter and John about to enter the Temple, was asking to take money. 4. And Peter with John, when he looked intently at him, said, "Look upon us." 5. And he fixed his attention on them, expecting to take something from them. 6. And Peter said, "I do not have silver and gold for myself, but what I do have, this I give to you: in the name of Y'shua Messiah of Nazareth you must rise and you must continually walk." 7. And as he took hold of him by the right hand, he was raising him: and immediately his feet and ankles were strengthened, 8. and leaping up he stood and was walking and entered the Temple with them, walking and leaping and praising God: 9. so all the people saw him walking and praising God: 10. and they recognized him because he was the one who was sitting for alms at the Beautiful Gate of the Temple and they were filled with astonishment and amazement after that happened to him.

The Ninth Hour was 3:00 PM, the time for afternoon prayer. Having been placed by the Beautiful Gate every day for years shows that Y'shua walked past him numerous times because the Beautiful Gate was the entrance to the Inner Court of the Temple. This was the First miracle after their Immersion in the Holy Spirit and it was very public, so everyone would know about it. The LORD* wanted the message known! The formerly crippled man immediately credited God which was what God wanted!

Peter and John before the Council

Acts 4.1. *And while they were speaking to the people, the* priests *and the* commander of the Temple guard *and the* Sadducees *stood by them. 2. They were greatly disturbed because they taught the people and proclaimed the* resurrection *from (the) dead in* Y'shua, *3. so they* arrested *them and put (them) in prison for the next day in the morning: for it was already evening. 4. And, when many of those (people) heard the Word, they believed and the number of the men was about* five thousand.

The Sadducees did not believe in Resurrection of the Dead; not wanting teachings about Y'shua and Resurrection they put Peter and John in prison. The total number of people responding to the message by the Apostles was a lot more than five thousand because the crowd would have included women and children plus old men; those were not counted.

Acts 4:5. *And it happened on the next day, their **leaders** and **elders** and **scribes** gathered in **Jerusalem**, 6. and **Annas the High Priest** and **Caiaphas** and **John** and **Alexander** and as many as were of the **High Priest's family**, 7. and having placed them in the middle they asked, "By what **power** or in what **name** did you do this?" 8. Then **Peter**, because he was filled with the **Holy Spirit**, said to them, "**Leaders** of the people and **elders**, 9. if we are judged this day because of a good deed (for) an infirm man by means of which (good deed) this one has been delivered, 10. it must be known to you all and to all the people in Israel that in the **name of Y'shua Messiah of Nazareth** Whom you crucified, Whom **God raised** from (the) dead, by means of Him, this one stands before you whole. 11. This is*

'The stone, the one who has been rejected by' you 'the builders,

the one who became the cornerstone.' (Ps. 118:22)

*12. And deliverance is **not** in any other, for there is no other name under heaven which was given to mankind by which it is necessary for us to be saved." (Isa. 43:11) 13. And when they saw the **boldness** of **Peter** and **John** and understood that they were **unlearned** and **unskilled** men, they were **astonished** and recognized them, because they had been with **Y'shua**, 14. and when they saw the man who was **standing with them**, the one who had been **healed**, there was no way to contradict, (**deny the miracle**). 15. And after they commanded them to go outside the **Sanhedrin** they were conferring with one another 16. saying, "What will we do with these men? Because indeed a very notable sign has come through them, known, **visible** to all those who live in **Jerusalem** and we are not able to deny it: 17. but in order that it would not be spread further among the people we should* *warn them **not to speak any longer** to anyone in **this name.**" 18. Then after they called them, they warned them not to speak and not to teach at all on the name of **Y'shua**. 19. And **Peter** and **John** said to them, "You must judge if it is **just before God** to hear from **you, rather than God**: 20. for we are not able to speak except what we **saw** and **heard.**" 21. And after they were threatened further they set them free, for they did not find a way they could punish them, because of the people, because **all** were **glorifying God** on account of what happened: 22. for the man, for whom this miracle of healing happened, was more than **forty years** old.*

This meeting was with the powerful council, the Sanhedrin, before the civic and Temple leadership. Those leaders knew that Peter and John had not been to a Jewish School known as a Yeshiva, which is why they were called "Unlearned." Warning them not to speak in His Name was useless and powerless, which the leaders quickly realized, there were simply too many witnesses to the miracle. Now we know why Y'shua walked past the cripple so many times without healing him.

Ananias and Sapphirah Set as an Example

*Acts 5.1. And a certain man named **Ananias**, with his wife **Sapphirah**, sold **property** 2. and **kept back** from the **payment**, while his **wife** was also **fully aware**, and then he brought **part** (and) placed it beside the feet of the **apostles**. 3. And **Peter** said, "**Ananias**, by what means did **Satan** fill your heart, for you to have lied to the **Holy Spirit** and to have **kept back** from the **price of the property**? 4. While it remained (unsold) was it not remaining yours until you sold it by your authority? Why did you place this deed in your heart? You did not lie to men but to **God**." 5. And when **Ananias** heard these words, as he **fell** down he **breathed his last**, and great fear came upon all those who heard. 6. Then the young men got up, covered him and after they carried him out, **buried** (him).*

Peter saw into the Spirit Realm to learn that they held back. Although Ananias and Sapphirah were not required to sell the property; they could have kept it with no criticism or guilt attached, but once sold they were expected to bring all the money.

*Acts 5:7. And it was about a three-hour interval when his **wife** came in, not knowing what had happened. 8. And **Peter** declared to her, "You must tell me, if you sold the field for so much?" And she said, "**Indeed, so much.**" 9. And **Peter** (said) to her, "Why was it agreed between you to test the **Spirit** of (the) **Lord**? Behold the feet of those who **buried your husband** are at the* *door and they will carry you out.*" *10. And she **fell** at once at his feet and* ***expired***: *and when the young men came in they found her dead and after they carried (her) out, they **buried** (her) beside her husband, 11. and great fear was upon the whole congregation and upon all those who heard these things.*

Ananias and Sapphirah being killed by the LORD* was indeed severe punishment for their crime of lying and holding back money!

Apostles Do Many Signs and Wonders

Acts 5:12. *And many **signs** and **wonders** were being **done among the people** through the hands of the **apostles**. And they were all together on **Solomon's Colonnade**, 13. but none of the rest was daring to join with them, but the people were holding them in high esteem. 14. And more believing in the Lord were being added, a **multitude** of both **men** and **women**, 15. so that they even **brought** the **sick** out into the streets and placed (them) on stretchers and cots, so that when **Peter** was passing his **shadow** would fall on some of them. 16. And the **multitude** was also gathering from the cities around **Jerusalem**, bringing (the) **sick** and (those) troubled by **unclean spirits**, who were **all healed**.*

This series of Miracles brought a Multitude of Believers!

Growth of the Congregation Brings Persecution of the Apostles

Acts 5:17. *Then the **High Priest** and all those with him, which is the sect of the **Sadducees**, rose up, filled with **jealousy** 18. and they **arrested** the **apostles** and put them in the public **prison**. 19. But an **angel** of the Lord, having **opened** the doors of the **jail** by night, after he led them **out** then said, 20. "**You must** go and when you stand in the **Temple you must** continually speak the words of this (**eternal**) **life** to all the people." 21. Then after they heard (this) they entered the **Temple** before **dawn** and they were **teaching**. And when the **High Priest** arrived he and those with him summoned the **Sanhedrin**, even all the **council of elders** of the children of Israel, and they sent to the **jail** to have them brought. 22. But when the attendants arrived they did **not** find them in the **jail**. And when they returned they reported 23. saying, "We found the **prison** secured in every certainty and the **guards** standing by the doors, but when we opened (the doors), we found **no one** inside." 24. And as the captain of the **Temple** guards and the **high priests** heard these words, they were **perplexed** about these things, whatever this* *might be. 25. And then someone approached (and) reported to them that "Behold the **men whom you put in prison are standing in the Temple and teaching** the people." 26. Then when the captain left with the attendants, he was leading them, (but) not with force, because (the attendants and guards) were afraid that the people would stone (them).*

Think about so many People being in the Temple before Dawn! They were excited and inspired by the Kingdom Preaching! Kingdom Preaching with Signs and Wonders is needed today to bring the same Excitement and Inspiration!

Philip Preaches Kingdom in Samaria

*Acts 8:4. Therefore those who were **scattered** went through **(Judea and Samaria)** preaching the Word. 5. And when **Philip** came down to the city of **Samaria** he proclaimed the **Messiah** to them. 6. And the crowds paid attention to those things which were spoken by **Philip**. Of one mind in this, they listened and saw the **signs** which he was doing. 7. For then many of them had **unclean spirits** (and) they, **(unclean spirits)**, were coming out shouting in a **loud voice**, and many **paralytics** and **lame** were being **healed**: 8. and there was much joy in that city.*

Voice in the singular, here with a plural verb, is a Hebraism called the collective singular, which is very common in Scripture. Casting out Evil Spirits and healing of Paralytics and Lame are demonstrations of Kingdom Preaching!

Philip and the Ethiopian Eunuch

*Acts 8:26. Then an **angel** of the Lord spoke to **Philip** saying, "Rise and go down south on the road that descends from Jerusalem to Gaza." This is wilderness. 27. And when he got up he went. And there was a man, an **Ethiopian eunuch**, of great authority under Candace queen of the Ethiopians, who was over all her royal treasury, who had come in order to worship in Jerusalem 28. and was returning. And while he was sitting in his chariot he was reading the prophet **Isaiah**. 29. And the **Spirit** said to **Philip**, "You must approach and join this one in the chariot." 30. And as he was running up **Philip** heard him reading **Isaiah** the prophet and said, "Do you really understand what you are reading?" 31. And he said, "How indeed would I be able unless someone would guide me?" He urged **Philip** to come up to sit with him.*

The Angel brought an assignment to Philip. Ethiopian is the translation of the Hebrew word Cushi in the Greek text.

The LORD* Summons Saul

Acts 9.1. *And **Saul**, still breathing threat and murder among the disciples of the Lord, when he went to the **High Priest**, 2. Asked from him letters to the synagogues in Damascus, to the end that if he would find any who were of the **Way**, both men and women, he would lead them bound to Jerusalem.*

The Way refers to those who are totally committed to God. Way is used more than sixty times in the Hebrew Scriptures referring to being committed to the LORD*, with its first use in Genesis 18:19.

Acts 9:3. *And it happened while he was going as he drew near to **Damascus**, a light from heaven suddenly shone around him 4. And as he fell to the ground he heard a voice saying to him, "**Saul. Saul!** Why are you persecuting Me?"*

The Double Name in Hebrew is a stern rebuke, really getting Saul's attention.

Acts 9:5. *And he said, "Who are You, Lord?" And He said, "I AM **Y'shua** Whom you are persecuting: 6. But you must now **rise** and enter the city and it will be told to you what is necessary for you to do." 7. And the men traveling with him had stood speechless, hearing the **voice** on the one hand but on the other hand not **seeing** anyone. 8. Then **Saul** got up from the ground, but when he opened his **eyes** he was **not** seeing anything: and taking him by the hand they were leading him to **Damascus**. 9. And he was **without sight** three days and he was neither **eating** nor **drinking**.*

Y'shua appeared to Saul, then Saul became blind for several days.

Acts 9:10. *And there was a certain disciple in **Damascus** named **Ananias**, and the **Lord** said to him in a vision, "**Ananias**." And he said, "**Here I am, Lord**." 11. Then the **Lord** said to him, "When you get up you must be going to the street called **Straight** and you must at once seek in the house of **Judas** someone named **Saul of Tarsus**: for behold he is praying 12. And he saw in a vision a man named **Ananias** who had entered and after he laid his hands on him then he would regain his **sight**." 13. But **Ananias** answered, "**Lord**, I have heard from many about this man who did **evil** to Your **saints** in **Jerusalem**: 14. And here he has **authority from the high priests** to bind all those who call on Your name."*

The news about Saul's mission in Damascus traveled very quickly!

Acts 9:15. *Then the **Lord** said to him, "**You must be going**, because this one is a **chosen vessel for Me**, to carry **My name** before **heathens** and even* *kings and children of Israel: 16. For I shall show him how much it is necessary for him to suffer on behalf of My name." 17. Then Ananias left and entered the house and when he placed his hands on him said, "Saul, brother, the Lord has sent me, Y'shua the One Who set upon you on the way while you were coming, so that you would regain your sight and you would be filled with the Holy Spirit." 18. And immediately there fell away from his eyes something like scales, and he regained sight and then when he got up he immersed 19. And when he took food he regained strength.*

The Miracles of the appearance of Y'shua coupled with Saul's temporary blindness surely reinforced the Faith of all the believers. Saul had immersed many times over the years because Jewish people immerse any time they have been touched by profane things or impure people. Saul repented for his persecution of the followers of Y'shua and is now prepared to Preach Kingdom, going to synagogues in Damascus.

Saul Preaches at Damascus

Acts 9:19b. *And he was with the disciples in Damascus some days 20. and right away he preached Y'shua in the synagogues, that He was the Son of God. 21. And all those who heard were amazed and were saying, "Is this not the one who devastated those who called on this name in Jerusalem, and has he (not) come here for this, so that after he bound them he could lead (them to) the high priests?" 22. And Saul was becoming stronger and threw the Jewish people living in Damascus into dismay by proving that (Y'shua) was the Messiah.*

Saul escaped from Damascus, going to Arabia for a season.

Galatians 1:13. *For you have heard about my earlier conduct when in Judea, that I persecuted beyond measure the congregation of God and was destroying it, 14. and I was advancing in Judea over many contemporaries in my generation, since I was a zealot of the traditions of my ancestors to a much greater degree. 15. But when God chose, the One Who appointed me from my mother's womb and Who called (me) through His grace, 16. to have revealed His Son to me, so that I would proclaim Him to the heathens, I did not immediately consult flesh and blood 17. and I did not go up to Jerusalem to those (who were) apostles before me, but I went to Arabia, then again returned to Damascus.*

Judea is the translation of the Greek word, Ioudaismos, commonly translated Judaism, but it means "of or pertaining to Judea." The modern use of the word "Judaism" came centuries later.

Galatians 1:18. *Then **after three years** I went up to **Jerusalem** to get to know **Cephas** and I stayed with him fifteen days, 19. but I did not see another of the apostles except Jacob, the brother of the Lord. 20. And (about) which I write to you, behold before God that I am not lying. 21. Then I went through the regions of Syria and Cilicia: 22. but I was not known in person by those congregations of the Jewish people in Messiah.*

Paul spent three years before returning to Jerusalem. Cephas is the Latin spelling of Kefa, which is an Aramaic word for a small, hand sized "Rock." The Hebrew word is Kaf. The letter C is the giveaway that the word Cephas is from the Latin Bible, source of the early English translations. Only Latin has the letter C. Hebrew and Greek have no letter C.

The Healing of Aeneas

Acts 9:32. *And it happened (that) **Peter** was going through all those (cities) to go down also to the saints living in Lud. 33. And he found some man there named **Aeneas**, who was **paralyzed**, lying on a pallet for eight years. 34. And **Peter** said to him, **Aeneas**, **Y'shua** Messiah is **healing** you: **you must rise** and **you must immediately take care of your own pallet**. And he **got up** at once. 35. And all who lived in **Lud** and **Sharon** saw him (and) **returned** to the Lord.*

Peter simply told Aeneas that he was being healed – and Aeneas believed it and got up!

Gazelle Restored to Life

Acts 9:36. *And in Joppa there was a certain disciple named Tabitha, which when it is translated means Gazelle: she was rich in good deeds and charities that she was doing.*

The Greek word for gazelle is dorkas. To be Rich in Good Deeds is to do Mitsvot.

Acts 9:37. *And it happened in those days, that she became sick (and) died: and when they had washed her they placed her in an upstairs room.*

The Jewish people still prepare a body for burial by washing it.

Acts 9:38. *And because **Lud** was near **Joppa**, the **disciples**, having heard that **Peter** was in (**Lud**), sent two men to him urging, "Do **not delay** to come to us." 39. And then **Peter** got up (and) went with them: after they arrived they led him up to the **upstairs** room and all the widows came to* *him crying and pointing out how many tunics and garments **Gazelle** used to make when she was with them. 40. Then after he put all those outside and knelt, he prayed and when he turned to the body he said, "**Tabitha**, you must immediately get up." And she **opened her eyes**, and when she saw **Peter** she sat up. 41. And then he gave her a hand (and) stood her up: and, after he called the **saints** and the **widows**, he presented her **alive**. 42. And it became known throughout the whole of **Joppa** and many believed in the Lord. 43. And it happened he stayed many days in **Joppa** with a certain tanner, **Simon**.*

The LORD* Appears to Paul a Second Time

*Acts 22:17. "And it happened, when I returned to **Jerusalem** and while I was praying in the **Temple**, I became **entranced** (in a state of ecstasy) 18. And **saw Him saying to me, 'You must hurry and come out quickly from Jerusalem**, because they will not accept your testimony about Me.' 19. And I said, 'Lord, they understand that throughout the synagogues I was imprisoning and beating those who believe in You, 20. And, when they were pouring out the blood of your witness Stephen, I was standing by and agreeing and guarding the prayer shawls of those who were killing him.' 21. And He said to me, 'You must be going, because I shall send you out far away to the heathens.'"*

God warns Paul to leave Jerusalem quickly.

Peter was demonstrating Kingdom wherever he went.

Peter and Cornelius

*Acts 10.1. And a certain man in **Caesarea** named **Cornelius**, a centurion from a cohort called Italian, 2. devout and **God-Revering** with all in his house, doing many charitable things for the people and praying to God for everything, 3. about the **ninth hour** of the **day** saw clearly in a vision an **angel of God** coming to him and saying to him, "**Cornelius**." 4. Then, after he looked intently at him, he became terrified and said, "What is it, Lord?" And he said to him, "**Your prayers** and **your charities** came up as a **memorial** before **God**. 5. And now you must send men at once to **Joppa** and summon a certain **Simon** who is called **Peter**: 6. this one is staying with a certain tanner, **Simon**, with whom he is in a house by (the) sea." 7. And as the **angel**, the one who was speaking to him, left, then he called two of the household (**servants**) and a devout **soldier** of those attached to him 8. and after he described everything to them he sent them to **Joppa**.*

Caesarea was fifty miles north of Joppa. God-Reverer was the name given to non-Jewish believers who attended a synagogue and learned Judaism, but were not full converts. The Ninth Hour was 3:00 PM, the time of afternoon prayer, with the group travelling fifty miles in a day and three quarters to arrive by 3:00 PM.

Acts 10:9. *And the next day, as those traveling were nearing the city, about the sixth hour Peter went up on the roof to pray. 10. And he became very hungry and was wanting to eat. And while they were preparing (a meal) a trance came over him*

The Sixth Hour was Noon. The Trance was a state of ecstasy brought about by God, in which consciousness is wholly or partially suspended.

Acts 10:11. *and he saw heaven opening and something lowering, like a great sheet, being let down by four corners upon the ground, 12. in which were all the four-footed (animals) and reptiles of the earth and birds of the sky. 13. And a voice came to him, "Rise, Peter, you must right now kill and eat." 14. But Peter said, "Certainly not, Lord, because I never ate anything defiled or unclean." (Ezek. 4:14) 15. And again a second time a voice said to him, "What God has cleansed, you must not declare unclean." 16. And this happened three times, (and) then the object was immediately taken up into the sky.*

What God has cleansed does not refer to the animals on the sheet, but to the non-Jewish people to whom Peter is to minister. Cornelius, his family, and his co-workers were the ones who had been cleansed by their seeking God and by their obedience.

Acts 10:17. *And as Peter was greatly perplexed with himself whatever could be (the meaning) of the vision (See Acts 10:28,29; 11:5-12) which he saw. Behold, the men who were sent by Cornelius, as they found out by asking about the house of Simon, stood by the gate, 18. and when they called they asked if Simon, the one called Peter, was a guest here. 19. And while Peter was pondering about the vision the Spirit said to him, "Behold three men are seeking you, 20. so after you get up you must go down and you must go with them, not doubting that I have sent them." 21. And when Peter went down he said to the men, "Behold I am (the one) whom you are seeking: what is the reason for which you are here?" 22. And they said, "Cornelius, a centurion, a righteous and God-Revering man, who is well spoken of even by the whole nation of the Jewish people, was directed by a holy angel to summon you to his house and to hear what you have to say." 23. Then, having invited them in, he entertained (them).*

And the next day when he got up he left with them, and some of the brothers from **Joppa** *came with him. 24. Then the day after that he entered* **Caesarea***. And* **Cornelius** *was waiting for them, having called together his kin and close friends. 25. And as* **Peter** *happened to come, when* **Cornelius** *met him he fell at his feet (and)* **paid homage** *to him. 26. But* **Peter raised him** *saying, "You must get up: for I also am a man." 27. And conversing with him he entered and found many gathered, 28. and he said to them, "You believe that it is contrary to law and justice for a* **Jewish person to associate with or to approach a foreigner***: but* **God explained to me not to say in any way that a man is common or unclean***:*

When Cornelius Bowed before Peter, Peter showed the appropriate Humility and raised Cornelius immediately.

Acts 10:29. *for this reason then I came without raising any objection when I was sent for. Therefore I ask for what reason did you send for me?" 30. And* **Cornelius** *said, "From four days ago to this (very) hour (of) the afternoon I was praying at the* **ninth hour** *in my house, and behold a* **man** *stood before me in shining clothing 31. and he said, '***Cornelius***, your prayer has been heard and your charities have been remembered before God. 32. Therefore you* **must now send to Joppa** *and summon* **Simon***, who is called* **Peter***. He is staying in the house by (the) sea, of* **Simon***, a* **tanner***.' 33. Therefore I immediately sent for you, and you did well by coming. Now then we all are* **present before God** *to hear everything that has been ordered to you by the* **Lord***."*

The ninth hour is 3:00 PM, the time for afternoon prayer when the second lamb was offered at the Temple.

Peter Speaks in Cornelius' House

Acts 10:34. *Then when* **Peter** *opened his mouth he said, "In truth I understand that God does not show* **partiality***, (Deut. 10:17, 2 Chr. 19:7, Mark 12:14) 35. but in every nation the one who* **reveres Him** *and* **works righteousness** *is acceptable to Him. 36. (The) message, which He sent to the children of Israel, when He proclaimed* **Good News** *of peace through* **Y'shua Messiah***, this One, is Lord of All. 37. You know the report, what happened throughout the whole of* **Judea***, beginning from Galilee after the* **immersion** *which* **John** *preached, 38. as God anointed this* **Y'shua***, the One from Nazareth, in (the)* **Holy Spirit** *and power, Who came through doing good and healing all those who were oppressed by the devil, because God was with Him. 39. And we (are) witnesses of all that He did in both the* **country** *of the **Jewish people** and in **Jerusalem**. And Whom they **killed**, by **hanging** Him on **wood**. 40. **God raised Him** on the **third day** and caused Him to be revealed, 41. not to all the people, but to **witnesses chosen beforehand by God**, to **us**, we who **ate** and **drank** with **Him** after **He was raised** from (the) dead: 42. and He commanded us to **preach** to the people and to **testify** earnestly that He is the One Who has been appointed by God (as) **Judge** of (the) living and (the) dead. 43. All the **prophets testify**; everyone who **believes** in Him takes **forgiveness of sins** through His name.*"

To not show Partiality is Literally, "does not look at the face," which is a Hebrew idiom commonly translated "not a respecter of persons." Testifying about the Immersion of John, then the Immersion of the Holy Spirit, brings the Immersion of the Holy Spirit to those gathered at Cornelius' home. Testimonies can be very powerful! To the Jewish people to "Believe" required a change in behavior; if you really did Believe you would be transformed, so you could not just say idle words and be saved, but your behavior had to demonstrate that you were different.

Heathens Receive the Holy Spirit

Acts 10:44. *While **Peter** was still speaking these words the **Holy Spirit** fell upon all those listening to the message. 45. And the faithful from the circumcision who came with **Peter** were amazed, because the **gift of the Holy Spirit** fell even **upon the heathens**: 46. for they heard them **speaking in tongues** and **glorifying God**. Then **Peter** responded, 47. "No one can deny (the) water, can they, (for) any of these to be **immersed**, who took the **Holy Spirit** like we (did)?" 48. And he ordered them to be **immersed** in the name of **Y'shua Messiah**. Then they asked him to spend some **days** (with them).*

Peter's testimony was certainly powerful, bringing the first Heathens into the Jewish Faith with the sign of Speaking in Tongues. Their Immersion sealed that committed state for the former Heathens! That brought Cornelius and his guests to ask for more, with Peter and those with him staying longer for more Kingdom Preaching!

An Angel Brings Peter Out of Prison

Acts 12:6. *But when Herod was going to bring him out (the next morning), that night **Peter** was sleeping between **two soldiers**, **bound** by **two chains**, and there were **guards** by the door, guarding the prison. 7. And behold an **angel** of (the) Lord **stood** and a **light** shone out in the **prison**: and as **he struck Peter's side**, he **woke** him up saying, "**You must get up quickly**."*

*And his **chains fell off** from his hands. 8. And the **angel** said to him, "You must immediately **gird yourself** and put on your **sandals**." And so he did. Then he said to him, "You must put on your **cloak** and follow me." 9. Then after they went out he was following and he was **not knowing** that what was happening through the **angel** (was) **real**: but he was thinking he was seeing a vision. 10. And then they came through (the) first **guard** then a second (and) they came upon the iron **gate** leading into the city, which was **open to them by itself** and after they came out they went down one alley, then immediately the **angel** left him. 11. And when **Peter** came to himself he said, "Now I know truly that the **Lord sent out His angel** and delivered me from Herod's hand and every expectation of the Jewish (leaders)." 12. And when he understood (what was going on) he went to the house of **Miriam**, the **mother of John**, the one called **Mark**, where many were gathering and praying. 13. And when he knocked on the door of the vestibule a maid named **Rhoda** came to open, 14. and when she recognized **Peter's** voice, on account of her joy she did not open the gate, but running in reported that **Peter** was standing at the gate. 15. But they said to her, "You are mad." But she insisted it was so. And they were saying, "It is his **angel**." 16. And **Peter** was continuing to knock: and when they opened they saw him and they were amazed. 17. Then after he made a sign to them with his hand that they should be silent he described to them how the Lord led him out from the jail and said, "Report these things to **Jacob**, (the brother of Y'shua), and to the brothers." Then when he came out he went to a different place.*

When the Angel told Peter to get up, the chains just fell off his hands. He put on his Prayer Shawl because that was the outer garment of every Jewish man, then he was led out of the prison and down an alley. At Miriam's house a maid opened the door, showing that not all members of the congregation in Jerusalem sold their property; Miriam also had enough money that she had at least one maid but might have had more servants than just Rhoda. Peter went into hiding because he was still a wanted man and Herod was eager to have a prisoner to kill like he had executed Jacob, Y'shua's brother.

The Death of Herod Agrippa

*Acts 12:20. And he was very angry with the people of Tyre and Sidon: (who) of one mind were present with him and after they persuaded Blastus, the officer of the king, they were asking peace because their country (was) to be fed from that which belonged to the king. 21. At the appointed time of day **Herod** put on his royal robe and when he sat on the judicial bench he was delivering an address to them, 22. and the people were crying out, "**A voice*** *of a god and not of a man."* 23. *And immediately an* **angel** *of (the) Lord hit him because he did not give the* **glory to God**, *and then he became eaten by worms and* **expired**.

This was in 44 AD that Herod Agrippa died, killed by an Angel.

Barnabas and Saul Preach in Cyprus, Saul Named Paul

Acts 13:4. *Then indeed as they were sent out by the* **Holy Spirit** *they went down into Seleucia, from there they sailed to* **Cyprus** 5. *and while they were in* **Salamis** *they were proclaiming the Word of God in the* **synagogues** *of the* **Jewish people**. *And they had* **John** *as a servant.* 6. *And after they went through the whole island as far as* **Paphos** *they found a certain man, a* **sorcerer**, *a* **false prophet**, *a Jewish man by the name of Bar-Jesus* 7. *who was with the proconsul* **Sergius Paulus**, *an intelligent man. Then after he summoned* **Barnabas** *and* **Saul**, *he sought diligently to hear the* **Word of God**. 8. *But the sorcerer,* **Elymas**, *for thus his name was translated, was opposing them, seeking to turn the proconsul away from the faith.* 9. *And when* **Saul**, *or* **Paul**, *having been filled with (the)* **Holy Spirit**, *fixed his eyes on him* 10. *he said, "O you, full of every deceit and every villainy, a son of the devil, enemy of everyone righteous, would you stop perverting the right* **Ways** *of the Lord?* 11. *And now behold (the) hand of (the) Lord (is) upon you and you will be* **blind**, *not seeing the sun for a time." And immediately mistiness fell upon him, then darkness, and he was seeking someone (to) lead him about by the hand.* 12. *Then, when the* **proconsul** *saw what happened, he* **believed**, *being* **amazed** *at the* **teaching** *of the Lord.*

The Holy Spirit let Saul know about the treachery of Elymas so that the Power of God would be shown to the proconsul, blinding Elymas for a time. Notice that going from Jerusalem, someone always goes down, even when going north because Jerusalem is on the heights, going to Jerusalem is always going up from any place in Israel.

Paul Sees that a Man Who Never Walked has the Faith to be Healed

Acts 14:8. *And in Lystra a certain* **man who never walked**, *without strength in his feet, was sitting,* **lame** *from his mother's womb.* 9. *He heard* **Paul** *speaking: who when (***Paul***) fixed his eyes on him, since he* **saw** *that (the man) had* **faith to be delivered**, 10. *he said in a loud voice, "***You must get straight up on your feet*** right now." And he did* **spring up** *and he was* **walking**.

Paul saw into the Spirit Realm, then knew that the Man was Healed.

Paul Stoned!

> Acts 14:19. *But Jewish people came from Antioch and Iconium, and then they persuaded the crowds (**to stone Paul**), then after they **stoned Paul** they were **dragging** (him) outside the city **thinking he had died**. 20. But, after the **disciples circled him**, he **got up** (and) entered the city. And the next day he went out with Barnabas to Derbe.*

Could it be that Paul had died, and when the disciples circled him, praying, that he was restored to life? Stoning is such a brutal, horrifying act, with victims terribly disfigured, often with broken bones, making walking improbable; it certainly seems impossible that someone taken for dead could simply get up and walk away. Years ago, I read the autobiography of James Jacob, a pastor in India who had been stoned by Hindu zealots, his autobiography telling of his lengthy recovery. This could be the out of body experience described by Paul in 2 Corinthians 12:2.

> 2 Corinthians 12.1. *It is necessary to boast, even though it doesn't help, but I shall go on to visions and revelations of (the) Lord. 2. I know a man (who was) in **Messiah** more than **fourteen years ago**, whether in (the) body I do not know, God knows, or outside the body I do not know, this one was taken away up to the **third heaven**.*

The visit to Heaven could well have been Paul himself fourteen years after he and Barnabas ministered in Lystra when Paul was stoned, Acts14:19,20. The Third Heaven does not mean there are just three levels in Heaven because the Hebrew language has seven words describing Heaven, which Paul certainly knew. See *Heavens* in the One New Man Bible Glossary for the full description of the Seven Levels of Heaven.

Paul's Vision of the Man of Macedonia

> Acts 16:6. *And they went through the regions of Phrygia and Galatia because they had been prevented by the **Holy Spirit** from speaking the **Word** (of God) in Asia: 7. and when they came down to Mysia they were trying to go into Bithynia, but the **Spirit of Y'shua** did not let them: 8. and after they went through Mysia they went down to Troas. 9. And during the night a **vision was seen** by **Paul**, a man of **Macedonia** who was standing and urging him and saying, "**You must now come over** into **Macedonia** (and) help us right away." 10. And when he saw in the vision, **we** immediately left to go out into **Macedonia** because we concluded that God had called us to evangelize them.*

The LORD* directed every step for the Apostles' successful missions. This is the first time Luke writes "we" so he apparently joined Paul's group in Mysia. Notice that Mycia and Macedonia, having the letter C is evidence of the translations and transliterations coming from Latin texts, because both Hebrew and Greek do not have the letter C. The Holy Spirit inspired Paul to see a Vision, calling him to Macedonia.

The Imprisonment at Philippi

> Acts 16:16. *And it happened while we were going into prayer, a certain servant girl (who) had a spirit of divination met us, who, acting as seer, was bringing a lot of profit to (her) masters. 17. She, following **Paul** and us, was crying out saying, "These men are servants of the **Most High God**, who are proclaiming a way of salvation to you." 18. And she was doing this over many days. And since **Paul** was disturbed, then, after he turned, he said to the **spirit**, "I command you in (the) name of **Y'shua Messiah** to come **out from her:**" and it came out from her at (that) moment. 19. And when her owners saw that the hope of their profit came out, having caught hold of **Paul** and **Silas** they dragged them into the market place to the officials 20. and bringing them they said to the chief magistrates, "These men, who are **Jewish**, are agitating our city 21. and they are proclaiming customs which are not lawful for us since they are not for Romans to accept or to do." 22. And the crowd rose up together against them, and the magistrates, having torn off their prayer shawls, were commanding (that) they beat (them) with rods, 23. and after they put many strokes on them they threw (them) in **jail**, having given orders to the jailer to keep them under guard. 24. He, when he received such a command, then took (them), threw them into the **inner prison** and secured their **feet** in the **shackle**.*

The Servant girl has a Familiar Spirit giving her the words she was speaking referencing the Most High God. Demons are evil spirits who know Who God is! Just imagine how Paul and Silas felt, being in severe pain from being beaten with rods, then having their feet in shackles, but not feeling sorry for themselves; they were singing Psalms, praising God.

> Acts 16:25. *And at midnight while **Paul** and **Silas** were **praying**, they were **singing hymns of praise** (to) God, (Psalms), and the prisoners were listening to them. 26. Then suddenly there was a great earthquake so as to shake the foundations of the prison: and all the doors were immediately opened and the bonds of all were loosed. 27. And as the **jailer** became aroused and when he saw the **doors** of the **jail** were **opened**, after he drew a **sword** he was going*

*to **kill himself** because he thought the **prisoners** had **escaped**. 28. But **Paul** cried out in a loud voice saying, "**Do not do** (this) evil to yourself, for **we are all here**." 29. Then after he asked for lights he rushed in and he fell down trembling before **Paul** and **Silas** 30. and leading them outside he said, "Sirs, what **must I do so that I would be saved**?" 31. And they said, "You must **believe** at once in the **Lord Y'shua** and **you** and **your household** will be **saved**." 32. And they spoke the word of the Lord to him with all those in his house. 33. And then he took them along in that hour of the night (and) he washed their wounds, and immediately he himself and all those of his (household) were **immersed** 34. and when he led them into the house he set a table before them and he **rejoiced** with (the) whole family because they had believed in God.*

Singing Psalms brings an anointing in our services today as we become adorned in His Holiness! The Jewish understanding of the word "believe" requires a change in behavior, providing evidence of belief. These converts were immersed in the Jewish tradition! They were now Jewish!

*Acts 16:35. And when it became day the **magistrates** sent the **policemen** saying, "**Release those men**." 36. And the **jailer** reported these words to **Paul** that "The **magistrates** sent so that you would be **released**: therefore now as you leave, go in peace." 37. But **Paul** said to them, "After they **beat us publicly** without trial, men who are **Roman**, they threw (us) into **jail**, and now they throw us **out secretly**? **No indeed**, but when they come to us **they must lead us out**." 38. And the **policemen** reported these words to the **magistrates**. And they were **afraid** when they heard that they were **Romans**, 39. and so when they came they called (**Paul** and **Silas**) and when they led (them) out, they asked (them) to go away from the city. 40. And when they left the **jail** they went to **Lydia** and when they saw (her) they encouraged the **brothers** (who met there), then they left.*

The Magistrates were afraid because they broke the law when they Beat, then imprisoned the Roman citizens, Paul and Silas, without a trial. The word Brothers shows that the house congregation of Lydia's contained both men and women.

The Sons of Sceva vs. Anointing for Casting out Demons

*Acts 19:11. **God** was doing extraordinary **miracles** by the hands of **Paul**, 12. so that even **face cloths** or **aprons** were taken away from **his skin** (and placed) upon those who were **sick** and their **diseases** left from them, and the **evil spirits departed**. 13. And also some of the **Jewish** exorcists who were going around tried to speak the name of the **Lord Y'shua** over the ones who*

*had **evil spirits** saying, "I implore you by **Y'shua Whom Paul** preaches."
14. And seven sons of a certain **Sceva**, a high priest of Judea, were doing
this. 15. But when the **evil spirit** answered it said to them, "Indeed **I know
Y'shua** and **I am acquainted with Paul**, but yourselves, who are you?" 16.
And the man in whom was the **evil spirit**, leaping upon them, was strong,
overpowering all of them so that as they were wounded and nearly naked,
(they had) to flee away from that house. 17. And this became known to all,
both **Jewish** and **Greeks**, who were living in **Ephesus**, and fear fell upon
them all and the name of the **Lord Y'shua** was being **glorified**. 18. And
many of those who believed were coming, confessing and reporting their (evil)
doings. 19. And many of those who had been practicing magic, after they
brought their scrolls (of the magic) they were burning (them) before everyone,
and they counted up the value of them and found it **fifty thousand pieces
of silver**. 20. In this manner the **word** of the **Lord** was increasing mightily
and growing in strength.*

Commanding Evil Spirits to leave actually healed diseases, released demonic
prisoners, opened blind eyes, deaf ears, and was done by Jewish Exorcists as well
as by the early Apostles and other Disciples. Jewish exorcists prayed in the name
of the LORD*.

*Matthew 12:22. Then a **blind** and **deaf demonized** (man) was brought
to Him, and He **healed** him, so that the **deaf** one **spoke** and **saw**. 23. And
all the crowds were amazed and were saying, "Is this not the Son of David?"
24. And when the Pharisees heard they said, "This One does **not cast out
demons** except by **Beelzebub, leader** of the **demons**." 25. And because
He knew their thoughts He said to them, "Every kingdom divided against
itself is made desolate and not one city or house divided against itself will
stand. 26. And if **Satan** casts out **Satan, he is divided against himself**:
therefore how will his kingdom stand? 27. And if I cast out demons **by means
of Beelzebub**, <u>by whose (authority) are your sons casting (them) out</u>?
Because of this they will be your judges. 28. But if I cast out demons by (the)
Spirit of God, then the **Kingdom of God** has come **upon you**.*

There were Jewish Exorcists in Y'shua's day, so the sons of Sceva were in that
ministry, but using the name of Y'shua without being covered by Him caused
them some misery. Beelzebub is the Greek spelling of Baal Zevuv, Lord of
Flies. The name Sceva is another example of the Latin origin of the early
English translations, with the letter C giving it away. Those names are in our
Bibles by Tradition! Skeua is the Greek spelling.

Fifty Thousand pieces of Silver was about $10,000. Exorcism exemplifies Kingdom!

Paul Knows by the Spirit that He will go to Jerusalem, then be Taken to Rome

> Acts 19:21. *And as these things were finished, Paul resolved in his spirit to go through Macedonia and Achia, (then) to go to Jerusalem, saying that "After I am there, it is then necessary for me to see Rome." 22. And after he sent two of those who served him, Timothy and Erastus, to Macedonia he stayed a time in Asia.*

Paul's Imprisonment Prophesied

> Acts 21:10. *And while we were staying more days a certain prophet named Agabus (Acts 11:28) came down from Judea, 11. and when he came to us he took Paul's belt, and after he bound his own feet and hands he said, "The Holy Spirit says these (things), 'The man whose belt this is, the Jewish people in Jerusalem will bind (him) in this manner and will give him over into (the) hands of (the) heathens.'" 12. And as we heard these things, both we and those from Caesarea were begging him not to go up to Jerusalem. 13. Then Paul answered, "What are you doing, weeping and breaking my heart? For I am not only in readiness to be bound, but also to die in Jerusalem on behalf of the name of the Lord Y'shua." (Acts 20:23) 14. And when he was not persuaded, we fell silent saying, "The Lord's will must continually be done."*

Paul had already been told by the LORD* what was coming.

Paul Restores Eutuchus to Life

> Acts 20:7. *And after sundown at the end of the Sabbath, (with a service called Havdalah), when we gathered to break bread, Paul was speaking with them because he was planning to go on a journey the next day, and he was prolonging the message until midnight. 8. And there were many lamps in the upper room in which we were gathered. 9. And while a certain youth named Eutuchus was sitting in the window, as he became overwhelmed by deep sleep while Paul was discoursing more and more, he fell down from the third story window and was taken away dead. 10. But when Paul went down he fell upon him and after embracing (him) said, "Do not be troubled for his life is in him." 11. And then he went up and broke bread and ate, talking for a long while until dawn, (and) then he left. 12. And they were leading the living child and they were greatly comforted.*

The Havdalah service makes the transition from the holy Sabbath to the secular work-a-day world. The service starts two hours after sundown on Saturday evening. The Greek text says "On the first day of the week," the Hebrew expression for Sunday, which starts at sundown on Saturday. See Havdalah under *Seasons* in the One New Man Bible Glossary. Midnight does not mean 12:00 AM on the dot; with no clocks; this refers to the middle of the night.

An Angel Tells Paul That All on board will be Saved

Acts 27:21. *And since many had gone without eating, **Paul** then stood in their midst and said, "Men, you ought to have followed my advice not to sail from Crete and to be spared this hardship and the loss. 22. And now I urge you to be of **good cheer**: for there is to be **no loss of life among you**, except the ship (will be destroyed). 23. For this night an **angel from God**, to Whom I belong and Whom I serve, **stood beside me** 24. saying, 'You must not be afraid, **Paul**, it is necessary for you to **stand** before **Caesar**, and behold **God** has granted to **you all** those who are sailing with **you**.' 25. For this reason, men, be of **good cheer**: for I trust in **God** that it will be just as it has been spoken to me. 26. And it is necessary for us to run aground on some island."*

The Angel standing beside him is quite a sign for those on the Ship; everything Paul says happens!

Paul Demonstrates the Spirit Realm to His Shipmates and the People of Malta

Acts 28.1. *And after we were saved we then understood that the island was called **Malta**. 2. And the **natives** were granting uncommon hospitality to us, for after they kindled a fire, they accepted us all because it had begun to rain and because of the cold that had set in. 3. And when **Paul** gathered some quantity of sticks and placed (them) upon the fire, a **viper** (that) came out from the heat **seized his hand**. 4. And when the **natives** saw the **beast** hanging from his **hand**, they were saying to one another, "Certainly **this man is a murderer**, whom, although he was saved from the sea, **justice does not permit to live**." 5. However, **he just shook the beast into the fire** and **suffered nothing evil**, 6. and they were expecting that he would become swollen from it, and then suddenly fall down **dead**. And yet many of them, expecting and watching, when nothing unusual was happening to him, they changed (their minds), saying **he** was a **god**. 7. And among the (farms) around that place was land of the **chief** of the island, named **Poplio**, who, having welcomed us (into his home), showed us hospitality in a friendly manner for three days. 8. And it happened that the **father** of **Poplio** was suffering, lying down from a **fever** and **dysentery**, for whom **Paul**, when* *he came and **prayed**, **laid hands** on him (and) **healed** him. 9. And after this happened the rest (of the **people**) of the island, those who were **sick**, were coming to (**him**) and being **healed**, 10. and they were rewarding us with much honor and when we put to sea they gave us the things we needed.*

Paul brought the Spirit Realm prominently to the attention of the Natives, bringing much honor to the LORD* Y'shua.

The Earthly Body is Sown in Corruption, but Raised in Magnificence

1 Corinthians 15:42. *So also the **resurrection** of the **dead**. It is **sown in corruption**, it is **raised incorruptible**: 43. it is **sown** in **dishonor**, it is **raised in magnificence**: it is **sown in weakness**, it is **raised in power**: 44. a body is **sown fleshly**, it is **raised** a **spiritual body**. If there is a **fleshly body**, there is also a **spiritual**. 45. And so it has been written, "The first man was Adam in living life," (Gen. 2:7) the last Adam (has become) a life-giving **spirit**. 46. But the **spiritual** was **not first** but the **physical**, then the **spiritual**. 47. The first man is from **dust** of the earth, the second man out of **heaven**. 48. What sort of **earthly** (man), and such as these **earthly** (ones), and what sort of the **heavenly** (One), then such as these born of the **heavenly** nature: 49. and just as we bore constantly the image of the **earthly**, we will bear constantly also the image of the **heavenly** One.*

Heaven is a Spiritual state of Being; it is Not Physical, but it is Real. Each Saint will be Transformed from the Physical to the powerful Spiritual Body!

1 Corinthians 15:50. *But I say this, brothers, that **flesh and blood** are **not** able to inherit (the) **Kingdom of God**, nor does corruption inherit incorruption. 51. Behold I am telling you a mystery: we will not all be asleep (in death), but we will all be **transformed**, 52. in a moment, in a twinkling of an eye, at the last **shofar**: for a **shofar** will sound and the **dead** will be **raised incorruptible** and we will be **transformed**. (Isa. 26:19, Dan. 12:13, Rev. 20:5) 53. For it is necessary to clothe this **corruptible** (with the) **incorruptible** and to clothe this **mortal** (with the) **immortal**. 54. And when this **mortal** will be clothed **immortal** and this **corruptible** will be clothed **incorruptible** then the written word will happen,*

*"**Death** was swallowed up in victory." (Isa. 25:8)*

*55. Where, O **Death**, is your victory?*

*Where, O **Death**, is your sting?" (Hos. 13:14)*

*56. But **sin** is the **sting** of **death**, and the power of **sin** (is taken from) the*

*Torah (Teaching): 57. but thanks to God, to the One Who gives us victory through our **Lord Y'shua Messiah**. 58. Thus, my beloved brothers, **you must continually be steadfast, immovable, abounding** in the **work** of the **Lord** always, since you have known that your labor is not without result in (the) Lord.*

There will be no skin and bones in our Spirit Beings. ETERNAL LIFE is Real, but not Physical.

The Spirit Realm Awaits Us! The Spirit Realm is ETERNAL LIFE!

2 Corinthians 4:16. *We do not despair on account of this, yet if indeed our **outer man is corrupted**, then the **one within us is being renewed day by day**. 17. Truly our affliction for the moment (is) insignificant beyond all measure and proportion into eternal fullness, a weight of **glory eternally** working out in us, 18. we do not notice what we are seeing but the things we do **not see**: for the things we **see** (are) **temporary**, but the **things we do not see** (are) **eternal**.*

What we see is physical, Temporary; What we do not see is the Real, the Spiritual. The Brick and Mortar with which we are so familiar does not exist in the Spiritual – in Heaven. The Coming World is infinitely better than the world we know!

2 Corinthians 5.1. *For we know that if our **earthly house** (we live in of this) tent would be **destroyed**, we have a **building** from **God**, an **eternal house** in the **heavens not** made by **(human) hands**. 2. For indeed we sigh in this our dwelling, longing to put on, for ourselves, the one from heaven, 3. then indeed, if we have been **clothed** we will not be found naked. 4. For indeed we, who are in the **tent**, sigh, being oppressed, because of which we do not wish to be unclothed but to be **clothed**, so that our mortal (being) would be swallowed up by life. 5. And the One Who has worked this same thing in us (is) God, the One Who gave us the pledge of the **Spirit**.*

2 Corinthians 5:6. *Therefore, since we are always confident, and knowing that when **we are at home in the body we are getting away from the Lord**: 7. because we are **walking by faith, not by sight**: 8. but we are confident; we even rather prefer to leave from the body and to **be at home with the Lord**. 9. For this reason then we strive earnestly, whether when we are at home or when we are away, to be **well pleasing to Him**. 10. For it is necessary for us all to be revealed before the **judgment seat of the Messiah**, so that each would receive the things according to what he **accomplished with his body**, whether **good** or **evil**.*

The Spirit Realm is very Real, but hard to imagine; it is like the Spirit Army seen by Elisha and his servant – real, but not physical! That Army was Effective although not seen by the Syrian Army! The Syrian Army was struck blind, then led to Samaria! So will be our World in the Hereafter; Real, but not Physical! New Jerusalem, which John saw, is Real, but it is Not Physical, not Brick and Mortar! Our bodies will be REAL, but not physical, not Flesh and Blood!

THE BOOK OF REVELATION

Revelation 1:8. *"I AM the* Alef *and the* Tav, *says the Lord God, the One Who* is *and Who* was *and Who* is coming, *the* Lord of Hosts. *"* (Isa. 44:6)

Alef is the first letter of the Hebrew alphabet, Tav is the last; together they spell ET, the Hebrew word that directly precedes the direct object of the verb, so Y'shua is saying that He was the object of God's love brought to Earth, that He had completed His assignment, that now the LORD*and Y'shua are truly One.

Judgment Day

> Luke 17:20. *And having been asked by the Pharisees when the Kingdom of God is coming He answered them and said,* **"The Kingdom of God does not come by means of, or in company with, close observation,** *21. And will they not say, 'Behold it is here,' 'There it is,' for behold* **the Kingdom of God is within you.** *"*

The Kingdom of God is within you! Judgment Day is within you! That means His coming is Spiritual! It is not a natural Day but is individual and spiritual for each one of us! The LORD* setting foot on the Mount of Olives is allegorical, not natural. The Greek preposition meta in verses 20 and 21 can be translated either 'by means of,' 'in company with,' or just 'with.' Another way of saying it is that watching for Messiah will not bring Him any sooner. The Kingdom of God is within you or among you. Paul wrote in 1 Corinthians 15:50. *"But I say this, brothers, that* flesh and blood *are not able to inherit the* Kingdom of God.. *"* The Kingdom is spiritual. See *Kingdom* in the One New Man Bible Glossary. Judgment Day is described fully in the Book of Revelation. There is nothing physical in Heaven! The trumpets, the vials, the robes, the horses, the living creatures, and the streets of gold are all spiritual, not physical.

A Vision of Messiah

> Revelation 1:9. *I **John**, your brother and partner in affliction and in **kingdom** and in patient expectation in **Y'shua**, I was on the island called **Patmos** because of the Word of God and the testimony of **Y'shua**. 10. I was in the **Spirit** on the **Lord's Day** and I heard behind me a loud voice like a trumpet 11. saying, "You must write in a scroll what you see and you must send it to the seven congregations, in **Ephesus** and in **Smyrna** and in **Pergama** and in **Thyatira** and in **Sardis** and in **Philadelphia** and in **Laodicea.***"

Patmos is an island in the eastern Mediterranean Sea where ancient Rome sent prisoners; criminals were put in prison but political prisoners were released to fend for themselves. The apostle John was ordered there by Emperor Domitian after he had been sentenced to death by Domitian for not worshipping Domitian on Lord's Day. Lord's Day when John transcribed Revelation was the first day of each month, established by Domitian for everyone in the Roman Empire to worship Domitian, so Lord's Day in the Book of Revelation refers to the first day of each month. John had been sentenced to death for not worshipping Domitian, so he was thrown into a vat of boiling oil, but to Domitian's chagrin, John was not killed and was never in pain coming out of the boiling oil unscathed, not a mark on him. Some months later in 93 AD John was sent to Patmos, released on the island to fend for himself. John was probably around ninety years old and Prochoros, Bishop of northwestern Asia Minor went to Patmos to take care of John. Living in a cave, John was able to transcribe the Book of Revelation at the dictation of Y'shua. Domitian was assassinated in 96 AD, to be succeeded by Nerva who released John and other political prisoners from Patmos. John returned to Ephesus where he resumed leadership of the congregations of Asia Minor, with Prochoros returning to his office of bishop in Nicomedia.

John was in the Spirit to receive the message, which began with the messages to seven congregations of Asia Minor. Those messages are reviewed in *Every Prophet in the Bible; Genesis to Revelation* by this author.

> Revelation 1:12. *And I turned to see the voice that was speaking with me, and when I turned I saw seven golden menorahs 13. and in the middle of the menorahs I saw someone **like a Son of Man** (Dan. 7:13) clothed to His feet and girded at the chest with a golden belt. (Ezek. 9:2, Dan. 10:5) 14. And His head and hair were white as wool, white as snow, (Dan. 7:9) and **His eyes as flame of fire** (Gen. 49:12) 15. and His feet like a metal **more precious than gold** (Dan. 10:6) as heated thoroughly in a furnace and His*

voice as a sound of many waters, (Ezek. 1:24; 43:2) 16. and Who had in His right hand seven stars and there was going out from His mouth a large sharp two-edged sword (Isa. 49:2) and His face was as the sun shines in its power at noon.

His eyes as flames of fire is from Jacob's personal prophecy over Judah in Genesis 49, well over one thousand five hundred years earlier. The metal more precious than gold is not named but today we know of several metals more precious than gold! This metal is Spiritual though, not physical metal.

*Revelation 1:17. And when I saw Him, I fell toward His feet as dead, and He placed His right hand upon me saying "Stop being afraid! I AM the First and the Last (Isa. 44:6; 48:12) 18. and the One Who is living. And I died, but look! I am living forever and **I have the keys of death and Hades**. 19. Therefore, you must write what you have seen and what is happening and what is going to happen after these things. (Isa. 48:6, Dan. 2:28,29,45) 20. The mystery of the seven stars which you saw in My right hand and the seven golden **menorahs**: the seven stars are **messengers** of the seven **congregations** and the seven **menorahs** are the seven **congregations**."*

With the keys of death and Hades **Y'shua** has brought **Eternal Life** for each believer! **Each church member** is to be like each of these **messengers**, a **light** in the **darkness**, whose **light** is to be seen by those in **darkness**. Although not perfect, each one of us is to be a good example to others. Each **congregation** is to be like these **menorahs**, which represent the **Holy Spirit** and the **Torah**, empowering **each member** to shine like a **beacon**, filled with the **Spirit** and the **Word of God**.

The letters to the Congregations are in the natural, then the Revelation returns to the supernatural.

Heavenly Worship, to which we all look forward eagerly!

John Sees into Heaven

*Revelation 4.1. After these things I **looked**, and there was a **door** that was opened in heaven, and the first voice which I heard speaking with me was like a **shofar** saying, "You must **come up here**, (Exod. 19:20,24) and I shall show you what must happen (Dan. 2:28,29,45) after these things."
2. I immediately was in the **Spirit**, and there was a **throne** standing in heaven, and **(One)** seated upon the **throne**, (1 Ki. 22:19, Isa. 6:1, Ezek. 1:26,27, Ps. 47:8, 2 Chr. 18:18) 3. and the **One** Who was seated had an appearance like a jasper and sardius stone. And a rainbow, like an emerald*

in appearance, surrounded the throne. 4. And all around the throne were **twenty-four thrones,** *and upon the* **thrones twenty-four elders** *sitting (Isa. 24:23), clothed in white garments and with gold crowns on their heads. 5. And lightnings and voices and thunders (Exod. 19:16, Ezek. 1:13) were going out from the* **throne,** *and in front of the* **throne** *seven* **lamps** *of fire were burning, (Ezek. 1:13, Zech. 4:2) which are the* **seven Spirits of God,** *6. and in front of the throne like a sea of glass, like crystal. (Ezek. 1:22)*

The One Who is seated on the Throne is the LORD* and Y'shua – Who are One. The twenty-four Thrones are for the Twelve Tribes of Israel and the Twelve Apostles, which are the gates and the foundations of New Jerusalem. The seven Lamps of Fire represent the Seven-fold Holy Spirit as described in Isaiah 11. The Throne, the LORD*, and Y'shua are Spiritual, not physical.

Isaiah 11:1. And there will come forth a **shoot** *out of the trunk of Jesse, and a* **Branch** *will grow out of his roots: (Matt. 2:23, Rev. 5:5; 22:16) 2. and the* **Spirit** *of the LORD* will rest upon Him, the* **Spirit** *of 1)* **wisdom** *and 2)* **understanding,** *the* **Spirit** *of 3)* **counsel** *and 4)* **might,** *the* **Spirit** *of 5)* **knowledge** *and of the   6)* **reverence** *and 7)* **awe** *of the LORD*.* (Rev. 5:6)

The Shoot and the Branch are both Y'shua.

Revelation 4:6b. And in the middle of the throne and around the throne were **four living creatures full of eyes before and behind.** *7. And the* **first** *living creature was like a* **lion,** *and the* **second** *living creature like a* **calf,** *and the* **third** *living creature having a face like a* **man,** *and the* **fourth** *living creature like a flying* **eagle.** *(Ezek. 1:5-10; 10:14) 8. And the* **four living creatures,** *each one of them having six wings, (Isa. 6:2) all around and within they were* **full of eyes,** *(Ezek. 1:18; 10:12) and they do not have* **rest** *day and night saying,*

"Holy, holy, holy,

Lord God of Hosts, *(Isa. 6:3)*

Who was and Who is and Who is coming." (Exod. 3:14)

The Living Creatures are in the Spirit; not needing sleep, their Rest would only be a brief break if they had a Rest. Worshipping the LORD* refreshes them, obviating any need for Rest.

Revelation 4:9. And whenever the **living creatures** *give* **glory** *and* **honor** *and* **thanksgiving** *to the* **One** *Who sits on the* **throne,** *(1 Ki. 22:19, Isa.*

6:1, Ezek. 1:26,27, Ps. 47:8, 2 Chr. 18:18) to the **One** *Who* **lives forever and ever**, *(Dan. 4:34; 6:26; 12:7) 10. the twenty-four* **elders** *fall down before the* **One** *Who sits upon the* **throne** *and they* **worship** *the* **One** *Who* **lives forever and ever** *and they* **cast their crowns** *before the* **throne** *saying,*

11. *"*Worthy *are* You, *our* Lord *and our* God

to receive glory *and* honor *and* power,

because You *did* create *all things*

and by Your will *they indeed were* created.*"*

Everything that has been created was created by the LORD*, our Creator, the One Who lives forever and ever! There is One Throne with One sitting on the Throne, the LORD* and Y'shua, Who are One!

The Scroll and the Lamb

Revelation 5.1. *And I saw in the right hand of the* **One** *Who sits upon the* **throne** *(1 Ki. 22:19, Isa. 6:1, Ezek. 1:26,27, Ps. 47:8, 2 Chr. 18:18) a scroll that had been written within and on the back, (Isa. 29:11, Ezek. 2:9,10) and had been sealed with seven seals. 2. And I saw a strong* **angel** *proclaiming in a loud voice, "Who is worthy to break its seals and to open the scroll?" 3. And no one in heaven and no one on earth and no one under the earth was able to open the scroll and to see it. 4. And I was weeping copiously, because no one was found worthy to open the scroll and to see it. 5. And one of the elders said to me, "Stop weeping! Look!* **He** *was victorious, the* **Lion of the Tribe of Judah**, *(Gen. 49:9,10) the* **Root of David**, *(Isa. 11:1) so* **He** *can* **open** *the* **scroll** *and its* **seven seals**.*"*

The Lion of the Tribe of Judah was in the awesome personal prophecy by Jacob over Judah! (Genesis 49:9) Only He could open the Scroll! All this is in the Spirit!

Revelation 5:6. *And I also saw in the midst of the* **throne** *the four living creatures and in the midst of the elders a* **Lamb** *standing as* **having been slain**, *(Isa. 53:7) having* **seven horns** *and* **seven eyes** *(Zech. 4:10) which are the* **seven Spirits of God** *that were sent into all the earth. (Isa. 11:1,2)*

Throne is sometimes a metaphor referring to the authority of the Ruler of the Universe or here it may be a semi-circle, with the four living creatures partially enclosed. It could also be that the throne is surrounded by the four living creatures, the elders, and the Lamb. This Lamb in death in verse six could not share the Throne with the LORD*; His Resurrected body does share the Throne with the LORD*. All this exists only in the Spirit; it is not physical.

Revelation 5:7. *And **He** came and took the scroll from the right hand of the **One** Who sits on the throne. 8. And when **He** took the scroll, the four living creatures and the twenty-four elders fell before the **Lamb**, each having a harp and a gold bowl filled with burning incense, which are the prayers of the saints, (Ps. 141:2) 9. and they were singing a new song saying,*

> *"Worthy are **You** to take the scroll*
>
> > *and to open its seals,*
> >
> > > *because **You** were slain and **You purchased mankind for God by means of Your blood***
> > >
> > > > *from every **tribe** and **tongue** and **people** and **nation***
> > >
> > *10. and You made them a **kingdom** and **priests** for our God,*
> > >
> > > *(Exod. 19:6, Isa. 61:6)*
> > >
> > > *and they will **reign** upon the **earth**."*

Their Reign will be in the Hereafter where all the Saints will be Priests. Their Reign will be to administer and teach under God.

Revelation 5:11. *And I looked, and I heard a sound of many angels surrounding the **throne** and the living creatures and the elders, and the number of them was ten thousand of ten thousands and a thousand of thousands (Dan. 7:10) 12. saying in a loud voice,*

> *"**Worthy** is the **Lamb** that was slain to take*
>
> *the **power** and **wealth** and **wisdom** and **strength***
>
> *and **honor** and **glory** and **blessing**." (Isa. 53:7, 1 Chr. 29:11)*

This Worship is in Heaven, a Perpetual Rejoicing!

Revelation 5:13. *And **every living thing** that is in the sky and on the earth and under the earth and in the sea and I heard them all saying,*

> *"To the **One** Who sits upon the **throne** and to the **Lamb***
>
> * **blessing** and **honor** and **glory** and **power** forever and ever."*

*14. And the four living creatures were saying, "**Amen**." And the elders fell down and worshipped.*

The action in chapters five and six makes us long for this awesome worship!

One Hundred Forty-Four Thousand of Revelation Seven: Who are these? What do they represent?

The second question must be answered first, because John wrote in a style that used symbols and metaphors. The number 144,000 represents Perfection of Divine Government and Perfect Reign. One hundred forty-four represents Perfection of Divine Government. One thousand represents Perfect Reign. This is a description of two things: Heavenly Reign and Messianic Reign. Thus, Revelation Chapter Seven is about those two governments, which are ONE, not about Jewish young men.

> Revelation 7.1. *After these things I saw* **four angels** *standing upon the* **four corners** *of the earth, holding the four winds (Jeremiah 49:36, Ezekiel 37:9, Zechariah 6:5, Daniel 7:2) of the earth so that the wind could not blow upon the earth and not upon the sea nor even upon any tree. 2. And I saw another* **angel** *going up from the east, having a seal of the Living God, and in a loud voice he cried out to the* **four angels** *to whom it was given to destroy the earth and the sea 3. saying, "Do not harm the earth or the sea or the trees, until we could* **seal** *the* **servants of our God** *upon their* **foreheads***. (Ezekiel 9:4, Revelation 9:4; 14:1; 22:4) 4. Then I heard the number of those who had been* **sealed***, a* **hundred forty-four thousand***, that they had been* **sealed** *from every* **tribe** *of the children of* **Israel***:*

Twelve Jewish tribes, 12,000 each: 12 is perfect government, 1,000 is perfect reign, so this is not about the number of people, but all about the two Perfect Reigns.

> Revelation 7:9. *After these things I looked, and there was an enormous crowd, which no one was able to number, from all* **nations** *and* **tribes** *and* **peoples** *and* **languages***, standing before the* **throne** *and before the* **Lamb***, who had been clothed with* **white robes** *and they had date palms in their hands.*

The Crowd had all been clothed with White Robes.

Revelation 7:13. *And one of the elders answered, saying to me, "Who are these clothed in white robes and where did they come from?*

So, who are these people?

> Revelation 7:14. *And I said to him, "My lord, you know." Then he said to me, "***These are those who came out of the Great Affliction** *(Daniel 12:1) and they washed their robes and they made them* **white** *in the* **blood of the Lamb***."*

The Great Affliction is all that transpires in the chapters describing the fate of the

Sinners, the Heathens. The order of the Chapters in this book is now changed, with the fate of the Sinners listed first, then the fate of the Saints is listed.

FOR THE SINNERS, HEATHENS

The Seven Seals: The First and Fifth Seals are Good, the Rest, for Sinners

> **1.** Revelation 6.1. *And I looked when the* **Lamb** *opened* **one of the seven seals***, then I heard* **one** *of the* **four living creatures** *saying in a voice like thunder, "You must come." 2. And I looked, and there was a* **white horse***, (Zech. 1:8; 6:3,6) and the one who sat upon it had a bow, and a* **crown** *was given to him and he came out* **conquering***, so he could* **overcome every enemy***.*

The Lamb gets the Crown then goes on to conquer, overcoming every enemy, riding the White Horse. All that is explained later in this chapter in the section on the Saints.

> **2.** Revelation 6:3. *And when He opened the* **second seal***, I heard the* **second living creature** *saying, "You must come." 4. And another* **horse** *came out, B, (Zech. 1:8; 6:2) and to the one who sat upon it, it was given to him to* **take peace from the earth** *so that they will slay one another and a great small* **sword** *was given to him.*

First, Peace is taken from the earth. What the great small sword is, is not known, but some scholars think it resembled a Saber.

> **3.** Revelation 6:5. *And when He opened the* **third seal***, I heard the* **third living creature** *saying, "You must come." And I looked, and there was a* **black horse***, (Zech. 6:2,6) and the one who sat upon it had a balance (***scale***) in his hand. 6. And I heard like a voice among the four living creatures saying, "A* **quart of wheat** *for a* **denarius** *and* **three quarts of barley** *for a* **denarius***, and do not harm the olive oil and the wine."*

The Balance Scale is for Judgment! These Living Creatures do not relate to any living creatures on Earth because they are not physical Creatures, but Spiritual. Spiritual Creatures are Real, just not physical. A Denarius was a day's pay.

> **4.** Revelation 6:7. *And when He opened the* **fourth seal***, I heard (the) voice of the* **fourth living creature** *saying, "You must come." 8. And I looked and there was a* **pale horse***, like the pallor of a sickly person, and the one who sat upon it was named* **Death***, and* **Hades** *was following in company with him and authority was given to them over a fourth of the earth to kill with a*

broad sword and with famine and with death, and by beasts of the earth. (Jer. 14:12; 15:3, Ezek. 5:12,17; 14:21; 33:27)

The Pale Horse carried the Spirit of Death to kill Heathens throughout the world, having no pity, which makes this Spirit like Satan – cruel, enjoying inflicting the pain of famine and other cruel deaths. The Broad Sword is the very heavy Sword needing a strong arm to wield it.

5. Revelation 6:9-11 is listed later, because it is about Martyrs who are Raised.

6. Revelation 6:12. *And I looked when He opened the **sixth seal**, and there was a great earthquake and the **sun** became black like sackcloth made of hair and the whole moon became like blood (Jl. 3:4) 13. and the stars of the sky fell to the earth, as the fig tree shaken by a strong wind casts its summer figs, (Isa. 13:10, Ezek. 32:7,8, Jl. 2:10; 4:15) 14. and the **sky** was separated like a scroll rolling up (Isa. 34:4) and every **mountain** and **island** was moved out of its place. 15. And the kings of the earth and the great men and the military leaders and the rich and the powerful and every slave and the free people hid themselves in caves and in the rocks of the mountains (Isa. 2:10,19,21, Jer. 4:29) 16. and they were saying to the mountains and to the rocks, "You must **fall** on us and you must **hide** us (Hos. 10:8) from the face of the **One Who sits upon the throne** and from the **wrath of the Lamb**, 17. because the great **Day** of **Their wrath** has come, and who is able to stand?"* (Jl. 2:11, Nah. 1:6, Mal. 3:2)

The Sixth Seal is Judgment Day! This is the end of the World, the Universe as we know it. The Saints are gone, many Heathens are now killed. The Martyrs already have their White Robes and have entered the Hereafter. There is only the Spiritual Realm. Judgment Day is a process, not one Zap and it is over. But in the natural it takes time to take each step. The testimony and preaching of the Two Witnesses are bringing in new Saints.

The Seventh Seal

7. Revelation 8.1. *And when He opened the* seventh seal, *there was* silence in heaven *for about* half an hour. *2. And I saw the* seven angels *who stood before God, and* seven trumpets *were given to them.*

In the Spirit, which means in Heaven, Time is a different dimension, not like we know Time in the world, so we cannot view this as literal. The Earth has not yet been destroyed, so the Sun and Moon are still there to set times by, but the Day is no longer twenty-four hours. The Seven Trumpets are introduced:

The Golden Fire-pan

> Revelation 8:3. *And another **angel** came and stood by the altar of incense, he had a **golden fire-pan** and much incense was given to him, so that he could present the **prayers** of all the **saints** upon the **golden altar** which is before the **throne**. (Exod. 30:1-3, Ps. 141:2) 4. And the **smoke** of the **incense** ascended from the **angel's hand** with the **prayers** of the saints to the **presence** of God. 5. And the **angel** took the **fire-pan** and filled it up from the **coals** of the **altar** (Lev. 16:12) and **cast them to the earth**, and there were **thunders** and **sounds** and **lightnings** and an **earthquake**.* (Exod. 19:16-19)

The Golden Altar is the one that was copied from Moses' view of the Heavenly Tabernacle with the Golden Altar standing before the veil, except on Yom Kippur. On Yom Kippur the Golden Altar was taken into the Holy of Holies to be in the Presence of God. Since this is before the Throne this could well be on Yom Kippur in earthly time, but what it is in Heavenly time is not known. The prayers of Saints do go to God, Who is in us even now! The Thunders and Sounds and Lightnings and the Earthquake are Spiritual.

The Trumpets

Revelation 8:6. *And the **seven angels** who had the **seven trumpets** prepared themselves so that they could **sound** them.*

The text saying the **Angels** could **Sound** the **Trumpets** is technically correct! Often spoken of as blowing Shofars, **Sound** is the correct term! **Shofars** are to be **Sounded**, not **Blown.**

> **1.** Revelation 8:7. *And the **first trumpeted**: and there was **hail and fire mixed in blood** and it was **cast to the earth**, and a **third of the earth was consumed by fire** and a **third of the trees were consumed by fire** and all **green grass was consumed by fire**.* (Exod. 9:23-25, Ezek. 38:22)

Judgment Day will see this destruction in slow-motion as the Day progresses!

> **2.** Revelation 8:8. *Then the **second** angel **trumpeted**: and something like a **great fiery mountain** was cast **burning** into the **sea**, and a **third of the sea became blood**. (Exod. 7:20,21) 9. And a **third of the creatures in the sea that had life died** and a **third of the ships were destroyed**.*

Time will hang heavy as destruction flows steadily. The Martyrs are gone, having been taken in the Fifth Seal of chapter 6, so only the Heathens see this, being killed off slowly. They are being prepared for the Second Death!

3. Revelation 8:10. *And the **third** angel **trumpeted**: then a great **star** fell from **heaven**, **burning like a lamp** and it fell upon the **third of the rivers** and **upon the springs of the waters**, 11. and the name of the star was called* **Apsinthos**. *A **third of the waters** were made into **apsinthos** and **many people died from the waters that were made bitter**.* (Jer. 9:15)

Apsinthos means Wormwood, Absinth, Bitter. The Second Death will be excruciatingly slow. Each believer must be careful to walk in Repentance all day every day in order for the Man with the Inkhorn (Ezekiel 9) to mark each one's forehead. Be sure you are marked! The marked do not go through this!

4. Revelation 8:12. *Then the **fourth** angel **trumpeted**: and a **third of the sun** was **struck** and a **third of the moon** and a **third of the stars**, so that a **third** of them would be **dark** and a **third** of a **day** could not be made **visible** and the **night likewise**.* (Isa. 13:10, Ezek. 32:7,8, Jl. 2:10; 4:15)

The sequence goes on.

Revelation 8:13. *Then I looked and I heard one **eagle** flying in the middle of the **sky**, saying in a loud voice, "**Woe, woe, woe**, to those who **live** on the **earth**, (because) of the remaining sounds of the **trumpet** which are about to be sounded by the **three angels**."*

These are the last three of the Seven Angels who have the Trumpets. The Seventh Angel is not identified.

5. Revelation 9.1. *Then the **fifth** angel **trumpeted**: and I saw a **star** that had **fallen out from heaven** to the **earth**, then the **key** of the **pit** of the **abyss** was given to (**the star**) 2. and it opened the **pit** of the **abyss** and **smoke** rose from the **pit** like **smoke** of a great furnace, (Gen. 19:28, Exod. 19:18) and the **sun** and the **air** were **darkened** by the **smoke** from the **pit**. 3. And **locusts** came out from the **smoke** to the **earth**, (Exod. 10:12,15) and **authority** was given to them as the **scorpions** have **authority** over the earth. 4. And it was said to them that they could not **injure** the grass of the earth nor any green thing and not any tree, **only the people who do not have the seal of God** on their **foreheads**. (Ezek. 9:4, Rev. 7:3; 14:1; 22:4) 5. And it was given to them that **they could not kill them**, but that they would be **tormented** (for) five months, and their **torment** will be like a **torment** of a **scorpion** when it would sting someone. 6. And in those days people will seek death but they will **not** find it, and they will desire to die but death flees from them.* (Jer. 8:3, Hos. 10:8, Job 3:21)

The Star that fell was Satan, Isaiah 14:12. The Authority given to the Locusts was the power to Sting. The Locusts are Spiritual, not Locusts that have swarmed over parts of the world. The Spiritual Locusts as described in verse seven do not at all resemble the earthly Locusts. Those who have the Mark of God during these disasters are those who have Repented, when they saw the beginning of the destruction of Judgment Day. The Martyrs were taken at the very beginning of Judgment Day, but God is patient, allowing those last heathens to Repent and escape the Second Death. The months in verse five are Spiritual Months, giving no hint to what that is in Earthly time.

> Revelation 9:7. *And the appearance of the* **locusts** *(was) like horses when they had been prepared for battle, (Jl. 2:4,5) and upon their heads (were)* **crowns** *like gold, and their faces were like faces of men, 8. and they had hair like women's hair, and their teeth were like* **lions'** *(teeth), (Jl. 1:6) 9. and they had* **breastplates** *like* **iron breastplates**, *and the* **sound** *of their* **wings** *like a* **sound of many chariot horses** *running in battle, (Jl. 2:5) 10. and they had* **tails** *like* **scorpions** *and stings, and in their* **tails** *was their power to* **injure** *people (for) five months. 11. they had for their king the* **angel** *of the* **abyss**, *(whose) name in Hebrew (is)* **Abaddon**, *and in the Greek it has the name* **Apollyon**.

The Locusts are not Physical but they are Real. Abaddon and Apollyon mean Destruction, Hell.

Revelation 9:12. *The* one woe *has passed. Behold! Two woes are still coming after these things.*

Those awaiting the Second Death still have a chance to Repent to become Saints.

> **6.** Revelation 9:13. *And the* **sixth** *angel* **trumpeted**: *and I heard one voice from the four horns of the* **golden altar** *that is in front of God, 14. saying to the* **sixth angel**, *the one who had the* **trumpet**, *"You must release by the great river Euphrates the* **four angels** *who have been bound." 15. And the* **four angels** *who were prepared for the* **hour** *and* **day** *and* **month** *and* **year** *were* **released**, *so that they could* **kill** *the* **third of mankind**. *16. And the number of the cavalry troops (was)* **twenty thousand of tens of thousands**, *I heard their number. 17. And then I saw the* **horses** *in my sight and* **those who** *sat upon them, having* **fiery breast-plates** *also dark blue and sulfurous, and the* **heads** *of the* **horses** *like* **lions' heads**, *and* **fire** *and* **smoke** *and* **sulfur** *were going out from their* **mouths**. *18. And a* **third of mankind** *was* **killed** *by these* **three plagues**, *by means of the* **fire** *and the* **smoke** *and the* **sulfur** *going out from their* **mouths**. *19. For the* **power** *of the* **horses** *was in their* **mouths**

*and in their **tails**, for their **tails** were like **snakes**, having **heads** and they **injure** with them.*

Like the Locusts the Horses and their Riders are spiritual, not like any that have been seen on Earth. The Death is also Spiritual, leading to the Second Death. Spiritual Death is when a person's Spirit Dies, so that person's Spirit cannot go to ETERNAL LIFE.

Revelation 9:20. *And the **rest of mankind**, those not killed by these three plagues, did **not repent** from the deeds of their hands, so they would not (any longer) be paying homage to the demons and idols of gold and silver and brass and copper and wood, (Deut. 32:17) which things are not able to see or to hear or to walk, (Ps. 115:4-7; 135:15-17, Dan. 5:23) 21. and they did **not repent** from their **murders** nor from their **witchcraft** nor from their **idolatry** nor from their **thefts**.*

The Greek word translated witchcraft is pharmakon, referring to the use of drugs to cause visions and messages from spirits. See *Sorcery* in the One New Man Bible Glossary. Idolatry is a metaphor for Immorality as in the Book of Hosea.

The Angel and the Little Scroll; A Different Angel – not one of the Seven

Revelation 10.1. *Then I saw **another mighty angel** descending from heaven clothed in a **cloud**, and a **rainbow** upon his **head** and his **face** like the **sun** and his **feet** like **pillars of fire**, 2. and having in his **hand** a **little scroll** (that) had been **opened**. And he placed his **right foot** upon the sea, and the **left** upon the **ground**, 3. and he cried out in a **loud voice** as a **lion roars**. And when he **cried** out, the **seven thunders spoke** their own **voices**. 4. And when the **seven thunders spoke** I was going to write, then I heard a voice from heaven saying, "**You must seal** what the **seven thunders** were **speaking**, and do not write these things." (Dan. 8:26; 12:4,9) 5. And the **angel**, whom I saw standing upon the **sea** and upon the **earth**, raised his right hand to the sky 6. and he **swore by the One Who lives forever and ever**, (Deut. 32:40, Dan. 12:7)*

***Who created the sky** and the **things** in it and the earth and the things on it and the sea and the things in it, (Gen. 14:19,22, Exod. 20:11, Ps. 146:6, Neh. 9:6) that **there will be no more delay**, (Ezek. 12:28) 7. but in the days of the voice of the **seventh angel**, when he would be going to blow the **trumpet**, then the mystery of God was fulfilled as He brought the **Good News** by His servants the prophets. (Amos 3:7, Zech. 1:6, Dan. 9:6,10)*

The huge Angel is Spiritual as are the Seven Thunders, whose words are Sealed, not written. Saying There will be no more Delay! Judgment Day will proceed on schedule! With the sun no longer determining a twenty-four hour day, Judgment Day is an unknown time. There is no point in debating the length of the Day, whatever it will be it will be, with the hope that no one who reads this will see the Day. Everyone who reads this should have the mark on the forehead by the Man with the Inkhorn and be in Heaven.

> **1.** Revelation 10:8. *And the **voice** from heaven which I again heard was speaking with me and saying, "**You** must go. **You** must take the **opened scroll** in the hand of the **angel**, the one who stands upon the sea and upon the earth." 9. And I went to the **angel** telling him to give the little scroll to me. And he said to me, "You must take it and you must devour it, and it will make your stomach bitter, but in your mouth it will be sweet as honey." (Ezek. 2:8; 3:1-3) 10. Then I took the little scroll from the hand of the **angel** and I devoured it, and in my **mouth it was sweet as honey** but when I ate it, it became **bitter** in my **stomach**. 11. Then they said to me, "It is necessary for you to prophesy again to many peoples and nations and languages and kings." (Jer. 25:30)*

You are what you eat! So, eat the Word of God, which is how you get to know Him better. The Little Scroll tells of the painful end of certain sinners, so it turns bitter in the stomach. Unlike the Little Scroll, the Word of God does not get bitter in your stomach but gets sweeter and sweeter.

Second Angel

> **2.** Revelation 14:8. *And another, a **second angel**, followed saying, "**She has fallen, she has fallen! Babylon** the Great, by whom all the **heathens** had been given to drink from the **wine** of the **wrath** of her **idolatry**." (Isa. 21:9, Jer. 51:7,8)*

Babylon represents all of modern society, seeking riches and political control. Idolatry refers to all forms of idolatry; see Harlot in the One New Man Bible Glossary. The winecup of His fury is an idiom for dire prophecy. Wrath comes with Heat! Both the Hebrew Hamah and the Greek Thumos speak of heat, of great rage. See Rev. 16:19, Deut. 28:15ff, and Jer. 25:15.

Third Angel

> **3.** Revelation 14:9. *Then another, a **third angel**, followed them saying in a loud voice, "If someone **pays homage** to the **beast** and his **image** and takes*

*his **mark** on his **forehead** or upon his **hand**, 10. then he will **drink** from the **wine** of the **wrath** of **God** which has been poured undiluted in the **cup** of His **wrath** (Isa. 51:17,22, Jer. 25:15, Ps. 75:9) and he will be **tortured** in **fire** and **sulfur** before **holy angels** and before the **Lamb**. (Gen. 19:24, Ezek. 38:22, Ps. 11:6) 11. And the **smoke** of their **tormenting** (**fire**) ascends forever, (Isa. 34:10) and those who pay **homage** to the **beast** and his **image** do **not** have **rest** day or night, even if someone (just) takes the mark of his name. 12. Here is the (need for) **patient endurance** by the **saints**, those who **keep the commandments of God** and their **faith in Y'shua**."*

The Mark of the Beast is Spiritual, not a physical Mark, and it is taken by all who acknowledge the Beast - by the way they live, not obeying the commandments of the LORD*, not walking in Repentance, in Humility. Judgment Day is not over in our twenty-four-hour day, but goes on and on for a long time by our earthly time. Spiritual time is different and cannot be measured like Natural time. Those who pay homage to the Beast do not have any rest, not even a short break. The Saints need Patient Endurance until they are taken to heaven because they will see so much evil on the Earth as the Beasts, the Dragon, the Serpent, and all the versions of the Devil aka Satan work their things. Saints who are killed go straight to Heaven and are given their Eternal Martyrs' Rewards right away.

The Fifth and Sixth Angels; the Wine press of the Wrath of God

5. Revelation 14:17. *Then another **angel**, who also had a sharp **sickle**, came out of the **Sanctuary**, the one in heaven. 18. And still another (**6.**) **angel**, who had authority over fire, came out from the **altar**, and he called in a loud voice to the one who had the sharp **sickle** saying, "You must now send your sharp **sickle** and you must at once gather in the bunches of **grapes** of the vine of the earth, because its **grapes** have ripened." 19. Then the **angel** threw his **sickle** forcefully to the earth and he gathered in the **vine** of the earth and he cast it into the great **wine press** of the **wrath of God**. 20. And the **wine press** was trod outside the city and **blood** came out from the **wine press** as far as the bridles of the horses for **one thousand six hundred stadia**.* (Isa. 63:3, Lam. 1:15)

The vine is used to represent numerous things, but there are two kinds of vines: Holy and Strange. Strange represents Sodom, the evils with which the wrath of God is dealing in this passage. The wine press of the wrath of God is from Joel 4:13, while Joel 4:2 says the nations will gather at the Valley of Jehoshaphat, the Valley of God's Judgment, from verse twelve. This valley is about twelve miles south of Jerusalem in the natural; this is the Spiritual Judgment of God, not physically in that valley. One thousand six hundred stadia is about one hundred eighty miles in the natural, but this is Spiritual, showing that there will be quite a few people lost to Satanic forces. After this harvest of Evil people, there are still people left on Earth!

The Seven Angels with the Seven Last Plagues

Revelation 15.1. *Then I saw another great and marvelous miracle in heaven,* seven angels *having* seven final plagues, *(Lev. 26:21) because with them the* wrath of God is completed.

Completed means that the Wrath of God has been carried out.

> Revelation 15:5. *Then after these things I looked, and the* **Sanctuary of the Tabernacle of the Testimony** *in heaven opened, (Exod. 38:21; 40:34) 6. and* **seven angels**, *holding the* **seven plagues**, *came out from the* **Sanctuary** *clothed in* **pure brilliant linen**, *and* **gold belts** *had been fastened about their chests. 7. And* **one** *of the* **four living creatures** *gave to the* **seven angels seven golden vials** *filled with the* **wrath of God**, *the* **One** *Who lives forever and ever. (Isa. 51:17,22, Jer. 25:15,   Ps. 75:9) 8. And the* **Sanctuary** *was filled with smoke from the* **glory of God** *and from His* **power**, *(Exod. 40:34, 1 Ki. 8:10,11, Isa. 6:4, Ezek. 44:4, 2 Chr. 5:13,14) and no one was able to enter the* **Sanctuary** *until the* **seven plagues** *of the* **seven angels** *were* **completed**.

The Sanctuary seen here is not in New Jerusalem which does not descend until Judgment Day has been completed. As the Day continues on Earth we learn there are Seven more Plagues to be issued to the followers of Satan. Completed means that the Seven Plagues had been carried out, but Judgment Day is not over yet!

The Seven Vials of God's Wrath

> Revelation 16.1. *Then I heard a loud voice from the Sanctuary (Isa. 66:6) saying to the* **seven angels**, *"You must go and pour out upon the earth the* **seven vials** *of the* **wrath of God**.*" (Jer. 10:25, Ezek. 22:31, Zph. 3:8, Ps. 69:25)

> **1.** Revelation 16:2. *Then the* **first** *came and poured his* **vial** *to the earth, and* **very evil sores** *came upon mankind, those who had the* **mark of the beast**, *those who* **bowed down** *to his* **image**. (Exod. 9:10, Deut. 28:35)

Very Evil Sores is the correct translation of the Hebrew idiomatic text, commonly translated "vile and evil sores;" this is a Hebraism with two synonyms meaning "evil" making the superlative, very. The sores will be very painful, irritating constantly.

2. Revelation 16:3. *Then the* second *angel poured out his* vial *into the sea, and it became like the blood of a dead man, and* every living *being of the things in the* sea died. (Exod. 7:17-21)

Now, every living thing in the sea dies; the sea no longer provides food for the many people remaining.

> **3.** Revelation 16:4. *Then the **third** poured out his **vial** into the rivers and the fountains of the waters, and they became blood. (Exod. 7:19-24, Ps. 78:44) 5. And I heard the **angel of the waters** saying,*
>
>> *"You are **righteous**, the **One** Who **is** and Who **was**, the **Undefiled**,*
>>
>> *because You have judged these things,*
>
>> 6.   *because **they** poured out the **blood of saints** and **prophets** (Ps. 79:3)*
>>
>> *and You have given them **blood** to drink, (Isa. 49:26)*
>>
>> *of which they are deserving."*
>
>> 7. *Then I heard the **altar** saying,*
>>
>> *"Indeed, **Lord**, the **God of Hosts**,*
>>
>> **Your judgments** are **true** and **righteous**."* (Ps. 119:137)

Next, the domestic waters, the rivers and lakes are turned to Blood, the Blood of the Martyrs, so that all life in them is destroyed; another source of food is eliminated.

> **4.** Revelation 16:8. *Then the **fourth** poured out his **vial** upon the sun, and it was given to it to scorch **mankind** with **fire**. 9. And **mankind** was **burned** by a **great heat** and they **blasphemed** the **name of God**, the **One** Who had authority over these **plagues**, but they did **not** repent to give Him glory.*

The remaining people are tortured by the heat of the Sun! The Earth and the Sun have not yet been totally destroyed; but the Sun no longer measures twenty-four hour days, so perhaps prolonged days bring the heat or perhaps the heat of the Sun is ramped up for Judgment Day. Sinners still do not repent, but continue to Blaspheme God! See Revelation 12:1 with the Woman clothed with the Sun! That is described later in this chapter.

> **5.** Revelation 16:10. *Then the **fifth** poured out his **vial** upon the **throne** of the **beast**, and its **kingdom** became **darkened**, (Exod. 10:21, Isa. 8:22)*

and they chewed their tongues from the pain, 11. yet they **blasphemed** *the* **God of heaven** *because of their pain and because of their sores but they did* **not** *repent from their deeds.*

Those who are condemned by their relationship with the Beast, blaming God for their pain, continue to resist the LORD* even after torture, refusing to Repent!

6. Revelation 16:12. *Then the* **sixth** *poured out his* **vial** *upon the great river Euphrates and its water dried up, (Isa. 11:15; 44:27, Jer. 50:38; 51:36) so that the way of the kings from the east could be prepared. 13. And I saw* **three unclean spirits** *like* **frogs** *come from the* **mouth** *of the* **dragon** *and from the* **mouth** *of the* **beast** *and from the* **mouth** *of the* **false prophet***: 14. for* **spirits of demons** *were performing* **miracles***, which were going out over the* **kingdoms** *of the* **whole inhabited world** *to gather them into the* **war** *of the* **great Day** *of the* **God of the Hosts***. (Matt. 25:31) 15. "Behold I am coming like a thief. Blessed is the one who is awake and keeps his garments ready, so that he would not walk* **naked** *and they would see his shame." 16. And* **He** *gathered them into the place called in Hebrew* **Har Megiddo***. (Jdg. 5:19, 2 Ki. 9:27; 23:29, Zech. 12:11)*

In the Hebrew idiom, naked could be wearing a loincloth. Har Megiddo is a mountain in the Jezreel Valley, where the enemies will gather to fight Israel, but the battle is in the Valley of Jehoshaphat – also called the Valley of Blessing. This is a Spiritual Battle, not a Physical Battle and this battle is raging right now!

7. Revelation 16:17. *Then the* **seventh** *poured out his* **vial** *upon the air and a loud voice came out of the* **Sanctuary** *(Isa. 66:6) from the* **throne** *saying,* **"It is finished."** *18. And there were lightnings and sounds and thunders and there was a violent earthquake, such as had not happened since mankind came upon the earth, so powerful an earthquake as this. (Dan. 12:1) 19. Then the* **great city** *was (split) in three parts and the* **cities** *of the* **heathens** *fell. And* **Babylon** *the great was remembered before* **God***, to give to her the cup of the* **wine** *of the* **wrath** *of* **His punishment***. (Isa. 51:17,22, Jer. 25:15, Ps. 75:9) 20. Then every island fled and mountains were not found. 21. And great* **hail** *as heavy as* **talents** *came down from the sky on* **mankind***, and* **mankind blasphemed God** *because of the* **plague** *of the* **hail***, because this plague is exceedingly great.*

After all Seven Plagues come to the Earth, there are still people Blaspheming God. Each hail stone weighs seventy-five pounds! The population of the earth has been decimated, but not eradicated. Those living are in pain, but many still do not Repent.

The Great Harlot and the Beast

Revelation 17.1. *Then **one** of the **seven angels** who had the **seven vials** came and spoke with me saying, "Come here, I shall show you the **judgment of the great harlot** who sits upon **many waters**, (Jer. 51:13) 2. with whom the kings of the earth did fornicate and those who dwell on the earth did become **drunk** from the **wine** of her **idolatry**."* (Isa. 23:17, Jer. 51:7)

Many waters can be used as a symbol for an enormous crowd of people, as in Revelation 17:15 and 19:6. Idolatry refers to Immorality. The Leaders who are responsible for spreading Satan's work now are shown what God really thinks of them, of those who have been multiplying the evil works, leading their people in sin.

Revelation 17:3. *and **he carried me away in the spirit into the wilderness**. And I saw a **woman** sitting upon a **scarlet beast**, full of **blasphemous names**, which had **seven heads** and **ten horns**. 4. And the **woman** was clothed in **purple** and **scarlet** and adorned with **gold** and **precious stones** and **pearls**, (Ezek. 28:13) having in her hand a **gold cup** filled with **detestable** and **unclean things** of her **idolatry** 5. and a name had been written upon her forehead, "**Mystery**, **Babylon the Great**, the **Mother** of the **Fornications** and of the **Detestable Things** of the Earth." 6. And I saw the **woman** drunk from the **blood** of the **saints** and from the **blood** of those testifying about **Y'shua**.*

This Woman is the epitome of the evils in our modern world; evils that we see every day in the U.S. from drug addiction, murders, foul-speaking in public media, greed, and common-place immorality among every age group and every class of the population. The Blood of the Martyrs, both Jewish and Christian makes our persecutors drunk with their power.

Revelation 17:6b. *And I **marveled**, seeing her with great amazement. 7. And the **angel** said to me, "Why were you **astonished**? I shall tell you the **mystery** of the **woman** and the **beast** which is carrying her, the one that has the **Seven Heads** and the **Ten Horns**. 8. The **beast** you saw which was (earlier) and is not (any longer) then it is going to **ascend** from the **abyss** (Dan. 7:3) and go into **destruction**. Then those who **dwell** upon the **earth**, whose names are **not** written in the **Book of Life** (Exod. 32:32,33, Ps. 69:29, Dan. 12:1) from (the) foundation of (the) world, will be **amazed**, when they see the **beast**, because it was and it is **not** and it will be **present**. (Dan. 7:3) 9. Here is (the need) for a mind that has wisdom. The **seven heads** are **seven mountains**, where the **woman** is staying on them. And the* *(seven heads) are seven kings: 10. five fell, one is, the other has not yet come, and when he would come, it is necessary for him to remain (only) a little while. 11. And the beast who was and who is not, even he himself is (the) eighth (king) and is from the seven, and he is going into destruction. 12. And the ten horns (Dan. 7:24) that you saw are ten kings, who did not yet take a kingdom, but they take authority as kings for one hour with the beast. 13. These have one purpose and they impart their power and authority to the beast. 14. These will make war against the Lamb but the Lamb will conquer them, because He is Lord of Lords and King of Kings (Deut. 10:17, Dan. 2:47, 1 Tim. 6:15) and those with Him (are) called and chosen and faithful.*

The Modern, Evil System we now live in will be destroyed! But first, after the Beast is destroyed, it will rise and be Present, which Beast is present as this is written. The Ten Kings are the evils which are now so common-place; witchcraft, all sorts of immorality, gambling, greed, wars, globalism, attempts to obliterate nationalism, and more. All those evils are at war against the Lamb, the One Who will conquer all that the Beast stands for. This Spiritual Battle will definitely be won by the One Who created everything!

Revelation 17:15. Then he said to me, "The waters which you saw, on which the harlot is seated, are people and crowds and nations and languages. 16. Then the ten horns which you saw and the beast, these will hate the harlot and will make her desolate and naked and devour her flesh and will burn her in fire. (Lev. 21:9) 17. For God gave into their hearts to do His purpose and to make one judgment and to give their kingdom to the beast until the words of God will be fulfilled. 18. And the woman whom you saw is the great city, the one which reigns over the kings of the earth."

The Waters are the people of the world who remain at this time, those not killed by the previous plagues. The Ten Horns and the Beast will hate the Harlot because Satan is not capable of Love, so they will devour the Harlot. Then God causes them to do His will, making one judgment giving their kingdom to the Beast until the very end when the Great City, representing all the evils of the modern world, is destroyed.

The Fall of Babylon

Revelation 18.1. After these things I saw another angel, who had great authority, descending from heaven, and the earth was given light by his glory.

The Light is both the Light of His Glory and the Light of Understanding.

2. *And he cried out in a strong voice saying,*

>*"**She has fallen, Babylon the Great has fallen**, (Isa. 21:9, Jer. 51:8)*
>
>*and she has become a **dwelling place** of **demons***
>
>*and a **prison** of every **unclean spirit***
>
>*and a **prison** of every **unclean bird***
>
>*and a **prison** of every **unclean** and **hated beast**,*
>
>*(Isa. 13:21; 34:11, Jer. 50:39)*

3. *because all the nations (**Heathens**) have drunk from the **wine***

>*of the passion of her **idolatry** (Isa. 23:17, Jer. 51:7)*
>
>*and the **kings** of the earth committed **adultery** with her*
>
>*and the **merchants** of the earth became*
>
>***wealthy** from the **power** of her **excessive wealth**."*

The Evil system will fall, taking the Powerful and the Wealthy with it. The Immorality of the present time will be erased as the world turns to God.

Revelation 18:4. *Then I heard another voice from heaven saying,*

>*"**My people**, you must immediately **come out** from her*
>
>*(Isa. 48:20; 52:11, Jer. 50:8; 51:6,9,45)*
>
>*so that you would not share her sins,*
>
>*and so that you would not take any*
>
>*of her plagues,*

5. *because her sins reached as far as heaven (Gen. 18:20,21, Jer. 51:9)*

>*and **God** remembered her **crimes**.*

6. *You must now reward her as she also rewarded (Jer. 50:15,29, Ps. 137:8)*

>*and you must immediately pay back double (to her)*
>
>*according to her deeds.*
>
>*In the cup in which she mixed **you** must now*
>
>*mix **double to her**,*

At this late date, God doubles the punishment!

7.　　*who did glorify herself and live sensually,*

　　You must now give so much torment and mourning to her.

　　Because in her heart she says that

　　　'I sit as **Queen**

　　　and I am **not a widow**

　　　and I shall **never see mourning.***'*

8.　　*Because of this her* **plagues** *will come in one* **Day,**

　　　death *and* **mourning** *and* **famine,**

　　　and she will be **burned up** *in fire, (Lev. 21:9)*

　　　because the **Lord God Almighty** *(is) the* **One**

　　　　Who is judging her." (Isa. 47:7-9, Jer. 50:34)

Pride causes the attitude of superiority and never mourning seen here. Today there are people who promote Immorality and Idolatry; they will receive double the Punishment they deserve in the Judgment.

Revelation 18:9. *Then the* **kings** *of the earth, those who committed* **adultery** *with* **her** *and* **lived luxuriously** *(with her), will* **weep** *and* **mourn,** *when they see the* **smoke** *of* **her burning,** *(Ezek. 26:16; 27:30-35) 10. standing from afar because of fear of her torment, saying,*

　　"Oh! It can't be! The **great city,**

　　　Babylon *the powerful city,*

　　because your **judgment** *came in* **one hour."** *(Ezek. 26:17, Dan. 4:30)*

The Punishment will be prolonged for a time as the Powerful and the Wealthy endure their Punishment.

Revelation 18:11. *And the* **merchants** *of the earth were* **weeping** *and* **mourning** *over her, because* **no one** *is buying their cargo any longer, (Ezek. 27:36) 12. cargo of* **gold** *and* **silver** *and* **precious stones** *and* **pearls** *and* **fine linen** *and* **purple cloth** *and* **silk** *and* **scarlet,** *and every* **vessel** *of* **citron** *wood and every* **ivory vessel** *and every* **vessel** *of very precious* **wood** *and* **copper** *and* **iron** *and* **marble,** *13. and* **cinnamon** *and* **amomum** *and* **incense** *and* **perfume** *and* **frankincense** *and* **wine** *and* **olive oil** *and fine* **flour** *and* **wheat** *and* **cattle** *and* **sheep,** *and* **horses** *and* **carriages** *and* <u>**slaves,** *and* **lives of men.**</u>

Amomum was a spice from India. The Slaves are in the Greek and Roman sense of personal property with which the owner could treat any way he wanted, just like a piece of furniture or garbage. Lives of Men is a Hebrew idiom referring to Slaves in that same vein, doubling the reference to Slaves for emphasis. The last of the people will be the horribly mistreated, but many will still not respond to the Two Witnesses.

Revelation 18:14. *And the **ripe fruits** from your **craving** for life's **forbidden things***

have been taken away from you,

*and **all** the **luxuries** and **brilliance***

have been lost, (taken) from you

*and **no longer** will they find these things.*

*15. **Their merchants** who became rich from her will stand from afar **because of the fear of her torment, crying** and **mourning**, (Ezek. 27:36) 16. saying,*

*"**Woe. Woe!** The **great city**,*

*the one clothed in **fine linen***

*and **purple** and **scarlet***

*and adorned in **gold***

*and **precious stone** and **pearl**," (Ezek. 28:13)*

*17. because in **one hour** so much **wealth** was **laid waste**.*

"Woe. Woe!" is a gasp of Horror, doubled because this Gasp was exceptionally loud and long. The Powerful and the Wealthy are horrified to see all that they treasure going up in smoke; this is Spiritual, not literal, so it is the Spirits of the people crying over the destruction, which is done in the Spirit.

Revelation 18:17b. *And every (**harbor**) **pilot** and everyone who sails along the coast and sailors and as many as are working the sea stood from afar (Ezek. 27:27-29) 18. and they were crying out while they were watching the smoke of her burning saying, "What (other city) is like the **great city**?" 19. And they were throwing dirt on their heads and they were crying out weeping and mourning saying,*

*"**Woe. Woe!** The **great city**,*

in which all those who had ships in the sea

*had gained great **wealth** from her expensive things,*

*that in **one hour** she was laid waste."* (Ezek. 27:30-34)

The Spirits of those condemned to the Second Death mourn; the Spirits of the Saints Perpetually Rejoice!

ANOTHER ANGEL

Revelation 18:21. *And one **strong angel** brought a stone like a great millstone and cast it forcefully into the sea saying,*

"*Like this, the **great city Babylon***

*will be **cast** in **violence***

*and it would **never** again be found. (Jer. 51:63,64, Ezek. 26:21)*

Every sort of Evil has been eliminated!

*22. Then (the) **sound** of **harpists** and **musicians** and **flute players** and **trumpeters***

*will **never** again be heard in you, (Isa. 24:8, Ezek. 26:13)*

*and **no** craftsman of any skill*

*will **ever** again be found in you,*

*and a sound of a millstone will **never** again be heard in you,*

23. And a light of a lamp

*will **never** again be visible in you*

and a voice of a bridegroom and a bride

*will **never** again be heard in you, (Jer. 7:34; 16:9; 25:10)*

because your merchants were the great men of the earth, (Isa. 23:8)

*because all the **heathens** were **deceived** by your **sorcery**, (Isa. 47:9)*

*24. and in her was found (the) **blood** of **prophets** and of **saints***

*and all those who had been **slain** upon the earth."*

(Jer. 51:49, Ezek. 24:7)

There will be no Joy in the Second Death. All those who had been Slain are the Martyrs, who have great Rewards in the Hereafter.

THIS CLOSES THE CURSES OF THE SINNERS.

A SECOND ANGEL

The Thousand Years

Revelation 20.1. *Then I saw an **angel** descending from **heaven**, who had the **key** of the **abyss** and a large chain in his hand. 2. And he **arrested** the **dragon**, the **old serpent**, who is (the) **Devil** and **Satan**, then he **bound** him for a **thousand years** 3. and cast him into the **abyss** and **shut** and **sealed** (the abyss) above him, so that he could **not** deceive the **heathens** any longer until the **thousand years would be completed**. **After these things** it is necessary for him to be **loosed** for a **short time**.*

The Thousand Years is Spiritual Time, not time as we know it, so we do not have any idea how much time there will be, except it will likely be very long. This is during Judgment Day.

The Bride Now Makes Her Appearance

1/7. Revelation 21:9. *Then **one** of the **seven angels**, of those who have the **seven vials** full of the **seven last plagues**, came and spoke with me saying, "You must come, I shall show you the **bride**, the **wife of the Lamb**." 10. Then he took me away in the **spirit** to a great and high mountain, and he showed me the **holy city**, **Jerusalem**, (Ezekiel 40:2) **descending** out of the **sky** from God, 11. having the **glory of God**, her **radiance** like a precious stone as a crystal jasper stone. (Isaiah 60:1,2,19) 12. Having a great and high **wall**, which has **twelve gates** and upon the **gates twelve angels** and **names** that have been written upon the **gates**, which are the names of the **twelve tribes of the Children of Israel**: (Exodus 28:21) 13. on the east three **gates** and on the north three **gates** and on the south three **gates** and on the west three **gates**. (Ezekiel 48:30-35) 14. And the **wall** of the city had **twelve foundations** and upon them are **twelve names of the twelve apostles of the Lamb**.*

Each of the twelve Apostles of the foundation is Naturally Jewish. All who worship the God of Abraham, Isaac, and Jacob is Jewish, either Natural or Grafted in.

The New Jerusalem is founded on the Jewish Apostles of Messiah, and entry is only through the Jewish Gates, the twelve tribes of Israel. That is the reason for *Then I heard the number of those who had been sealed, a hundred forty-four thousand, that they had been sealed from every tribe of the children of Israel:* Revelation 7:4.

Each Gate has one or more Jewish Gate-Keepers who have a duty to admit only those who are qualified.

Revelation 21:15. *And the one who was speaking with me had a golden measuring rod, so that he could measure the city and its gates and its wall. 16. And the city is lying square, with its length as great as the width. And he measured the city with the reed to* **twelve thousand stadia**, *the* **length** *and the* **breadth** *and its* **height** *are equal*

The Spiritual Jerusalem is One thousand five hundred miles long, One thousand five hundred miles wide and One thousand five hundred miles high, which is no problem for the Spirit Realm. New Jerusalem is Spiritual, not physical.

Revelation 21:17. *Then he measured its wall one hundred forty-four forearms of a man, a measure men use, which the angel was using. (Ezek. 48:16,17)*

The Wall is two hundred sixteen feet wide and two hundred sixteen feet high.

Revelation 21:18. *And the material of its* **wall** *was* **jasper** *and the city pure* **gold** *like pure glass. 19. The* **foundations** *of the wall of the city were adorned with every precious stone: (Isa. 54:11,12) the first foundation* **jasper**, *the second* **sapphire**, *the third* **chalcedony**, *the fourth* **emerald**, *20. the fifth* **sardonyx**, *the sixth* **sardius**, *the seventh* **chrysolite**, *the eighth* **beryl**, *the ninth* **topaz**, *the tenth* **chrysoprase**, *the eleventh* **hyacinth**, *the twelfth* **amethyst**, *21. and the twelve gates were twelve* **pearls**, *in the midst of each one of the* **gates** *was a door made out of one* **pearl**. *And the wide street of the city was pure* **gold** *like translucent glass.*

No Evil can enter the Holy City. The elimination of Evil brings us to the passages regarding the Saints! The precious stones and the gold of the city are in the Spirit Realm. They are not physical, but they are Real!

THE BEGINNING OF THE SAINTS

The Seven Seals: The First and Fifth are good, the rest for Sinners, are cited above.

1. Revelation 6.1. *And I looked when the* **Lamb** *opened* **one of the seven seals**, *then I heard* **one** *of the* **four living creatures** *saying in a voice like thunder, "You must come." 2. And I looked, and there was a* **white horse**, *(Zech. 1:8; 6:3,6) and the one who sat upon it had a bow, and a* **crown** *was given to him and he came out* **conquering**, *so he could* **overcome every enemy**.

The first of these seals tells us that we overcome every enemy! The second, third and fourth seals are about the Heathens, the sinners, so, here we pick up with the Fifth Seal, starting with the Martyrs.

THE FIRST HARVEST OF THE SAINTS, THE MARTYRS:

The Martyrs are those who had their Lives, their breath taken away; they now receive their White Robes, the Robes of Righteousness. Read about them in the next Section on the Saints.

The Fifth Seal Takes the Martyrs to Heaven

> **5.** Revelation 6:9. *And when He opened the **fifth seal**, I saw under the altar the **lives** of those **slain because of the Word of God** and because of the **testimony** which they had. 10. And a loud voice cried out saying, "How long, the **Holy** and **True Lord**, are You not **judging** and **exonerating our blood** from those who live upon the earth?"* (Deut. 32:43, 2 Ki 9:7, Ps. 79:10)

How Long? How about instant! The Lives are the breaths of each one, those who have now expired; These are the Martyrs, the First Group taken to ETERNAL LIFE.

> Revelation 6:11. *And a **white robe** was given to each of them and it was told to them that they will **rest** yet a little time, until (the number of) their **fellow servants** and their **brothers** would be completed, (Gen. 48:19, Rom. 11:25) those who are going to be killed as also they (had been).* (Rev. 20:4)

The White Robe of Righteousness is Spiritual, not physical, but it is Real, given to each Martyr. Their Rest is just a short break as things can move quickly in the Spirit Realm. The Angel giving out the Robes could be the Sixth Angel. The Fellow Servants could also be translated Slaves, but that would not be appropriate because each Saint has a free will, so we are Servants not Slaves.

The Two Witnesses

> Revelation 11:3. *And I shall give My **two witnesses** (power), and they will prophesy one thousand two hundred sixty days clothed in sackcloth. 4. These are the **two olive trees** and the **two menorahs** that are standing before the **Lord of the Earth**.*

Zechariah 4:14 refers to the "two anointed ones" who are Joshua and Zerubbabel in the literal, restored second Temple. It is commonly accepted today that the two anointed ones are the spirits of Moses and Elijah. Their identity is less significant than their power and their duties in this passage, as this is all in the Spirit, not natural. The Two Spiritual Witnesses are not individuals, but the Congregations of the New Synagogue and the New Church. Both will be built from the ground up, not top leadership down to the people. Both will move in Power, preaching Kingdom, bringing Miracles and Healings through the Power of the Lamb of God. The bringing to Life of the unsaved will be explosive on Judgment Day.

Rabbi Shlomo Riskin, Chief Rabbi of Efrat, a suburb of Jerusalem, spoke at a meeting of Christian and Jewish Leaders in Jerusalem a few years ago, relating End Times to Genesis 15:

Covenant Between the Parts

> Genesis 15:9. *And He said to him, "Take a heifer for Me, three years old, and a three-year-old she-goat, and a three-year-old ram, a turtle-dove, and a young pigeon." 10. And he took all these to Him, and divided them down the middle, and laid each piece one opposite another, but **he did not divide the bird.***

The Bird, Tsipor in Hebrew, is a collective singular referring to both birds, showing the inherent lesson that Israel's generations (mother and child) are one unit, not to be divided. Rabbi Riskin said the birds were released, showing that the birds go out to spread God's love through the Earth, one bird representing Jews, the other representing Christians.

> Revelation 11:5. *If anyone determines to **injure them (the Two Witnesses) fire goes out from their mouth** and **devours** their **enemies:** (yes), if someone would **purpose to injure them**, it is necessary for him **to be killed in this way.** (2 Sam. 22:9, 2 Ki. 1:10, Jer. 5:14, Ps. 97:3) 6. These have the **authority** to **close the sky** so that rain would not fall the days of their **prophecy,** (1 Ki. 17:1) and they have **authority** upon the **waters** to turn them into **blood,** (Exod. 7:17,19,20) and to **strike** the earth with every **plague** (1 Sam. 4:8) as often as they would want. 7. And when they **finish** their **testimony,** the **beast** that ascends from the **abyss** (Dan. 7:3) will make **war** with them, and will **overcome** them (Dan. 7:7,21) and he will **kill them.** 8. And their **corpses** (will be) upon the streets of the great city, which is called **spiritually Sodom** and **Egypt,** where also their **Lord** was **crucified.** 9. And they from the **people** and **tribes** and **languages** and **nations** will see their **corpses three and a half days** and they will not allow their **corpses** to be placed in a tomb. 10. And **those who dwell upon the earth will rejoice over them** and they will be happy and they will send **gifts** to one another, because these **two prophets** tormented those who dwell upon the earth. 11. And after the **three and a half days** (the) **breath of life** from God entered them, and they stood upon their feet, (Ezek. 37:5) and great **fear** fell upon those who saw them. 12. Then (the two) heard a **loud voice** from heaven*

236

*saying to them, "**You must ascend to this place**." Then they **ascended** into **heaven** (2 Ki. 2:11) in the cloud, and their enemies watched them. 13. And in that hour there was a great **earthquake**, and a tenth of the city **fell** and seven thousand named of mankind were killed in the **earthquake** and the rest (of the people) became **terrified** and gave **glory** to the **God of heaven**.* (Ezek. 38:19,20)

This is the extended Judgment Day, during which people are saved, being given the Mark by the Man with the Inkhorn! Believers will be Persecuted! The Entire Time of this Day is in the Spirit, with each event being in the Spirit Realm, not the physical. The Two Witnesses are Congregations of Jews and Christians, physical people. At the very end, the Rest of the people gave Glory to the God of Heaven! The Prophetic Preaching of the Two Witnesses was quite effective even though not all the People were saved.

Revelation 11:14. *The* second woe *has passed. Behold the* third woe *is coming quickly.*

This is the only mention of the third woe although the third woe could be the destruction of Babylon in Revelation 18:10,15,19.

The Seventh Trumpet

7/7. Revelation 11:15. *Then the **seventh** angel **trumpeted**: and there was a loud voice in heaven saying,*

"*The **kingdom of the World of our Lord***
   *and of **His Messiah** has come*
   *and **He will reign forever and ever**.*"
(Exod. 15:18; 7:14, Ob. 21, Zech. 14:9, Ps. 10:16; 22:29, Dan. 2:44)

*16. Then the **twenty-four elders** who were sitting upon their **thrones** fell upon their faces before the **throne of God** and they paid **homage to God** 17. saying,*

"We give thanks to You, Lord God of Hosts,

   Who is and Who was,

Because You have taken Your great power

   and You have come to reign.

18.   And the heathens were enraged, (Ps. 2:1; 46:7)

   *and (now) Your **wrath** has come*

*and the **appointed time of the dead to be judged***

*and to give the **reward** to Your **servants the prophets***

(Amos 3:7, Zech. 1:6, Dan. 9:6,10)

*and to the **saints** and to those who **revere Your name**,*

(both) the small and the great, (Ps. 115:13)

*and to **destroy** those who **destroy** the earth."*

The Twenty-four Elders are the Twelve Leaders of the Twelve Tribes of Israel and the Twelve Apostles of the Lamb.

Revelation 11:19. *Then the **Sanctuary of God**, the **One** in heaven, opened and the **Ark of His covenant** (1 Ki. 8:1,6, 2 Chr. 5:7) was **seen** in His **Sanctuary**, and there were **lightnings** and **voices** and **thunders** and an **earthquake** (Exod. 19:18, Ezek. 1:13) and a violent **hailstorm**.* (Exod. 9:24)

Judgment Day is finally over, those Heathens having been judged and sentenced to the Second Death and the Saints having been rewarded. The Ark of the Covenant is Spiritual, not physical; the Spiritual Ark is real, just not physical.

The Twenty-four Elders are the Twelve Leaders of the Twelve Tribes of Israel and the Twelve Apostles of the Lamb.

Revelation 11:19. *Then the **Sanctuary of God**, the **One** in heaven, opened and the **Ark of His covenant** (1 Ki. 8:1,6, 2 Chr. 5:7) was **seen** in His **Sanctuary**, and there were **lightnings** and **voices** and **thunders** and an **earthquake** (Exod. 19:18, Ezek. 1:13) and a violent **hailstorm**.* (Exod. 9:24)

The Woman and the Dragon

Revelation 12.1. *And a great miracle was seen in **Heaven**, a **woman clothed with the sun**, and the **moon beneath her feet** and upon her head a **crown of twelve stars**, 2. and (she) was **pregnant**, and she **cried out in labor** and was **distressed** to give **birth**.* (Isa. 66:7, Mic. 4:10)

The Woman represents both Congregations of the LORD* about to come forth in Power to do the LORD*'s last bidding. Which was summarized in chapter eleven, with the Two Witnesses. This takes place in Heaven where there is Spiritual Sun, the Glory of God.

Jeremiah 3:14. *Return, O backsliding children, says the LORD*, for* I AM married to you *and I shall take you, one from a city, and two from a family, and I shall bring you to* Zion. *15. And I shall give you* shepherds *according to* My heart, *who will* feed *you with* knowledge *and* understanding. *16. And it will be, when you have multiplied and increased in the land, in those days, says the LORD*, they will no longer say, The* Ark of the Covenant of the LORD*. *Neither will it come to mind nor will they remember it, nor will they visit it, nor will that be done any more. 17. At that time they will call* Jerusalem, *The* Throne of the LORD* *and all the nations will be gathered to it, to the* name of the LORD*, *to* Jerusalem, *nor will they walk any more after the imagination of their corrupt heart.*

The Woman is the Bride, the Congregation, whom the LORD* Married to seal the permanent relationship of the Congregation with the God of Abraham, Isaac, and Jacob. He will appoint the Shepherds who will tend, teaching and feeding the flock. This is after Judgment Day has begun.

Revelation 12:3. *And another miracle was seen in heaven, and there was a great red like fire* **dragon** *which had seven heads and ten horns (Dan. 7:7) and seven crowns upon its heads, 4. and its tail was dragging a third of the stars of the sky and it cast them to the earth. (Dan. 8:10) And the* **dragon** *stood before the* **woman**, *the one about to give* **birth**, *so that when her* **child** *would be* **born** *he could* **devour** *(the child). 5. And she bore a* **son**, *(Isa. 7:14; 66:7) a male child, (the one) who is going to* **shepherd** *all the* **heathens** *with an* **iron rod**. *(Ps. 2:9) And her* **child** *was caught away to* **God** *and to* **His throne**. *6. And the* **woman** *fled into the* **desert**, *where she has a place there that was* **prepared by God**, *so that they could feed her there one thousand two hundred sixty days.*

The Dragon represents Satan with all the evil forces at his disposal. The Dragon is seen today in all the Anti-Semitic and Anti-Christian forces now attacking Jews and Christians all over the world. The Son born to the Congregation is those Jews and Christians now being attacked, with oppression of the Christians even in the U. S. as the government tries to force the Little Sisters of the Poor to provide funding for abortions in their health insurance. State governments in Colorado, Oregon, and Washington have forced bakeries to make cakes with LGBTQ messages against the beliefs of the bakers. Synagogues have been attacked in other states, so persecution is here! The Son goes forth in Power from millions of congregations throughout the world, bringing God's Love to all creation. This is not Revival; it is bringing Life for the first time with Kingdom

Preaching everywhere, truly bringing God's love to everyone. The Congregations representing the Son and the LORD* are the Two Witnesses of Revelation eleven.

> Revelation 12:7. *And there was a **war in heaven, Michael** (Dan. 10:13,21; 12:1) and his **angels** made **war** with the **dragon**. And the **dragon** and his **angels battled**, 8. but **he** (the **dragon**) was **not strong enough** and a **place** for them was still **not found** in heaven. 9. And the **great dragon**, the **old serpent**, the one called **Devil** and **Satan**, the one who **deceived** the entire **inhabited world**, was **cast** to the **earth**, (Isa. 14:12) and his **angels** were **cast with him**. 10. And I heard a loud voice in heaven saying,*
>
> > *"Now has come the **salvation** and the **power***
> >
> > *and the **kingdom** of our **God***
> >
> > *and the **authority** of His **Messiah**,*
> >
> > *because the **accuser** of our brothers has been thrown (down),*
> >
> > *the one who had **accused** them before our God*
> >
> > *day and night. (Zech. 3:1, Job 1:9-11)*

Satan being cast to the Earth is his being thrown out of Heaven. The Earth is no more, so Satan is cast into the Abyss. The words translated Accuser and Accused refer specifically to bringing formal charges in a court of law.

> 11. And they **overcame** him because of the **blood of the Lamb**
>
> > and because of the **word of their testimony**
> >
> > and they did not **love** their life (even) to the enduring of **death** itself.
>
> 12. Because of this you, the **heavens** and those who **dwell** in them,
>
> > must **constantly rejoice**.
> >
> > **Woe** to the **earth** and the **sea**,
> >
> > because the **devil** has come down to you
> >
> > having great **wrath**,
> >
> > since he has **known that he has little time**."

This is a picture of the present time throughout the world as persecution ramps up and evangelizing is forbidden in many countries.

> Revelation 12:13. *And when the **dragon** saw that he was thrown to the earth, he pursued the **woman** who gave **birth** to the **male child**. 14. And the two wings of the great **eagle** were given to the **woman**, so that she could*

fly into the desert to her place, where she was fed there a time and times and a half time, (Dan. 7:25; 12:7) away from the presence of the serpent.

This is a parallel to Exodus 19:4 when God said that He bore the children of Israel on the wings of eagles when He brought them out of Egypt. The wings of the eagle are Spiritual since there is no more Earth. God saved the Congregations to enable their anointed testimony, producing the miracles and healings so the Congregations would grow exponentially, taking God's love throughout the world. This shows that the Earth is not destroyed at the very beginning of Judgment Day, but slowly, deliberately during Judgment Day.

*Revelation 12:15. And the **serpent** spewed water like a **river** from its mouth behind the **woman**, so that it could make her be **swept away by a stream**, **drowned** in the waters. 16. Then the **earth** helped the **woman** and the **earth opened its mouth** and swallowed the **river** that the **dragon** cast from its mouth. 17. And the **dragon** was angered on account of the **woman** and left to make **war** with the rest of her seed, of those who keep the **commandments of God** and have the **testimony of Y'shua**. (Dan. 7:7,21) 18. Then he stood upon the sand of the sea.*

Testimony of Y'shua: The key verse is Revelation 19:10.

*Then I fell before his feet to pay homage to him. And he said to me, 'Stop! Don't do that: I am a fellow servant with you and your brothers who have the **testimony of Y'shua**: you must now pay homage to God. For the **testimony of Y'shua is the Spirit of Prophecy**.'*

The **testimony** means two different things. **One** is that <u>we are to testify about Him</u>. We certainly are to testify about Him in both word and deed. We are to show our family, friends, neighbors, co-workers, and everyone we meet that we are different, set apart from the world. We are to show by the way we live that we are committed wholeheartedly to the LORD*.

The Second and deeper meaning of Testimony of Y'shua speaks of <u>Y'shua as the Word of God</u>, as in John 1:1 *In the beginning was the Word, and the Word was with God, and the Word was God.* Revelation 1:2,9; 20:4 use the expression *the Word of God and the testimony of Y'shua,* using a Hebrew form of repetition to emphasize the statement, in effect saying "He is Scripture." Psalm 119:2 has *Happy are those who keep* His testimonies, *seeking Him with the whole heart.* Jewish Commentary says that "His testimonies" "refers to the Torah and mitzvot, which bear testimony to God's relationship to Israel." Those who serve Him wholeheartedly know His Scripture and do His mitsvot, which are His commandments. The phrase, "His testimonies," is used ten times in the Hebrew Scriptures, as in Psalm 25:10. *All the paths of the LORD* are loving kindness and truth for such as keep His covenant and His Testimonies.* John recorded in Revelation 19:10.

> *Then I fell before his feet to pay homage to him (the angel). And he said to me, "Stop! Don't do that: I am a fellow servant with you and your brothers who have the* **testimony of Y'shua***: you must now pay homage to God. For the* **testimony of Y'shua** *is the* **Spirit of Prophecy.***"*

Spirit of Prophecy is action, putting God's Word to work and turning **His commandments into deeds**. Doing His commandments is the **Spirit of Prophecy**; that is, the goal, the fulfilling of all prophecy, as His people are doing all that He has commanded, bringing His perfect will into being so that all He has spoken has come to pass. We are to be so committed to knowing His Word and to doing His will, that we move in perfect synchronization with Him, just as His Incarnate Body, Y'shua, did while He walked the earth. **Spirit of Prophecy** is a term used by Torah scholars from ancient times, so John would have understood the meaning when the messenger spoke this to him. Commentary lists many examples of people being led by the **Spirit of Prophecy**, with a few examples here:

- The seventy elders to help Moses carry the load in the wilderness
- The ten spies to the valley of Eshcol to get the grapes that they brought back
- Rahab to instruct the two spies that their pursuers would turn back in three days
- Ruth to the field of Boaz

The Testimony of Y'shua is the very Spirit of Prophecy. Each of us has been given the gift of prophecy and each of us is to live by that, to be so in tune with the perfect will of God that we follow the examples cited above to bring His perfect will here to earth. Romans 13:14. *but you will become so possessed of the mind of the Lord Y'shua Messiah that you will resemble Him and you must not be concerned for desires of the flesh.* To be possessed of or to have the mind of the Lord is to have your spirit so in tune with the Lord that you understand what He means, what He would have you do. That is also the primary meaning of 1 Corinthians 2:16, which ends with *But we have the mind of Messiah.* See Lord's Prayer in the One New Man Bible Glossary.

The following commentary is from June S. Rice, author of inspirational books:

> The Hebrew references all had one thing in common. In each instance cited, they relate to His Consummate Plan for the Ages. Each event

moves, and is prompted, according to Prophetic Time, so there are actually two Time Lines here, the natural and Prophetic Time (personal prophecy included) because both movealong according to and with God's Prophetic Time, with increasing frequency, like labor pains coming faster, toward the final crowning of that particular birth.

The testimony of Y'shua is Himself reigning now in us, and ultimately on the new earth. This shows me why we need one another, and why the move of the saints is so critical. In each of the Hebrew references cited in Hebrew Scriptures it had to do with others; such as the seventy elders (government of God) the ten spies getting the grapes (this can refer to the abundance of the final harvest, but not all are willing to step out in faith for it) or Ruth going to the field of Boaz that resulted in the birth of Y'shua, a daring new thing, and also bore witness to the New Man birthed from both Gentile and Jew which should be the new pattern birthed in the Church, which is also quite startling.

The Two Beasts

Revelation 13.1. *Then I saw a beast rising from the sea, (Dan. 7:3) which had ten horns and seven heads and upon its horns ten crowns and slanderous names upon its heads.*

The Beast is the epitome of greed; of pride in one's position, possessions, and reputation. The seven heads and ten crowns are the elements of the Pride, of the modern Idols worshipped by so many people. Those are the things that make it so hard for people to humble themselves before God.

> Revelation 13:2. *And the **beast** that I saw was like a **leopard** and its feet like a **bear** and its **mouth** like a **lion's mouth**. (Dan. 7:4-6) And the **dragon** gave to it its **power** and its **throne** and **great authority**. 3. And one of its **heads** was as if it had been **slain in death**, then its **fatal wound** was **healed**. And the whole **earth** was astonished and **followed** the **beast** 4. and they paid **homage** to the **dragon**, because he gave his **authority** to the **beast** and they paid **homage** to the **beast** saying, "Who is like the **beast** and who is able to **war against him?**" 5. And the **power of speech** was given to him, speaking loud and **blasphemous things**, (Dan. 7:8,20,25; 11:36) and authority was given to him to do **miracles** during forty-two months.*

The beast will even have authority to change times, affecting natural laws, Daniel 7:25. The Power of Speech is so the Beast will Deceive the people, which is one of Satan's Primary Weapons. Without the ability to Reason against God, the Beast resorts to Blasphemous Speech. That is very apparent today with the enemies of Righteousness attacking Righteous Judeo-Christian values; Obscene language being commonplace.

Revelation 13:6. *And his mouth opened in **blasphemies to God** to revile **His name** and **His Tabernacle**, those who **live** in **His Tabernacle in heaven**. 7. Then it was given to him to **make war** with the **saints** and to **overcome them**, (Dan. 7:7,21) and **authority** was given to him (the **Beast**) over every **tribe** and **people** and **language** and **nation**. 8. And all those who **live** on the **earth** will **pay homage to him**, whose name is **not** written (Exod. 32:32,33, Ps. 7:10; 69:28) in the **Lamb's Book of Life**, the book of the One Who has been slain from the foundation of the world. (Isa. 53:7)*

Persecution of believers around the world is not only common now, but growing each year! We see this in the United States, the European Union, the United Nations General Assembly, various UN organizations, and many other countries. This is the inter-face between the natural and the Spiritual realms.

Revelation 13:9. *If someone has an ear he **must now listen**.*

*10. "If someone is to go into **captivity**,*

*he is taken into **captivity**:*

*if someone is to be **killed** by means of a sword*

*he is **killed** by a sword." (Jer. 15:2; 43:11)*

*Here is the **patience** and the **faith** of the **saints**.*

Each one Must Listen so he or she will not be Deceived by the Beast who has power and authority to bring people into the godless, Satanic world view. Many are being Deceived, ignoring news of corruption and believing lies from the corrupt media which parrots the lies of the rich and famous, the corrupt and powerful.

Revelation 13:11. *Then I saw another **beast** rising from the earth, and he had **two horns** like a **lamb** and he was speaking (roaring) like a **dragon**. 12. And he carried out all the **authority** of the **first beast** before him, and he caused the earth and those **dwelling** in it to **bow down** and **pay homage** to the **first beast**, whose fatal wound was healed. 13. And he performed great **miracles**, so that he would make **fire descend from the sky** to the earth before mankind, (1 Ki. 18:24-39) 14. and he **deceived** those who lived on the earth by the **miracles** which were given to him to do in the sight of the* *beast, saying for those who lived on the earth to make an **image** to the **beast** (Deut. 13:2-4) that had the **wound** from the **small sword**, but **still lived**. 15. And it was given to him to give a **spirit** to the **image** of the **beast**, so that the **image** of the **beast** could also **speak** and could cause as many of those that would **not** pay homage to the image of the beast, that they would be **killed**. (Dan. 3:5,6) 16. And he forces **everyone**, the **small** and the **great**, and the **rich** and the **poor**, and the **free** and the **slaves**, so that he could give them a **mark** upon their **right hand or upon their forehead** 17. and so that **no one would be able to buy or to sell** except the one who had the **mark**, the **name of the beast**, or the **number of its name**. 18. Here is the wisdom. The one who has **understanding** must count the **number of the beast**, for it is a number of mankind, and its number is **six hundred sixty-six**.*

This Beast deceives with Miracles, including promises of money or other substance, promises not necessarily fulfilled. Promising unity while crafting destruction of his enemies, achieving unity only by destruction of opposition. Those who take the Mark of the Beast are immediately erased from the Book of Life, while those who do not take the Mark are Killed, but enter ETERNAL LIFE immediately being given a Martyr's Reward. The Mark of the Beast is Spiritual, not Physical so it is only visible in the Spirit.

The Messages of the Three Angels

1. Revelation 14:6. *And I saw **another angel** flying in mid-sky, having everlasting **Good News** to proclaim to those who are dwelling temporarily (sojourning) upon the earth, and for every **nation** and **tribe** and **language** and **people**, 7. saying in a loud voice, "You must now **revere God** and you must now give **glory** to **Him**, because the hour of **His judgment** has come, and you must immediately **pay homage** to the **One Who made heaven and earth and sea and fountains of waters**."* (Exod. 20:11, Ps. 148:5)

The First Angel proclaims the Good News throughout the world.

Good News, the Gospel message, translates the Hebrew word M'vaser, also translated Good Tidings. The M prefix makes this something planned by God, a blessing for all mankind. That noun comes from the root, a <u>verb</u>, bet-sin-resh, meaning to bear tidings. The <u>noun</u>, bet-sin-resh, means flesh, hinting at the relationship to Good News. M'vaser is in Isaiah 52:7. *How beautiful upon the mountains are the feet of Him Who brings Good News, Who is proclaiming peace, Who brings Good News of good, Who proclaims deliverance-salvation: Who says to Zion, Your God reigns!*

Isaiah 61.1. *The **Spirit of Adonai, the LORD*** is upon Me, because the* *LORD** has anointed **Me** to **preach Good News** to the **humble**. He has sent **Me** to bind up the **broken-hearted**, to proclaim **liberty** to the **captives**, and **opening of eyes** for those who are bound,* Nahum 2.1. *Behold, upon the mountains are the feet of him who brings **Good News**, who declares **Shalom**! O Judah, keep your solemn feasts! Perform your vows! For the **wicked one** will no longer pass through you. He is utterly cut off.*

The really Good News is John 1:14. *And the* Word *became flesh and lived among us, and we saw* His *glory, glory in the same manner as the only child of the Father, full of* grace *and* truth. The Living Word came to us to teach us and to show us how we are to live by every Word from the mouth of God, bringing us eternal life. 1 Peter 1:18. *Because* Messiah *also once suffered concerning sin, the* righteous One *on behalf of the* unjust, *so that He could bring you to* God *when* He *did indeed die in the flesh, but then was* made alive *by the* Spirit.. Y'shua is alive today, having entered that state (ETERNAL LIFE) that all of us will enter at the appropriate time.

Another relationship to Good News is from three points: First in Genesis 1:27 God made mankind and in verse 31 said it was very good; Second in Genesis 2:23 Adam said Eve was bone of his bones and flesh of his flesh; and Third in Genesis 2:24 Adam and Eve became one flesh. That is Good News for all mankind, establishing the foundation for Godly marriage, the most important element for Godly living.

Revelation 11:14. *The* second woe *has passed. Behold the* third woe *is coming quickly.*

Revelation 14:13. *Then I heard a voice from heaven saying, "You must now write: 'Blessed are the **dead**, those who die in the Lord from now on.'" "Indeed," says the Spirit, "that they will **rest** from their labors, for their works are following in company with them."*

The Dead are the Saints whose Righteous Deeds bring the Heavenly Rewards to each Saint. The Rest from their labors is just a short break, showing that Saints will have duties in Heaven that will really keep them busy.

THE SECOND HARVEST OF THE EARTH, the Fourth Angel

Revelation 14:14. *Then I looked, and there was a white cloud, and sitting upon the cloud like a **Son of Man**, (Dan. 7:13) Who had a gold crown on His head and a sharp sickle in His hand. 15. Then another **angel** came out of the **Sanctuary** crying in a loud voice to the **One** Who was sitting on the* *cloud, "You must now send your **sickle** and you must now **reap**, because the time to **reap** has come, because the **harvest** of the earth has **withered."** (Jl. 4:13) 16. Then the **One** Who was sitting on the cloud threw His **sickle** forcefully over the earth and the earth was harvested.*

This is the Second Harvest of Saints; the first harvest was the Martyrs. The time is well into Judgment Day showing that Judgment Day in Spiritual Time lasts considerably longer than in Natural Time. When the Sickle is thrown forcibly to the Earth, it shows that the End Time harvest will have great energy, with powerful enthusiasm bringing huge numbers into the Kingdom. That the Harvest had withered shows that the LORD* had been patient. Judgment Day will add many Saints to the Kingdom of Heaven; at the same time, the Day adds to Satan's followers! Every Saint except the Two Witnesses has now been taken to Heaven, each one has been given the Robe of Righteousness! The Two Witnesses are still out there preaching Kingdom!

After the Seven Last Plagues of Revelation 15:1 Good Things Come to the Worshipping Saints:

Revelation 15:2. *And I saw like a glassy sea that had been mixed with fire, and those who overcame the beast and his image and the number of his name (were) standing upon the glassy sea with harps of God.*

Each Saint has conquered, Overcome the Beast, Satan! Each Saint has been given a Harp to accompany Worship of the LORD*.

Revelation 15:3. *And they were **singing** the **song of Moses**, the servant of God, and the **song of the Lamb** saying, (Exod. 15:1)*

"Great and wonderful are Your deeds, (Exod. 15:11, Ps. 92:6; 111:2; 139:14)

*Lord, the **God of Hosts**:*

***righteous** and **true** are **Your Ways**, (Deut. 32:4, Ps. 145:17)*

*O **King of the nations**: (Jer. 10:10)*

*4. who would **not** revere You, Lord,*

and will not glorify Your name? (Jer. 10:6,7)

*because **only You** are **undefiled by sin**,*

because all the nations will come

*and bow down to pay **homage** before You, (Mal. 1:11, Ps. 86:9)*

*because Your **righteous deeds** have been revealed."*

King of the Nations could also be translated King of the Heathens!

Rewards in the Hereafter.

> Revelation 18:20. *Heaven, and **saints** and **apostles** and **prophets**,*
>
> > *you must **perpetually rejoice** in her,*
> >
> > > *because God **condemned** her **judgment of you**. (He has vindicated you.)*

So, gang, we win at the End!

> Revelation 18:20. *Heaven, and **saints** and **apostles** and **prophets**,*
>
> > *you must **perpetually rejoice** in her,*
> >
> > > *because God **condemned** her **judgment of you**. (He has vindicated you.)*

Our Victory at last!

ANOTHER ANGEL

The Thousand Years

> Revelation 20.1. *Then I saw an **angel** descending from **heaven**, who had the **key** of the **abyss** and a large chain in his hand. 2. And he **arrested** the **dragon**, the **old serpent**, who is (the) **Devil** and **Satan**, then he **bound** him for a **thousand years** 3. and cast him into the **abyss** and **shut** and **sealed** (the abyss) above him, so that he could **not** deceive the **heathens** any longer until the **thousand years would be completed**. After these things it is necessary for him to be **loosed** for a **short** time.*

The Thousand Years is Spiritual Time, not time as we know it, so we do not have any idea how much time there will be, except it will likely be very long, coming at the End of Judgment Day.

> 2 Peter 3:8. *But this one thing must not escape your notice, beloved, that **one day** with the Lord (is) as a **thousand years** and a **thousand years** as **one day**. (Ps. 90:4) 9. (The) Lord does not tarry with His promise, as some consider slowness, but He is patient with you, not wanting any to be destroyed but all to come to repentance. 10. But (the) **Day of the Lord** will come like a thief, on which (**Day**) the sky will pass away with a roar and the elements from which all things are made will be destroyed, being burned up, and the earth and the deeds (of all) on it will be laid bare in this (Day).*

Psalm 90:4. *For a **thousand years** in Your sight are but **as yesterday** when it is past, and as a watch in the night: (2 Pe. 3:8) 5. You carried them away as with a flood. They are as asleep, in the morning they are like grass (which) grows up.*

The Thousand Years will have to remain an unknown quantity until we get there. We may have to learn how days are measured when there is no sun, but maybe it just will not matter.

Revelation 20:4. *Then I saw **thrones** and (those that) sat upon them and **judgment** was given to them, (Dan. 7:9,22,27) and (I saw) the **lives** of those who had been **beheaded** because of the **testimony of Y'shua** and because of the **Word of God** and who did **not** worship the **beast** or his **image** and did **not** take the **mark** upon their **foreheads** or upon their **hands.** (Rev. 6:9-11)*

The Lives are the Spirits of the Martyrs, not their Souls. When the body dies the Soul ceases to exist, and the Spirit goes to be with the LORD*. The word translated Lives is Psuchas which means Lives or Breaths not Soul.

*Revelation 20:4b Then they became **alive** again and **reigned** with the **Messiah one thousand years.** 5. The **rest** of the **dead** did **not** become **alive** again until the **thousand years were completed.** This is the **first resurrection.** 6. **Blessed** and **holy** (is) the one who has a part in the **first resurrection**: the **second death** has **no** power to destroy them: but they will be **priests of God** and of the **Messiah** and they will **reign** with **Him** (Exod. 19:6, Isa. 61:6) the **thousand years.***

Heaven is and will continue to be a theocracy, with God the only King and the officials will be priests. The time is generally understood to be **one thousand**, but this word, **xilia**, was also used in a **general sense**, referring to any **very large number**. There were no numbers like Billions or Trillions in the first century and with one day as a thousand years and a thousand years a one day we have to wait until we get there to understand what is meant.

The Defeat of Satan

Revelation 20:7. *Then when the **thousand years are completed,** Satan will be loosed from his **prison** 8. and he will come out to **deceive** the **heathens** who are in the **four corners** of the **earth,** (Ezek. 7:2) **Gog** and **Magog,** (Ezek. 38:2-39:10) to **gather** them for the **war,** whose **number** is as the **sand of the sea.** 9. And they went up upon the breadth of the earth and they **surrounded** the **army** of the **saints** and the **beloved city,** and **fire** descended from the **sky** and **consumed** them. (1 Ki. 18:38, 2 Ki. 1:10,*

*Ezek. 38:22; 39:6) 10. Then the **devil**, the one who was **deceiving** them, was thrown violently into the **lake of fire** and **brimstone** (Isa. 30:33, Gen. 19:24, Ezek. 38:22, Ps. 11:6) in which place also the **beast** and the **false prophet** (had been cast), and they will be **tormented** day and night **forever and ever.***

The War is not on earth, but in the Heavenlies, taking care of Satan once and for all time. The LORD* and Y'shua zap the armies of the Devil, killing them all.

The Judgment at the Great White Throne;

THE THIRD AND FINAL RAISING OF THE SAINTS

Revelation 20:11. *Then I saw a **great white throne** and the **One** Who sits upon it, from Whose presence the **earth** (Ps. 114:3,7) and the **sky** fled and a place was not found for them. 12. Then I saw the **dead**, the **great** and the **small**, standing before the **throne**. And **scrolls** were opened, and another **scroll** was opened, which is of **life**, (Exod. 32:32,33, Ps. 69:29, Dan. 12:1) and the **dead** were judged according to their **deeds**, (Isa. 59:18, Jer. 17:10, Ps. 28:4; 62:13, Pro. 24:12, Rom. 2:6, 1 Cor. 3:8) by what had been **written** in the **scrolls**. (Dan. 7:9,10) 13. Then the **sea** gave up the **dead** that were in it and **Death** and **Hades** gave up the **dead**, those in them, and each was **judged** according to his **works**. 14. Then **Death** and **Hades** were thrown violently into the **lake of fire**. This is the **second death**, the **lake of fire**. 15. And if someone was not found written in the **Book of Life**, he was cast into the **lake of fire**. (Isa. 30:33)*

Those Written in the Book of Life have spotless records because of their Repentance. This Judgment is the Third Raising of the Saints.

Isaiah 43:25. I AM, I AM *He Who* erases *your* transgressions *for My own sake, and I will not remember your sins!*

Isaiah 44:22. *I have* erased *your* transgressions *as a thick cloud and your sins as a cloud. Return to Me, for I have redeemed you.*

When your sins, iniquities, and transgressions are erased from your record, that means that they never happened! So, do Not stew over past sins! God's record says they never happened, that He has erased them, bringing you into Eternal Life!

Forgiveness of Sins: While many Hebrew Scriptures proclaim forgiveness of sins, there is an order, a formula to obtaining forgiveness.

1. Forgiveness of others

There is one precondition, without which no amount of repentance can bring forgiveness. That is, the sinner must forgive every one of every little thing and every big thing before God will accept the sinner's repentant heart. Y'shua taught in the Lord's Prayer, *You must right now forgive our sins for us, in the same manner as we have completed forgiving everyone of everything, big and little, against us:* (Matt. 6:12) Verses 14 and 15 then continue this theme, *14. For if you would forgive all other people their transgressions, your heavenly Father will also forgive you: 15. but if you would not forgive all other people, neither will your Father forgive your sins.* Mark 11:25 and Colossians 3:13 reaffirm this principle.

2. Forgive yourself

As you forgive others include yourself among those you forgive, to remember God's great miracle of erasing your sin. You cannot make things right with God until you make things right with everyone; including yourself. Do not beat yourself over past mistakes, but forgive yourself. It is not possible for you to give your love to other people if you do not love yourself. A parent who does not love himself or herself is not able to give love to spouse or children. Forgive yourself and love yourself, then, with repentance, all of God's love and forgiveness can flow through you. See Ephesians 5:28.

3. Seek forgiveness from others

Y'shua says:

And I say to you that everyone who is angry with his brother will be guilty in the judgment. And whoever would say to his brother 'Empty-headed,' that one is guilty to the Sanhedrin: whoever would say, 'Stupid' is guilty in the Gehenna of the fire. 23. If therefore you would present your gift at the altar and there you would remember that your brother has something against you, 24. you must right away leave your gift there in front of the altar and go. You must first become reconciled with your brother, and then, after you come back, present your gift. (Matt. 5:22-24)

The Talmud makes clear the need to seek forgiveness of those sins committed unintentionally. It also makes clear that the sinner must make things right with the offended party before going to God. See *Gossip/Slander* in the One New Man Bible Glossary.

In seeking forgiveness from someone you are automatically confessing to that person.

And if your brother sins against you, you must go, you must show him the error between you and him alone. If he listens to you, you have gained your brother: (Lev. 19:17) 16. but if he would not listen, you must take with you yet one or two, so that 'by a mouth of two or three witnesses every word would stand:' (Deut. 19:35) 17. and if he refuses to listen to them, you must speak at once to the congregation: then if he refuses to listen to the congregation, he must be to you even as the heathen and the tax collector. (Matt. 18:15-17)

Confessing to a third party is not called for aside from the above sequence. Confessing to a group is not called for unless that group is the injured party.

Therefore you must continually confess your sins for yourselves with one another and you must continually pray for yourselves on behalf of one another so that you would be healed. The plea of a righteous person is very powerful, working effectively. (Jcb. 5:16)

Confession here is to the injured party. This verse has been misunderstood, but Jacob was not talking about public confession, nor was he talking about confessing the same sin over and over. After all, once repented that sin has been erased by God, Isa. 43:25.

4. Repent

Therefore I shall judge you, O House of Israel, each one according to his ways, the word of Adonai, the LORD*. Repent! Turn from all your transgressions so iniquity will not be your ruin. (Ezek. 18:30) The Bible frequently uses the word return to express repentance, as *Go! Let us return to the LORD*! For He has torn and He will heal us. He has smitten and He will bind us up.* (Hos. 6:1)

Return is appropriate because repentance requires action, much more than just regretting something. Without action, a change in behavior, there is not true repentance. The sinner must resolve not to repeat the mistake. See Psalm 51 for a model prayer of repentance.

5. Forgiveness from God

There are three verses that clearly state God's position. Exodus says, ..*keeping loving kindness for thousands, forgiving iniquity, transgression, and sin,* (Exod. 34:7) Isaiah wrote, *I AM, I AM He Who erases your transgressions for My own sake and I shall not remember your sins!* (Isa. 43:25) Jeremiah wrote, *They will no longer teach – each man his fellow, each man his brother – saying Know the LORD*! For all of them will know Me, from their smallest to their greatest – the* *word of the LORD* – when I shall forgive their iniquity (avon) and will no longer recall their sin (hata-ah).* (Jer. 31:33)

6. Clean slate

From the following verses we see that with repentance all sins are forgiven, even those committed with the intention of angering God. All forgiven sins are then deleted from God's computer.

The person who sins will die. The son will not bear the iniquity of the father, nor will the father bear the iniquity of the son. The righteousness of the righteous will be upon him, and the wickedness of the wicked will be upon him. But if the wicked will turn from all his sins that he has committed, and keep all My statutes and do that which is lawful and right, he will surely live, he will not die. 22. All his transgressions that he has committed, they will not be mentioned against him. He will live in his righteousness that he has done. 23. Have I any pleasure at all that the wicked should die? Says Adonai, the LORD*, and not that he should return from his ways and live? (Ezekiel 18:20-23) So Ezekiel removes all doubt about remembering sins, even those that are not mentioned in other verses about remembering. Our merciful heavenly Father forgives and forgets. Our All-Knowing Father is not forgetful, but He deletes forgiven sin from His computer. Ezek. 33:11 says, *Say to them, As I live, says the Lord, the LORD*, I have no pleasure in the death of the wicked, but that the wicked would turn from his way and live. Turn. Turn from your evil ways! For why will you die, O House of Israel?* Forgiven sins are erased, they never happened. Isa. 43:25 says, *I AM, I AM He Who erases your transgressions for My own sake, and I shall not remember your sins!*

A rabbi wrote many years ago that the greatest miracle of all happens when a sinner repents; because then God takes that person back in time to when the sin was committed – only this time the person does not commit the sin. Therefor the sin was never committed. So each of us needs to know that any remorse over past sin is not from God, but from the Accuser. Satan is the one who wants you to wallow in guilt. God says that any repented sin was never committed. (Isa. 43:25, et al.) Accept God's forgiveness, knowing that you are never again to dwell on that past mistake. That sin's being erased is the greatest of all miracles.

The New Sky and the New Earth

Revelation 21.1. *Then I saw a new sky and a new Earth. (Isa. 65:17; 66:22) For the first sky and the first land passed away, fading from sight, and the sea was no longer.*

The New Sky and New Earth are Spiritual, not physical. That is difficult for many of us to grasp because all we really know about is this present physical planet and sky. It stretches our imaginations to envision the New Jerusalem that is described next. The New Sky and New Earth are Spiritual, not Physical.

> Revelation 21:2. *Then I saw the **Holy City**, (Isa. 52:1) **New Jerusalem**, descending from heaven, from God, prepared like a **bride** when she was adorned for her husband. (Isa. 61:10) 3. Then I heard a loud voice from the throne saying, "Behold the **dwelling of God with mankind**, and He will **dwell** with them and they will be **His people**, and **God Himself, Emanuel**, will be with them, **their God**, (Lev. 26:11,12, Isa. 7:14, Ezek. 37:27, Zech. 2:9, 2 Chr. 6:18) 4. and He will wipe away every tear from their eyes and **death** will **no longer be**, there will be **neither mourning nor crying or pain**, because the first things went away." (Isa. 25:8; 35:10; 65:19)*

The Spiritual, Eternal Life will be amazing to us:

> Revelation 21:5. *Then the One Who sits on the throne said, "Behold I am making all things new," then He said, "You must now write, because these words are faithful and true." 6. Then He said to me, "It has been done! I AM the **Alef** and the **Tav**, the Beginning and the End. (Isa. 44:6; 48:12) I shall give freely from the fountain of the water of life to the one who thirsts. (Isa. 55:1) 7. The one who conquers will inherit these things and I shall be God to him and he will be a son to Me. (2 Sam. 7:14) 8. But for the cowardly, (those of little faith), unbelieving, abominable, murderers, immoral, sorcerers, idolaters, and all the liars – their part is in the lake that burns fire and sulfur, (Isa. 30:33, Gen. 19:24, Ezek. 38:22, Ps. 11:6) this is the **second death**."*

The Second Death is the reward of the lost, the Heathens, so be sure to be part of the Bride.

> 1/7-Revelation 21:9. *Then **one** of the **seven angels**, of those who have the **seven vials** full of the **seven last plagues**, came and spoke with me saying, "You must come, I shall show you the **bride**, the **wife of the Lamb**." 10. Then he took me away in the spirit to a great and high mountain, and he showed me the **holy city, Jerusalem**, (Ezekiel 40:2) **descending** out of the **sky** from God, 11. having the **glory of God**, her **radiance** like a precious stone as a crystal jasper stone. (Isaiah 60:1,2,19)*

The Holy City is radiant with the Glory of God, with His light shining on everything.

Revelation 21:12. *Having a great and high* **wall***, which has* **twelve gates** *and upon the* **gates twelve angels** *and names that have been written upon the* **gates***, which are the* **names** *of the* **twelve tribes of the Children of Israel***: (Exodus 28:21)* 13. *on the* **east three gates** *and on the* **north three** *gates and on the* **south three gates** *and on the* **west three gates***. (Ezekiel 48:30-35)*

All twelve Gates are the Twelve Tribes of the Children of Israel, so they are completely Jewish! Those who expect to enter Heavenly Jerusalem must be certain to understand their Jewish heritage, because the Gatekeepers will be responsible to see that only those qualified will be allowed to enter the Holy City.

Revelation 21:14. *And the* wall *of the city had* twelve foundations *and upon them are* twelve names *of the* twelve apostles of the Lamb.

Remember, all twelve Apostles of the foundation are Jewish.

The New Jerusalem is founded on the Jewish apostles of Messiah, and entry is only through the Jewish gates, the twelve tribes of Israel. That is the reason for Revelation 7:4. *Then I heard the number of those who had been sealed, a hundred forty-four thousand, that they had been sealed from every tribe of the children of Israel:*

Each Gate has one or more Jewish Gate-Keepers who have a duty to admit only those who are qualified.

The Church needs to return to its Jewish Roots, including honoring the Seasons of the LORD*. In the Last Days the Church will have to cease honoring of the Pagan holidays that have been enshrined since 325 AD, around one thousand seven hundred years ago – calling the Pagan Feasts Christmas and Easter. Christmas was originally Saturnalia honoring the Sun god, and Easter was the celebration of Ishtar, the fertility Goddess. Ishtar written in Greek and in Latin is spelled Istar and pronounced Easter! Those will not be celebrated in the Holy City!

Here are the physical dimensions of the Spiritual Holy City:

Revelation 21:15. *And the one who was speaking with me had a golden* **measuring rod***, so that he could* **measure the city** *and its* **gates** *and its* **wall***.* 16. *And the* **city** *is lying* **square***, with its* **length** *as great as the* **width***. And he* **measured the city** *with the* **reed** *to* **twelve thousand stadia***, the* **length** *and the* **breadth** *and its* **height** *are* **equal***.*

Twelve Thousand Stadia equals One Thousand Five Hundred MILES, in every direction – Length, Width, and Height. That is so immense it would cover half the United States and would be much higher than the atmosphere, which rises between fifty-three and six hundred twenty-one miles, making the Holy City at least eight hundred seventy-nine miles higher than the highest point of the atmosphere. That is no problem with the Spiritual City which will be elsewhere in some Heavenly Cove chosen by God. New Jerusalem is Spiritual – and Real!

Revelation 21:17. *Then he measured its* wall one hundred forty-four forearms *of a man, a measure men use, which the* angel *was using. (Ezek. 48:16,17)*

The measure of a forearm is the standard ancient Cubit of eighteen inches, so the Wall is two hundred sixteen feet high and two hundred sixteen feet wide.

Revelation 21:18. *And the material of its* wall *was* jasper *and the* city pure gold *like* pure glass.

The Jasper and the Gold are REAL but not physical. Jasper makes the wall very entertaining.

> Jasper is an opaque variety of Chalcedony, and is usually associated with brown, yellow, or reddish colors, but may be used to describe other opaque colors of Chalcedony such as dark or mottled green, orange, and black. Jasper is almost always multicolored, with unique color patterns and habits.[1]

That gives us an idea of the awesome appearance of the spiritual Wall. The City, all made of Pure (Spiritual) Gold will be even more awesome than the Wall!

> Revelation 21:19. *The foundations of the wall of the city were adorned with every precious stone: (Isa. 54:11,12) the first foundation jasper, the second sapphire, the third chalcedony, the fourth emerald, 20. the fifth sardonyx, the sixth sardius, the seventh chrysolite, the eighth beryl, the ninth topaz, the tenth chrysoprase, the eleventh hyacinth, the twelfth amethyst, 21. and the twelve gates were twelve pearls, in the midst of each one of the gates was a door made out of one pearl. And the wide street of the city was pure gold like translucent glass.*

New Jerusalem is immense, with twelve thousand stadia equaling one thousand five hundred miles in length, width, and height. That would cover around half the United States and extend far beyond our atmosphere. The Wall is two hundred sixteen feet in width and two hundred sixteen feet in height. This is a Spiritual city, not a physical city so how the numbers relate to the Spiritual is not known. God is Spirit as John wrote in John 4:24. *God is spirit, and it is necessary for those who*

1   https://www.minerals.net/

worship Him to worship in spirit and in truth. In our experience a pearl is a bead, often used as part of a string of beads in a necklace, but in Spiritual Jerusalem one pearl is a door in a city gate. In the natural a pearl that size would requires some heretofore unknown specie of giant oyster to make that pearl. The gold in the streets is translucent, not transparent as some translations say. Transparent is from the Latin text, not the Greek. The Translucent Gold of the Heavenly street glows with the radiant Light of the Glory of God, which permeates the Holy City. Again, what Spiritual Gold is will remain a mystery until we see it for ourselves.

No Temple in New Jerusalem

Revelation 21:22. *And I did not see a **Sanctuary** in it for the **Lord God of Hosts** and the **Lamb** are its **Sanctuary**. 23. And the city has no need of the sun or of the moon, that they would give **light** to (the city), for the **glory** of God, and the **light** of the **Lamb**, did illuminate it. (Isa. 60:19,20) 24. And the multitudes will walk by its **light**, (Isa. 60:3) and the **kings** of the earth will bring their **glory** into it, 25. and its **gates** would **never** be shut (all) day, for there will **not be night** there, (Isa. 60:11, Zech. 14:7) 26. and they will bring the **glory** and the **honor** of the **nations** into it. (Ps. 72:10,11) 27. And **no unclean thing and no** one doing a detestable (thing) or (telling) a lie could enter it, (Isa. 52:1) only those whose (names) have been written in the **Scroll of Life** of the **Lamb**.* (Exod. 32:32, Ps. 69:29, Dan. 12:1)

The Sanctuary of the Tabernacle in the Wilderness and the Temple was the place where God sat on the Ark of the Testimony in the Holy of Holies, but in Heaven He will not have that. In the Spirit Realm there will be no night, no physical food; our food will be the Word of God! The Lord God of Hosts and the Lamb are portrayed as ONE from here on because they are ONE! See the Chapter *The Immortal* in *Every Prophet in the Bible* by this author. Heavenly Jerusalem will be Heavenly, completely free of Sin! Because no unclean thing and no one doing a detestable (thing) or (telling) a lie could enter it. Revelation 21:27. Since there is only one King, the kings in verse twenty-four must refer to the Priests who reign with God. This is at the end of Judgment Day because no unclean thing or anyone doing a detestable thing, or telling a lie can enter.

River of Life

Revelation 22.1. *Then (the* angel*) showed me a* river of water of life *(*Torah*), bright as* crystal, *going out from the* throne *of* God *and the* Lamb. *(Ezek. 47:1, Jl. 3:18, Zech. 14:8)*

The Water of Life represents Torah, the Word of God flowing from the Throne to teach all mankind. In our spiritual bodies, mankind will use one hundred percent of our brains so the meaning of every Word of God will be Crystal Clear!

Revelation 22:2. *In (the) middle of its street, also on each side of the river, (is) a* **tree of life** *making twelve fruit, yielding its fruit each month, and the* **leaves** *of the tree (are used) for (the)* **healing of the multitudes***. (Gen. 2:9; 3:22, Ezek. 47:12)*

What does this mean? Every one of the Spirits in Heaven will be free, totally free! There will not be any oppression by Satan!

Revelation 22:3. *And there will no longer be anything there (that is) cursed. And the* **Throne of God and of the Lamb** *will be in it, and His servants will serve Him 4. and they will see His face, (Ps. 17:15; 42:2) and His name (will be) upon their foreheads. (Ezek. 9:4, Rev. 7:3; 9:4; 14:1) 5. And there will no longer be night and they will not need (the) light of a lamp or (the) light of (the) sun, (Zech. 14:7) because the* **Lord God** *will give* **light** *upon them, and (those whose names are written in the Book of Life) will reign forever and ever. (Isa. 60:19,20, Dan. 7:18,27)*

There is one Throne for God and the Lamb because the two are One. We all, everyone, will see the Face of the LORD* and the Lamb. All those whose names are written in the Book of Life will reign with Him as Priests to administer the edicts of the King (Revelation 20:6); there is One King, the rest are Priests. Hebrew Scholars say the Name on the foreheads will be Emmet, Truth.

The Coming of Messiah

Revelation 22:6. *Then he said to me, "These words (are) faithful and true, and the Lord God of the spirits of the prophets sent His angel to show to His servants what must happen in a* **short time.***" (Dan. 2:28,29,45) 7. "So behold!* **I am coming quickly***. Blessed is the one who keeps the words of the prophecy in this scroll."*

For a sense of Spiritual Time vs. Natural Time, look at the statements; "It must happen in a Short Time." And "I am coming quickly." Those statements were made around 95 AD and we are still waiting.

Revelation 22:8. *And I am John, the one who heard and saw these things. And when I heard and I saw, I fell to pay homage before the feet of the* **angel***, the one who showed me these things. 9. But he said to me, "Stop! I am a fellow servant of yours and of your brothers the prophets and those who keep the words of this scroll: you must now* **pay homage to God***." 10. And he said* to me, "Do not seal the words of prophecy in this scroll, for the **time is near**. *(Dan. 12:4) 11. Let the one who does wrong still do wrong and the one who is filthy still be filthy and let the **righteous still do righteousness** and let the **holy still be holy**."*

Those words were written to those of us on earth. Each one of us must be ready at every turn, so walk in Repentance, still be Righteous, and still be Holy!

Revelation 22:12. *"Behold! I am **coming quickly**, and **My reward** is with Me (Isa. 40:10; 62:11), to **reward** to each one according to his **deeds**. (Isa. 59:18, Jer. 17:10, Ps. 28:4; 62:13, Pro. 24:12, Rom. 2:6, 1 Cor. 3:8, Jcb. 2:14) 13. I am the **Alef** and the **Tav**, the **First** and the **Last**, the **Beginning** and the **End**. (Isa. 44:6; 48:12)*

The Priests will Award the Rewards, which are determined according to the deeds, the Mitsvot which are all the commandments, statutes, ordinances, observances, teachings, and testimonies.

Alef is the First letter of the Hebrew Alphabet, Tav is the last letter. Together they spell ET, a Hebrew word placed immediately in front of the direct object of the verb, so Y'shua is saying that He is the object of God's Creation.

Revelation 22:14. *"Blessed are those who are washing their robes, so that He will give them permission to use the **tree of life** (Gen. 2:9; 3:22, Ezek. 47:12) and they could enter the gates of the city. 15. And outside (will be) the dogs and the sorcerers and the immoral and the murderers and the idolaters and everyone loving and doing falsehoods.*

The Tree of Life is the same as the tree in Genesis 2:9. The leaves of this tree will not be used in the Spirit Realm because those who had been injured physically or emotionally in life will not carry their infirmities into the Spirit Realm. Heathens will be outside, not in Heaven. See *Sorcerers* in the One New Man Bible Glossary.

Revelation 22:16. *"I, **Y'shua**, did send My messenger to testify these things to you for the **congregations**. I AM the **Root** and the **Offspring of David**, (Isa. 11:1,10) the **Bright Morning Star**. (Num. 24:17) 17. And the **Spirit** and the **bride** are saying, 'You must come.' And the one who hears must now say, 'You must come.' And the one who **thirsts** must **come faithfully**, the one who wants must now take (the) **water of life** (John 4:14) as a free gift."* (Exod. 14:22, Isa. 55:1)

Water of Life is the Torah, which will be central to every Congregation and each Saint, both in the Synagogue and the Church. "You must come" here is a Greek phrase, but in 1 Corinthians 16:22 Paul uses a Greek spelling of the spelling of the Hebrew, "Maran Ata," Hebrew for the command, "You must Come!"

Revelation 22:18. *I am testifying to **everyone who hears the words of the prophecy** in this scroll: if someone would **add** to these things, God will **add to him** the **plagues** that have been written in this **scroll**, 19. and if someone would **cancel** from the words of the scroll of this prophecy, God will **cancel** his part in the **tree of life** and the **holy city**, of those things that have been written in this scroll.* (Deut. 4:2; 13:1)

Those who add to the Book of Revelation and those who cancel portions of Revelation are cancelled by God from having a part in the Heavenly Kingdom.

Revelation 22:20. *The **One Who testifies these things** says, "**Indeed, I am coming quickly.**" **Amen,** You must come, **Lord Y'shua.***

22:21. The grace of the Lord Y'shua be with all (of you).

CONCLUSION

From the very beginning mankind has interacted with the **Spirit Realm;** Adam and Eve, Enoch, and Noah walked with God. These encounters with the Spirit Realm are found throughout Scripture, with Abraham, Hagar, Elijah, Elisha, and then Zechariah, Elizabeth, and so many others. Those encounters show God's caring nature, His love for all. The encounters also show the power of God, that nothing is too difficult for Him. The LORD* can wipe out an entire army with one angel or He can dispatch a legion of demons with a word!

1 Timothy 1:17. *Now to the **Eternal King, Immortal, Invisible, (the) Only** God, (be) **honor** and **glory** forever and ever. Amen.*

We look forward to **Living** in the **Spirit Realm**. While there are some who now visit the **Spirit Realm** frequently, the vast majority of us do not have that pleasure, so we make do reading and thinking about that blessing, but realize Scripture does make those and more than those possible at any time. We all have the future of Praising the **KING**!

> Revelation 5:11. *And I looked, and I heard a sound of many angels surrounding the throne and the living creatures and the elders, and the number of them was ten thousand of ten thousands and a thousand of thousands (Dan. 7:10) 12. saying in a loud voice,*
>
> *"Worthy is the Lamb that was slain to take*
>
> *the **power and wealth and wisdom and strength***
>
> *and **honor and glory and blessing**." (Isa. 53:7, 1 Chr. 29:11)*

13. And every living thing that is in the sky and on the earth and under the earth and in the sea and I heard them all saying,

"To the One Who sits upon the throne and to the Lamb

blessing and honor and glory and power forever and ever."

14. And the four living creatures were saying, "Amen." And the elders fell down and worshipped.

We all need to walk in **Repentance** all day every day so we too can say:

*"To the **One** Who sits upon the throne and to the **Lamb***

blessing and honor and glory and power forever and ever."

ABOUT THE AUTHOR

Rev. William J. Morford graduated from Hobart College in 1953 and was a member of the 1955 class of the University of Minnesota's graduate school in hospital administration. Until 1989 Mr. Morford owned and operated a medical administration services company in South Carolina.

He was ordained in August 1988 by Christian International of Santa Rosa Beach, Florida, served on staff as student advisor for Christian International School of Theology and is a Certified Instructor to teach Christian International's series on the prophetic gifts.

From 1993 through 1999, Reverend Morford studied Hebrew under Rabbi Eliezer Ben-Yehuda, grandson of the Eliezer Ben-Yehuda whose lifetime work made Modern Hebrew the national language of Israel.

Reverend Morford and his wife, Gwen have traveled to Israel several times and expect their ministry to take them back for extended periods.

He is the editor of the popular One New Man Bible translation and the translator of The Power New Testament. He has written five books; God's Rhythm of Life, This God We Serve, and One New Man Bible Companion Volumes I, II, III, and IV.

Please visit *www.onenewmanbible.com* to explore the world of the *One New Man Bible*.